Hittite Diplomatic Texts

Society of Biblical Literature
Writings from the Ancient World

Simon B. Parker, General Editor

Associate Editors

Harry A. Hoffner, Jr.
Anne D. Kilmer
Theodore J. Lewis
Peter Machinist
William J. Murnane
David I. Owen
Robert R. Ritner
Choon Leong Seow

Volume 7
Hittite Diplomatic Texts
SECOND EDITION
by Gary Beckman
Edited by Harry A. Hoffner, Jr.

Hittite Diplomatic Texts

SECOND EDITION

by

Gary Beckman

Edited by
Harry A. Hoffner, Jr.

Society of Biblical Literature
Writings from the Ancient World Series

Scholars Press
Atlanta, Georgia

The Society of Biblical Literature gratefully acknowledges a grant from the National Endowment for the Humanities to underwrite certain editorial and research expenses of the Writings from the Ancient World series. Published results and interpretations do not necessarily represent the view of the Endowment.

Library of Congress Cataloging-in-Publication Data

Beckman, Gary M.
    Hittite diplomatic texts / by Gary Beckman ; edited by Harry A. Hoffner, Jr. — 2nd ed.
        p.   cm. — (Writings from the ancient world ; no. 7)
    Includes bibliographical references and index.
    ISBN 0-7885-0551-3 (alk. paper).
    1. Hittites—Treaties. 2. Law, Hittite—Sources.   I. Hoffner, Harry A. II. Title. III. Series.
KL4712.2.A4   1999
341'.0264392—dc21   99-14347
                                                                                    CIP

Printed in the United States of America
on acid-free paper.

99 00 01 02 03 04 05 06 07 08 — 10 9 8 7 6 5 4 3 2 1

Contents

v

II. DIPLOMATIC CORRESPONDENCE

III. MISCELLANEOUS TEXTS

Series Editor's Foreword

Writings from the Ancient World is designed to provide up-to-date, readable, English translations of writings recovered from the ancient Near East.

The series is intended to serve the interests of general readers, students, and educators who wish to explore the ancient Near Eastern roots of Western civilization, or compare these earliest written expressions of human thought and activity with writings from other parts of the world. It should also be useful to scholars in the humanities or social sciences who need clear, reliable translations of ancient Near Eastern materials for comparative purposes. Specialists in particular areas of the ancient Near East who need access to texts in the scripts and languages of other areas will also find these translations helpful. Given the wide range of materials translated in the series, different volumes will appeal to different interests. But these translations make available to all readers of English the world's earliest traditions as well as valuable sources of information on daily life, history, religion, etc. in the preclassical world.

The translators of the various volumes in this series are specialists in the particular languages and have based their work on the original sources and the most recent research. In their translations they attempt to convey as much as possible of the original texts in a fluent, current English. In the introductions, notes, glossaries, maps, and chronological tables, they aim to provide the essential information for an appreciation of these ancient documents.

Covering the period from the invention of writing (by 3000 B.C.E.) down to the conquests of Alexander the Great (ca. 330 B.C.E.). the ancient Near East comprised northeast Africa and southwest Asia. The cultures represented within these limits include especially Egyptian, Sumerian, Babylonian, Assyrian, Hittite, Ugaritic, Aramean, Phoenician, and Israelite. It is hoped that Writings from the Ancient World will eventually produce translations of most of the many different genres attested in these cultures: letters—official and private, myths, diplomatic documents, hymns, law collections, monumental inscriptions, tales, and administrative records, to mention but a few.

The preparation of this volume was supported in part by a generous grant from the Division of Research Programs of the National Endowment for the Humanities. Significant funding has also been made available by the Society of Biblical Literature. In addition, those involved in preparing this volume have received financial and clerical assistance from their respective institutions. Were it not for these expressions of confidence in our work, the arduous tasks of preparation, translation, editing, and publication could not have been accomplished or even undertaken. It is the hope of all who have worked on these texts or supported this work that Writings from the Ancient World will open up new horizons and deepen the humanity of all who read these volumes.

Simon B. Parker
Boston University School of Theology

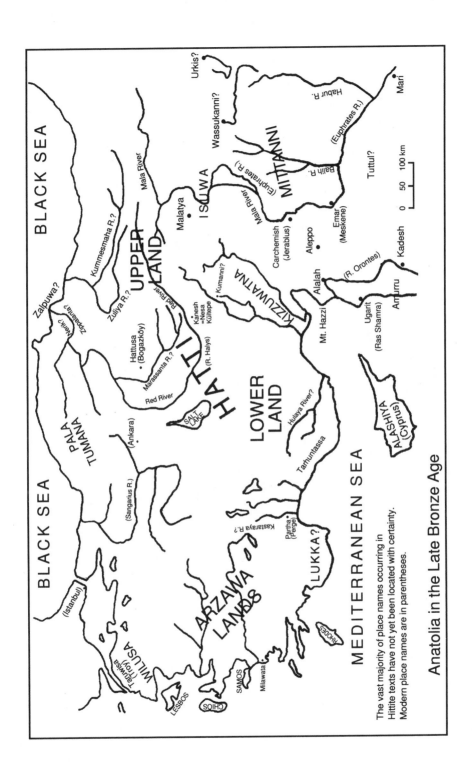

Anatolia in the Late Bronze Age

The vast majority of place names occurring in
Hittite texts have not yet been located with certainty.
Modern place names are in parentheses.

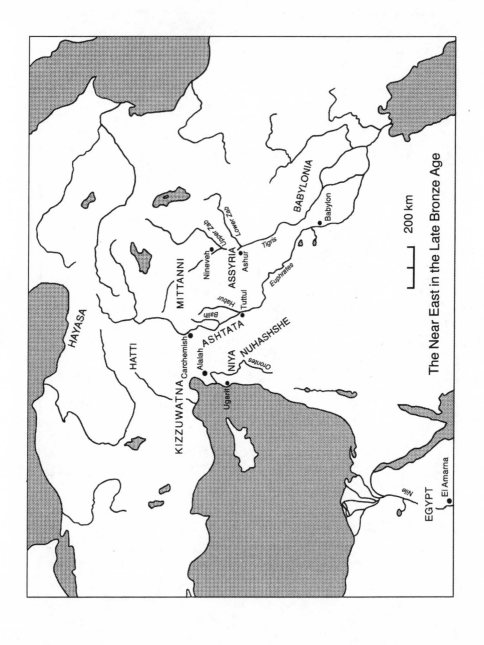

The Near East in the Late Bronze Age

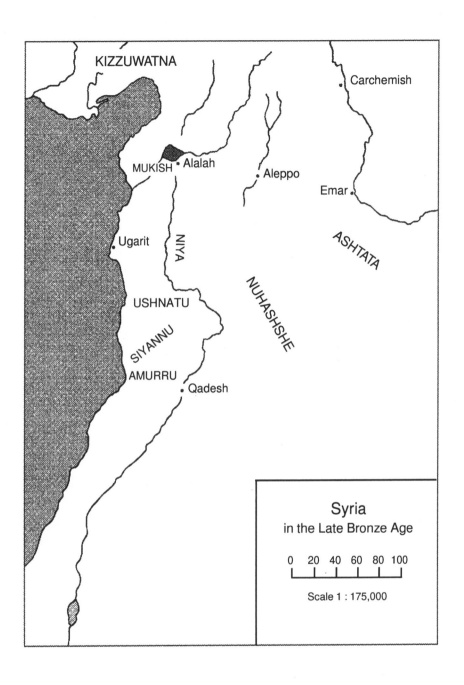

KIZZUWATNA

Carchemish

MUKISH · Alalah

Aleppo

Emar

Ugarit

NIYA

ASHTATA

USHNATU

NUHASHSHE

SIYANNU

AMURRU

Qadesh

Syria
in the Late Bronze Age

0   20 40 60 80 100

Scale 1 : 175,000

Chronological Chart*

Date	Hatti	Kizzuwatna	Carchemish	Aleppo
	Telipinu			
1500	Tahurwaili			
	Alluwamna			
	Hantili II	Paddatissu		
1450	Zidanta II			
	Huzziya II			
	Muwattalli I			
1400	Tudhaliya II	Sunashshura		
	Arnuwanda I			
	Tudhaliya III			
1350	Suppiluliuma I		Piyassili	Telipinu
	Arnuwanda II			
	Mursili II		Sahurunuwa	
1300	Muwattalli II			Talmi-Sharrumma
	Urhi-Teshshup			
	Hattusili III		Ini-Teshshup	
1250	Tudhaliya IV			
	Kurunta			
	Arnuwanda III		Talmi-Teshshup	
1200	Suppiluliuma II			

*Dates for the reigns of Hittite kings are known only approximately.

Chronological Chart

Ugarit	Amurru	Egypt	Assyria	Babylonia
Ammistamru I		Amenhotep III		
Niqmaddu II	Aziru	Akhenaten	Assur-uballit I	
Ar-Halba	Ari-Teshshup			
Niqmepa	Tuppi-Teshshup	Horemhab		
	Benteshina	Seti I	Adad-nirari I	
	Shapili	Ramses II		Kadashman-Turgu
	Benteshina		Shalmaneser III	Kadashman-Enlil II
Ammistamru II	Shaushga-muwa	Merneptah	Tukulti-Ninurta I	
Ibiranu				
Ammurapi				

Abbreviations

AfO	*Archiv für Orientforschung*
AJA	*American Journal of Archaeology*
AJSL	*American Journal of Semitic Languages*
AnSt	*Anatolian Studies*
AoF	*Altorientalische Forschungen*
ArOr	*Archiv Orientální*
AttiAccTosc	*Atti dell'Accademia Toscana di Scienze e Lettere "La Colombaria"*
BA	*Biblical Archaeologist*
BiOr	*Bibliotheca Orientalis*
CTH	*Catalogue des Textes hittites* (Laroche 1971). Numbers refer to entries, not pages.
IF	*Indogermanische Forschungen*
IM	*Istanbuler Mitteilungen*
JCS	*Journal of Cuneiform Studies*
JKF	*Jahrbuch für kleinasiatische Forschungen*
JNES	*Journal of Near Eastern Studies*
KZ	*Zeitschrift für vergleichende Sprachforschung* ("Kuhn's Zeitschrift")
MAOG	*Mitteilungen der Altorientalischen Gesellschaft*
MDOG	*Mitteilungen der Deutschen Orientgesellschaft*
MIO	*Mitteilungen der Institut für Orientforschung*
OA	*Oriens Antiquus*
OLP	*Orientalia Lovaniensia Periodica*
OLZ	*Orientalistische Literaturzeitung*
Or	*Orientalia*
PAPS	*Proceedings of the American Philosophical Society*

RA	*Revue d'Assyriologie et d'Archéologie orientale*
RHA	*Revue hittite et asianique*
RSO	*Rivista degli Studi Orientali*
SAK	*Studien zur altägyptischen Kultur*
UF	*Ugarit-Forschungen*
VT	*Vetus Testamentum*
WO	*Die Welt des Orients*
ZA	*Zeitschrift für Assyriologie und verwandte Gebiete*
ZDMG	*Zeitschrift der Deutschen Morgenländischen Gesellschaft*

Explanation of Signs

Single brackets [ ] enclose restorations.
Angle brackets < > enclose words omitted by the original scribe.
Parentheses ( ) enclose additions in the English translation.
A row of dots . . . indicates gaps in the text or untranslatable words.

Acknowledgments

First and foremost I must thank my editor, Professor Harry A. Hoffner, Jr., whose careful reading of my manuscript rooted out many an error and stylistic infelicity. The series editor, Professor Simon B. Parker, contributed greatly to the clarity of presentation. It goes without saying that any remaining blunders are solely my responsibility. Thanks are also due to Professor Heinrich Otten, who generously allowed me to utilize several unpublished Boğazköy fragments: 1472/u and 219/w (No. 6B) and 242/w (No. 11). Finally, I am grateful to Dr. Billie Jean Collins, who provided me with bibliographic assistance.

Introduction[1]

In concluding that account of his career which historians call his "Apology," the Great King Hattusili III relates:

> And those who were already kings before me and who were on good terms (with Hatti) remained on the same good terms with me. They began to send me messengers, and they began to send me gifts. Such gifts as they continue to send me they had by no means ever sent to my fathers and forefathers. The king who owed me respect, respected me. But I prevailed over those lands which were my enemies. I added district upon district to the lands of Hatti. Those who had been enemies of my fathers and forefathers concluded peace with me. (Otten 1981: 26–29)

This passage illustrates the Hittite belief that foreign lands were either enemies or friends. Neutrality was not an option. The goal of Hittite foreign policy, whether carried out by peaceful or military means, was to reduce the number of hostile countries, thereby promoting both internal and international stability. Depending on factors such as their distance from Hatti, their level of culture, and their own military and economic strength, foreign lands could be rendered harmless either by annexing them to the Hittite empire as vassals, or by drawing them into an alliance as equals.

In either case, beginning in the final years of the Hittite Old Kingdom (late sixteenth century B.C.E.), if not earlier, a written treaty setting forth the rights and obligations of both parties was routinely concluded with each new ally. The importance of such documents for Hittite statecraft is reflected by the fact that over half of the treaties now known from the ancient Near East are from the Hittite archives. We presently have the texts of approximately thirty-five records of this sort from Hatti, and several more treaties whose texts have not been recovered are mentioned in compositions of other types. (See Table 1 for a complete listing of preserved Hittite treaties.) The Hittites even concluded treaties with groups of

1

their troublesome Kaska neighbors (von Schuler 1965a: 109–45), although
experience demonstrated that the primitive level of social and political
organization of this people made such a practice fruitless, and their raids
on Hittite territory continued.

Many Hittite treaties were composed in the contemporary diplomatic
language of Akkadian (peripheral Middle Babylonian dialect), although
Hittite was also employed. As a general rule, diplomatic partners within
Anatolia received Hittite-language treaties, while those in Syria and
beyond were dealt with in Akkadian. In either language, these documents
were referred to by a pair of terms meaning literally "binding and oath"
(Hittite *išḫiul* and *lingai-*, Akkadian *rikiltu/rikištu/riksu* and *māmītu*). This
designation refers to the two most important constituent elements of the
agreements: the stipulations ("binding"), and the curses and blessings
("oath") by which the contracting parties invoked the gods as witnesses and
guarantors of these provisions. It is important to note that the formal written instructions issued to Hittite officials within Hatti itself — for instance
to the mayor of the city of Hattusa or to the members of the royal bodyguard — were also known as *išḫiul*. We may therefore conclude that the
Hittites made no fundamental distinction between internal and external
obligations to their king.

Since the Hittite monarch had to deal with many more subordinate
rulers than equals, by far the most commonly attested variety of diplomatic
agreement from Hatti is the vassal treaty, imposed by the Great King. (For
a thorough discussion of this type of document, see Korošec 1931.) Under
Mursili II, the Hittite ruler whose diplomatic activities are best attested,
such documents were issued for several states in western Anatolia (Nos.
10– 12), as well as for Amurru (No. 8) and Ugarit (No. 9) in Syria, and perhaps for other partners too.

A vassal treaty of this sort was composed by the chancellery of the Hittite king and presented to the subordinate ruler. The vassal was obliged to
swear in the presence of numerous deities to observe its provisions. Thus,
while the treaty text was a "binding" by the Great King, it was the "oath" of
the vassal. In one text we find the explicit statement: "These words are by
no means reciprocal. They issue from Hatti." (No. 13, §16). It must be
stressed that only the vassal — and not the Hittite overlord — swore an
oath in these instances. The text of the treaty presented to the subordinate
was engraved in cuneiform upon a tablet of metal (sometimes of silver, but
more often of bronze or iron). What archaeologists have recovered is in all
but one case (No. 18C) the file copies written on clay.

With some omissions and a certain variation in the order of components,
most of these vassal treaties follow a similar pattern:

I. *Preamble*: Here we find the name, titles, and genealogy of the Hittite
Great King. The vassal is not mentioned in this section.

II. Historical Introduction: This portion of the text sets forth the previous course of relations between Hatti and the vassal state, and especially between the individual Hittite king and the particular subordinate. Here it is demonstrated just why the latter should be loyal to Hatti — either because he had been favored by the Great King, having received, say, basic sustenance and military assistance (e.g., No. 6B, §§4–7), or because he had been spared the severe punishment he deserved (e.g., No. 11, §§4–8). Despite the certainty that their accounts of events are tendentious, these treaty prologues have served as a major source of information for modern students of Hittite history.

III. Provisions: These stipulations naturally vary greatly from text to text, but the primary duties imposed upon almost all vassals are the payment of tribute (Hittite *argamannu*; Akkadian *mandattu*) (e.g., No. 8, §5), the providing of military assistance when required — both in support of imperial campaigns in their vicinity and in the extreme case when the Hittite ruler is himself faced with internal revolt (e.g., No. 16, §§10–12), the renouncing of all independent foreign diplomatic contacts (e.g., No. 2, §58; cf. No. 27, §7), the extradition of Hittite fugitives who have entered their territory (e.g., No. 10, §6), and the guarantee of succession to the Hittite throne for the Great King's designated heir (e.g., No. 17, §6). In addition, Hittite vassals are forbidden to engage in warfare among themselves, but are rather required to present their differences to the Great King (or his deputy) for arbitration (e.g., No. 10, §§8–10). Occasionally it is demanded that the subordinate ruler make a yearly visit to the Hittite court to pay homage to His Majesty in person (e.g., No. 2, §9). Many treaty documents also delimit the frontiers of the vassal's realm (e.g., No. 18B, §§2–4).

IV. Deposition: The metal tablet upon which the treaty has been written is to be kept in the temple of the vassal's chief deity, where it will literally be under the oversight of the gods (e.g., No. 6A, §13). It is to be read aloud before the subordinate at stated intervals (e.g., No. 13, §16).

V. List of divine witnesses: The deities of both partners are summoned to act as witnesses to the provisions and oaths (e.g., No. 11, §§29–31).

VI. Curses and blessings: Here the vassal recites various self-curses before the deities guaranteeing the treaty, and the Great King pronounces a number of blessings upon the vassal, conditional of course upon his keeping his obligations (see No. 6A, §§15–16 for a colorful example).

These vassal treaties, with their explicit threats of divine retribution in case of violation, were the ideological glue which held the Hittite empire together. Nonetheless, some Hittite vassals were willing to risk the wrath of the gods and the might of the Hittite armies in order to achieve independence, as shown by the revolts which frequently broke out upon the death of a Hittite monarch. Therefore the Hittites also sought to bind their subjects to Hatti in other ways. The most important such expedient was the creation of personal bonds between vassal and overlord through diplomatic marriage (Pintore 1978: 71–78). Among others, rulers of Mittanni (No. 6A, §6), Hayasa (No. 3, §25), Amurru (No. 16, §5), and Ugarit (No. 38) all received Hittite princesses as wives. Other vassals were provided with a Hittite garrison for their capital (e.g., No. 10, §4). The duties of these Hittite units were no doubt as much to keep an eye on the activities of the local rulers as to protect them.

A special type of vassal treaty conferred what we might call "protectorate" status. We know that at various times rulers of Arzawa, Kizzuwatna, and Mittanni all occupied such a position, but the only protectorate documents that have come down to us are those concluded by Tudhaliya II with Sunashshura of Kizzuwatna (No. 2) and by Suppiluliuma I with Shattiwaza of Mittanni (No. 6). This type of treaty allowed the subordinate to save face by disguising his dependence. Thus, for instance, Sunashshura is promised that when he makes his annual visit to the Hittite court, all the courtiers of the Great King will rise to their feet upon his entrance (No 2, §9). Tribute was not collected from kings who ruled protectorates.

Relations of the Hittite Great Kings with rulers of equal status were codified in parity treaties. Although we know that the monarchs of Babylonia, Assyria, and perhaps Ahhiyawa in the Aegean were also considered to hold a rank equal to that of the King of Hatti (see No. 17, §11), and may have concluded written treaties with him, only two such agreements have survived: the very early treaty between a Hittite king whose name has been lost and Paddatissu of Kizzuwatna (No. 1) and that between Hattusili III of Hatti and Ramses II of Egypt (No. 15). Each of these documents is characterized by full equality between the parties. In contrast to vassal treaties, where the overlord imposes certain provisions upon the vassal and obliges him to swear to observe them, in these parity treaties neither party imposes anything on the other. Rather, each monarch in turn voluntarily assumes certain obligations. Then the other party takes on identical — or better, symmetrical — responsibilities. In particular, the Hattusili-Ramses agreement calls for the reaffirmation of former treaties, the mutual renunciation of aggression, a mutual defense pact, the guarantee of succession to the throne for the designated heir of the Hittite ruler, and the extradition of fugitives.

The absence of a guarantee for Ramses' succession is seemingly an exception to the rule of symmetry. But perhaps Ramses felt no need for such a provision, while as a usurper Hattusili feared that his offspring's claim to the throne might very well be challenged. In fact, the man supplanted by Hattusili, Urhi-Teshshup, was probably already living in Egypt at the time when this treaty was concluded, and Ramses was in a position to make sure that Urhi-Teshshup did not escape to Syria to cause trouble for his Hittite partner (see No. 22D, §§4–5).

In times of good relations among the great powers, there was a constant exchange of messengers among their courts. This may be illustrated by a line from the complaint of Hattusili III to the Babylonian King Kadash-man-Enlil II that he had made use of a flimsy pretext to cut off diplomatic traffic between their two realms (No. 23, §6): "[Only if two kings] are hostile do their messengers not travel continuously between them." Of course the Great Kings also on occasion sent envoys to their own vassals. Although their professional title may be literally translated as "messenger," the weighty responsibilities of war and peace shouldered by these ancient diplomatic travelers might justify for them the modern designation "ambassador." In order that the partner could be certain that the envoy was presenting his master's position accurately, he was also given a dispatch in Akkadian (see No. 2, §59; cf. No. 22F, §§10–14). Sixteen of these diplomatic letters have been translated in Part II of this work. Topics discussed in these documents include the conclusion of peace between empires (Nos. 22A–C), diplomatic marriage (Nos. 22D–F), the settlement of commercial claims (No. 23, §§12–13), the assumption of vassal status (No. 19), the payment of tribute (No. 21), and the extradition of fugitives (No. 28).

The messengers not only carried oral and written communications between royal courts, but also distributed presents among the rulers of highest rank. Indeed, in the Late Bronze Age much international trade in high-value goods was conducted under the guise of the exchange of diplomatic gifts (Liverani 1990: 205–82). Note that several of the letters included here close with an exact accounting of the precious materials that accompanied them. Also documented in this correspondence is the exchange among the Great Kings of various specialists, such as physicians (Nos. 22G and 23, §§12–13), magical experts (No. 23, §13), and artists (No. 23, §16) (Edel 1976; Zaccagnini 1983: 249–56).

Part III of this book presents edicts and other documents produced at the highest administrative levels of the Hittite empire. Primarily decisions elicited by the conflicts of Hittite vassals among themselves or by their relations with the central imperial authorities, these pronouncements were issued not only by the Great King and his chancellery in Hattusa, but also by the king of Carchemish, who served as a kind of viceroy for Syria. Among the matters dealt with in records of this sort are the assessment of tribute obligations (Nos. 28A–B, 31B, and 37), the drawing of borders (No. 31A), the adjudication of territorial disputes (No. 30, §§1–9), the extradition of fugitives (No. 33; cf. No. 30, §§10–11), the resolution of disputes of a commercial nature (Nos. 32 and 34), and even the inheritance and divorce of subordinate rulers (Nos. 35, 36A–B, and 38A–C).

Taken as a group, the documents collected in this book afford a glimpse of the complex system of imperial governance developed by the rulers of Hatti. In addition, along with the correspondence recovered from the ruins of the capital of the Egyptian kings Amenhotep III and Amenhotep IV/ Akhenaten (Moran 1992), they are our primary source of information concerning the conventions that structured international relations during the Late Bronze Age in western Asia.

On Translation, Transliteration, and Paragraph Divisions

The method of translation and transliteration employed here is basically that set forth in Hoffner 1990: 5–6. Note however, that while I follow Hoffner in rendering cuneiform "ḫ" as ordinary "h", I make a distinction in the treatment of cuneiform "š": When it appears in a Hittite-language context I have transliterated it as simple "s", but when "š" is found in an Akkadian or Hurrian proper name, where it was certainly pronounced as a palatal sibilant, I have rendered it as "sh".

For the most part, paragraph divisions in my translations correspond to horizontal rulings made by the scribes on the ancient tablets. However, in Nos. 15, 35, 36A, and 36B I have introduced the paragraphs myself. The numbering of the paragraphs runs consecutively through each text, even where gaps intervene, and is not necessarily identical to that found in the primary editions of these compositions. For the convenience of readers who wish to consult the cuneiform texts, I have given the lines of the original manuscripts (for a listing of which see "Sources") at the beginning of each paragraph. Of course, I have supplied the rubrics within the translations.

In the lists of divine witnesses to the treaties (e.g., No. 13, §§17–20) epithets directly follow the god or goddess to whom they belong, without definite article, as in "the Sun-god of Heaven, King of the Lands," or "Ishhara, Queen of the Oath."

SYNOPTIC TABLE OF HITTITE TREATIES[2]

CTH	Parties	Language	No. in this work
21	Telipinu of Hatti and Isputahsu of Kizzuwatna	Hittite and Akkadian	—
25	Zidanta II of Hatti and Pilliya of Kizzuwatna	Hittite	—
26	A king of Hatti and Paddatissu of Kizzuwatna	Akkadian	1

Notes

[1] For a brief general introduction to Hittite history and civilization, see Hoffner 1990: 1–4.

[2] These documents have been listed in chronological order, as far as this can be determined. The texts that have not been included in this volume are either mere fragments or too broken for connected translation.

Translations

1

Treaties

No. 1

Treaty between a King of Hatti
and Paddatissu of Kizzuwatna

During most of the Hittite Old Kingdom, Kizzuwatna (Cilicia of the Classical period on the southern coast of Anatolia) had been an integral part of Hatti known as the land of Adaniya. But by the late sixteenth century B.C.E. this region gained its independence, only soon to fall under the domination of the neighboring Hurrian state of Mittanni. Over the course of the fifteenth century, Hatti and Mittanni competed for hegemony over Kizzuwatna. The area ultimately returned to Hittite control once and for all under Tudhaliya II and was reabsorbed into the Hittite state under Suppiluliuma I. (On the history of Kizzuwatna, see Beal 1986; Desideri and Jasink 1990: 51–109). During the period when Kizzuwatna enjoyed full or partial independence, the Hittite kings contracted many of their earliest preserved treaties with its rulers.

Not translated in this volume because of their relatively poor state of preservation are accords between Telipinu of Hatti and Isputahsu of Kizzuwatna, between Zidanta II of Hatti and Pilliya of Kizzuwatna (Otten 1951), and between Tahurwaili of Hatti and Eheya of Kizzuwatna (Otten 1971: 66–68; del Monte 1981: 210–13). The latter document in particular is very similar to No. 1, itself a fragmentary treaty in which the personal name of the Hittite ruler is unfortunately not to be found among the recovered lines. It is clear, however, that this treaty is the last in the series of these early agreements and must be assigned to a Hittite king of the first decades of the fifteenth century, perhaps to Hantili II (Beal 1986: 431).

The primary concerns in what remains of this document, whose provisions are equal and reciprocal, are the extradition of political fugitives and the cross-border movements of transhumant populations.

Fugitives

§1 (lines 1'–5') [If a subject of the Great King plots against his lord and then enters the land of Kizzuwatna, and the Great King sends] after [the fugitive, saying thus: "He revolted against me. I will have him returned!" — If] the charge [is true, the fugitive must be returned. But if the fugitive denies it, claiming:] "I [myself] am not in revolt against him" — his word [is false. Whatever trustworthy Hittites] Paddatissu [may ask] for an oath [will swear an oath about this], and the fugitive must be returned.

§2 (lines 6'–10') If a subject of Paddatissu plots against his lord and then enters Hatti, [and] Paddatissu sends after the fugitive, saying as follows: "He revolted against me. I will have him returned!" — [If] the charge is true, the fugitive must be returned. But if the fugitive denies it, claiming: "I [myself] am not in revolt against him" — his word is false. Whatever trustworthy men of the land of Kizzuwatna [the Great King] may ask for an oath will swear an oath about this, and the fugitive must be returned.

Respect for Envoys

§3 (lines 11'–13') [If] the Great [King] sends either his son or his subject to Paddatissu, Paddatissu shall not harm him. And if Paddatissu sends either his son or his subject [to] the Great King, the Great King shall not harm him.

Reporting of Sedition

§4 (lines 14'–16') [If] a subject of the Great King plots against his lord while remaining in Hatti, and Paddatissu hears about it, he must report it to the Great King. If a subject of Paddatissu plots [against] his lord while remaining in the land of Kizzuwatna, and the Great King hears about it, he must report it to Paddatissu.

Transhumant Populations

§5 (lines 17'–20') [If the population of a settlement] of the Great King, including its women, its goods, and its large and small cattle, sets out and enters the land of Kizzuwatna, [Paddatissu] must seize them and return them to the Great King. And if the population of a settlement of Paddatissu, [including] its [women], its goods, and its large and small cattle, sets out and enters Hatti, [the Great King] must seize them and return them to Paddatissu.

§6 (lines 21'–29') [If some] Hittite falsely reports: "The population of a settlement, including its women [and its goods], has set out and has entered the land of Kizzuwatna," but the population of the settlement, including its women, has [by no means] set out, and if indeed there are those in the settlement who are busy with herding — [then whatever] trustworthy Hittite Paddatissu may ask for an oath [will swear an oath about this], and the women must be returned. And if someone of the land of Kizzuwatna [falsely] reports: "The population of a settlement, including its women and its goods, has set out and has entered [Hatti]," but the population of the settlement, including its women, has by no means set out, and if indeed there are those [in the settlement who] are busy with herding — then whatever trustworthy man of the land of Kizzuwatna [the Great King] may ask [for an oath] will swear an oath about this, and the women must be returned.

§7 (lines 30'–33') [If] ox[herds] go down from Hatti into the border districts of Kizzuwatna, a thief [among them(?)] who steals something must make full twofold restitution to his victim and pay thirty shekels of silver. [If he . . .] does not pay, then he is indeed a thief and must be . . . [If . . .] not, the oxherd will go to the thief, and he must be put to death.

§8 (lines 34'–37') [If oxherds] enter the border districts of Hatti from the land of Kizzuwatna, [a thief among them(?)] who steals something must make full twofold restitution to his victim and pay thirty shekels of silver. [If he . . .] does [not] pay, then he is indeed a thief and must be . . . [If . . . not], the oxherd will go to the thief, and he must be put to death.

§9 (lines 38'–40') [If a Hittite strikes a man of the land] of Kizzuwatna with a bronze spear, a bronze knife, or a bronze ax . . . [*The remainder of the preserved text, which seems to deal with the compensation due for the murder of a man of Kizzuwatna by a Hittite, or of a Hittite by a Kizzuwatnaean, is too fragmentary for translation.*]

No. 1A
Treaty between Arnuwanda I of Hatti and the Men of Ismerika

Renewed Hittite influence over Kizzuwatna was exercised in part through military colonists established in the region. This treaty concluded with soldiers from the southern Anatolian region of Ismerika shows that at least some of these colonists were not Hittites, but subject allies. Note §§13–15 where Ismerikans are identified both with their home towns and with the settlements in Kizzuwatna where they are stationed. In addition to demanding from these subordinates obedience and loyalty to Hatti and its royal family (§§3–8, 10–12), the text requires that they work closely with the local Hittite authorities in monitoring the Kizzuwatnaean population (§§9–10).

Unlike a typical Hittite treaty involving the Great King and a single monarch, this document was imposed upon a group of persons, referred to collectively as "the men of Ismerika." So that all of the vassals would be bound by the oath, each is listed by name (see von Schuler 1965b: 445–55).

Preamble; Divine Witnesses

§1 (obv. 1–5) Thus says Arnuwanda, [Great King, King of Hatti. I have placed the following matters] under oath [for the men of the land of Ismerika: You shall be well-disposed(?) to the King, to the Queen, to the sons of the King], and to the land of Hatti. [. . . I have] now [summoned] the Thousand [Gods to assembly for this oath, and I have called them to witness. They shall be] witnesses.

§2 (obv. 5–11) The Sun-god, the Storm-god, the Sun-goddess of [Arinna, . . .], the Storm-god [of . . .], the War-god, [. . .], the Storm-god of Aleppo, [. . .], Katahha of Ankuwa, [. . .], Teshshup of Aleppo, Hebat [of Aleppo . . .], the gods of heaven and earth, [. . .]

Loyalty to Royal Family

§3 (obv. 12–18) [All you men of the land of Ismerika shall be] justly and sincerely [well-disposed(?)] to the King, to the Queen, [and to the sons of the King]. No one [shall do] evil [to the King, to the Queen, or to the sons of the King. But if someone] does do evil [to them], these [oath gods shall seize] him [. . . and] destroy [him], together with his household, his fields, [his vineyards, his threshing-floors, his oxen, and his sheep, and together with] his renown, his progeny, [and his . . .]

§4 (obv. 19–22) [. . .] the King, the Queen, or the sons of the King [. . .] Or to him [. . . No] one shall seek [evil against them. If someone does seek evil against them, these oath gods shall destroy him, together with] his wife and [his] sons.

[*Only a few signs of the initial line of the next paragraph remain. A gap of 15–20 lines follows.*]

Alliance

§5 (obv. 3'–6') [. . .] let him be [. . .] And whenever an enemy(?) [. . . no one] will refuse (to go) into battle. And [. . .] No one shall send a message [to another land on his own authority. If a messenger comes to you from a foreign land], you shall not conceal him. Seize him and [send him off to My Majesty].

§6 (obv. 7'–12') [. . .] But whenever an enemy [penetrates(?)] into Kizzuwatna, and you [hear] of it, you will set [. . .] aright, and you will [thereby] put your mind at rest. [If you say to yourselves(?)], "He [will . . .] on our side; on our side [he will . . . ," then . . .] Then [you shall bring] the matter [immediately] to the attention of [the governor of the border province . . .] you shall not allow in. [. . .] you shall bring [to] My Majesty.

Fugitives

§7 (obv. 13'–16') If [a fugitive comes to you] from a neighboring land, [that] fugitive—[be he some] person's [relative by marriage], or either someone's father [or mother, or someone's brother, or] someone's [sister]—furthermore, [if] he comes as a fugitive, then he will take(?) [. . .] But no [one] shall take him for himself (as a slave).

§8 (obv. 17'–20') You shall [not] denigrate Hatti before fugitives, but [you shall] rather [praise(?)] it to them. Deploy the army . . . over your [. . .] they will be guarded. But you shall [not] protect them behind the others. Protecting your own [. . .] is correct.

Reporting of Sedition

§9 (obv. 21'–24') If someone speaks an evil word before you—whether he is a governor of a border province, [or he is a nobleman], or he is one of modest rank; or if he is a Hittite, or he is a Kizzuwatnaean, [. . .]; or if he is some person's father, mother, brother, sister, or his child or [his] relative by marriage—[. . .] No one shall conceal the one who speaks an (evil) word, but shall rather seize him and make him known.

Punishment of Rebels

§10 (obv. 25'–28') If within the land a single city commits an offence, you [men] of the land of Ismerika will intervene, and you shall defeat [that city], together with its men. You shall bring the civilian captives before My Majesty, but [take] the oxen and sheep for yourselves. If within a city a single household [commits an offence], that household, including its free men, shall perish. You shall bring its servants to My Majesty, but [take] the oxen and sheep for yourselves. [If] a single man commits an offence, [he alone shall die].

Military Obligations

§11 (rev. 1–6) In regard to your troops for the standing army—formerly one hundred fifty soldiers from the land of Ismerika reported regularly, but now I have made [a revised requirement] for you. Sixty of your regular soldiers shall be available. Only free men who [. . .] shall march. No servant or hired substitute shall report to the standing army. [This shall be placed] under oath. But even when the land becomes populous, the requirement will remain in effect concerning the troops for the standing army. In whatever unit of the standing army a servant or a hired substitute [is discovered]—it will be counted against you, the men of Ismerika, as an offence.

Loyalty to Hittite Dynasty

§12 (rev. 7–10) All you men of the land of Ismerika are now parties to his oath to [My Majesty]. In the future protect the King, the Queen, the sons [of the King], and the land of Hatti. And later your [sons] will be sworn allies of the sons of the King. And your grandsons too will be sworn allies of the grandsons of the King. [The sky] above [you] is free, and the earth beneath you is free (but you are constrained). In the future protect the King, the Queen, and the sons of the King to the first and second generation.

Participants

§13 (rev. 11–16) All [you] men of the land of Ismerika must stand by the oath. Ehalte, the Ismerikan—secondarily, Zazlippa is his city [in the land] of Kizzuwatna. He had been in Washshukanni. [. . .], the Ismerikan—Washshukanni is his city in Kizzuwatna. Warla-ziti, the Ismerikan—Ziyaziya is [his] city, [but] Washshukanni is [his] city in Kizzuwatna. [. . .], the Ismerikan—Ziyaziya is his city, but Washshukanni is his [city] in Kizzuwatna. [. . .], the Ismerikan—Zizziya is his city, but he is in Washshukanni.

§14 (rev. 17–21) [. . .] . . . , Nani, and Ali-wasu, four Ismerikans—[. . .] is [their] city in Kizzuwatna. Mazziya and Hurlanni, two Ismerikans—

Adara is their [city in Kizzuwatna], but Arana is their city. Akiya and Huha-nani, [two] Ismerikans—Terusa is their city [in Kizzuwatna]. Zardumanni and [. . .], two [Ismerikans— . . . is their city], but Uriga is their [city] in Kizzuwatna.

§15 (rev. 22–24) [. . .], from [. . .]—Urussa is his [city] in Kizzuwatna. [. . . of] Irrita—[Urussa(?)] is his [city] in Kizzuwatna. [. . .] and Pariya-muwa, two men from Zazlippa, and [. . .]—[. . . is their city in Kiz-zuwatna].

Oath

§16 (rev. 25–26) [You men of] Ismerika will come. You shall place your own wives, sons, [and relatives by marriage under this] oath. [You shall] all [. . .]

Curse

§17 (rev. 27–28) These oath gods [shall seize whoever] transgresses the oath, and [shall destroy him . . .], together with his household, his field, his vineyard, [his threshing-floor, his oxen, and his sheep].

§18 (rev. 29) They shall roast [his renown] and his [progeny . . . like grain(?)]. [*Text breaks off.*]

No. 2
Treaty between Tudhaliya II of Hatti and Sunashshura of Kizzuwatna

For years Hittitologists disputed the identity of the particular Hittite Great King to whom this treaty should be attributed, but a reexamination of its initial line has determined that it was issued by Tudhaliya II (Wilhelm 1988). Other recent scholarship has established that it is not necessary to posit more than one ruler of Kizzuwatna named Sunashshura, nor to assign the various Akkadian and Hittite-language tablets and fragments making up this text to different periods (del Monte 1981: 219–20; Beal 1986).

The textual history of No. 2 is complicated, reflecting the increasing domination of Hatti over Kizzuwatna during the reign of Sunashshura. The Akkadian-language text incorporates portions of an older document more or less verbatim: §§11–46 may be recognized as an earlier parity treaty (Korošec 1982), in contrast to the surrounding context in which Sunash-shura is clearly the subordinate of the Hittite monarch and must even pay a

visit of obeisance to the latter (§§9–10). In the description of frontiers
which closes the Akkadian treaty, §§62–64 retain the earlier designation of
Kizzuwatna as "the land of Adaniya" and also refer to the Hittite ruler as
"Great King," while the later title conventionally translated as "My/Your/
His Majesty" is employed throughout the remainder of the text.

The fragmentary Hittite-language composition is not a direct rendering
of the Akkadian, but rather a parallel text dealing with some of the same
topics. I have therefore translated it separately. It has come down to us in
two versions, one (Text B) seemingly slightly older than the other. That this
manuscript is also prior to all portions of the present Akkadian treaty is
suggested by its §§12–13, which allow for benevolent neutrality if one of
the partners goes to war with Mittanni, while the Akkadian text requires
that the enemy of one party equally be the enemy of the other.

Matters of security, both internal and external, and particularly the position of Kizzuwatna over against Mittanni, are the dominant concerns of
No. 2.

Akkadian Text

Preamble

§1 (A i 1–4) Seal of Tudhaliya, [Great King, King of Hatti(?)]. When with
[Sunashshura(?) . . .] They [swore] an oath to one another and concluded
this treaty with one another.

Historical Introduction

§2 (A i 5–7) Formerly, in the time of my grandfather, Kizzuwatna came
into the possession of Hatti, but afterwards the land of Kizzuwatna freed
itself from Hatti and turned to the land of Hurri.

§3 (A i 8–13) When the people of the land of Isuwa, [subjects] of My
Majesty, [commenced] hostilities against My Majesty, I, My Majesty, went
[in battle] against them. I overpowered the land of Isuwa, and [the
Isuwans] fled before My Majesty. They went down into the land of Hurri. I,
My Majesty, sent to the ruler of Hurri: "Return my subjects!" But the ruler
of Hurri sent back to My Majesty thus: "No!"

§4 (A i 14–19) "The populations of these cities had previously, in the
time of my grandfather, come to the land of Hurri and settled here. And
indeed they afterwards went as fugitives to Hatti. Now, finally, the cattle
have chosen their stable. They have definitely come to my land."

§5 (A i 20–24) The ruler of Hurri did not return my subjects to My Majesty, but dispatched his infantry and his chariotry. In the absence of My Majesty they plundered the land of Isuwa. They took to the land of Hurri whatever civilian captives, oxen, and sheep they captured, while I, My Majesty, remained elsewhere for battle [against] another enemy.

§6 (A i 25–29) The [ruler of] Hurri transgressed the oath, so I, My Majesty, sent as follows to the ruler of Hurri: "If some land were to free itself from you and turn to Hatti, then how would this matter be?" The ruler of Hurri sent to me as follows: "Exactly the same!"

§7 (A i 30–33) Now the people of the land of Kizzuwatna are Hittite cattle and have chosen their stable. They freed themselves from the ruler of Hurri and turned to My Majesty. The ruler of Hurri offended against Hatti, and he offended gravely against the land of Kizzuwatna.

§8 (A i 34–37) The land of Kizzuwatna rejoiced exceedingly over its liberation. Now Hatti and the land of Kizzuwatna are indeed freed from the oaths (to the ruler of Hurri). I, My Majesty, have now given the population of the land of Kizzuwatna its freedom.

Audience with Great King

§9 (A i 38–44) The Hurrians call Sunashshura a subject, but His Majesty has now made him a true king. Sunashshura must come before His Majesty and look upon the face of His Majesty. As soon as he comes before His Majesty, the noblemen of His Majesty <will rise> from their seats. No one will remain seated above him. As soon as <he wishes>, he may go back to the land of Kizzuwatna.

§10 (A i 45–48) Whenever His Majesty summons him, "Come before me!" — if he does not wish to come, whichever of his sons His Majesty designates must come before His Majesty. But he will definitely not have to pay tribute to His Majesty.

Succession

§11 (A i 49–54) His Majesty, the Great King, must not stir up revolt against Sunashshura nor be hostile to him. As His Majesty protects his own person and land, he must likewise protect the land and person of Sunashshura. His Majesty must protect for kingship whichever son of Sunashshura he designates as his successor.

§12 (A i 55–59) Sunashshura, the Great King, must not stir up revolt against His Majesty, nor be hostile to him. As Sunashshura protects his own land and person, he must likewise protect the person and land of His

Majesty. Sunashshura must protect for kingship whichever son <of> His Majesty he designates to Sunashshura as his successor.

Defensive Alliance against Revolt

§13 (A i 60–64) If someone revolts against His Majesty, [and he captures him], His Majesty shall do as he pleases (with him). [If the enemy is in] Hatti — if [he has seized or encircled a city — as] he is His Majesty's enemy, [he must likewise be Sunashshura's].

§14 (A i 65–ii 1) [If the Hittites] capture [this enemy, they will kill him. If] they give him [into the custody of Sunashshura, he must kill him. Sunashshura shall be at peace with Hatti. If His Majesty asks Sunashshura for help, he must restore him] to the throne. [If the Hittites do not kill that enemy or give] him [into the custody of Sunashshura so that he can kill him], Sunashshura [must conduct hostilities] against [Hatti] as far as he is able.

§15 (A ii 2–6) If someone [revolts] against Sunashshura, and he captures him, Sunashshura [shall do] as he pleases with him. If the enemy is in the land of Kizzuwatna — if he has seized or encircled a city — as he is Sunashshura's enemy, he will likewise be His Majesty's.

§16 (A ii 7–9) If the people of the land of Kizzuwatna capture this enemy, they will kill him. If they give him into the custody of His Majesty, he must kill him. His Majesty shall be at peace [with] the land of Kizzuwatna.

§17 (A ii 11–15) [If] Sunashshura asks His Majesty for help, he must restore him to the throne. If the people of [the land of] Kizzuwatna do not kill that enemy or give him into the custody of His Majesty so that he can kill him, His Majesty must conduct hostilities against the land of Kizzuwatna as far as he is able.

§18 (A ii 16–18) If someone, either a single man or a city, incites a revolt and begins war against His Majesty, Sunashshura must inform(?) His Majesty as soon as he hears of it.

§19 (A ii 19–21) If someone, either a single man or [a city], incites a revolt [and begins war] against Sunashshura, His Majesty must inform(?) [Sunashshura] as soon as he hears of it.

Defensive Alliance against External Enemies

§20 (A ii 22–23) If some other land begins war [against] His Majesty, Sunashshura must inform(?) [His Majesty] <as soon as> he hears of it.

§21 (A ii 24–25) If some other land begins war against Sunashshura, His Majesty must inform Sunashshura as soon as he hears of it.

§22 (A ii 26–28) If any city in the land of His Majesty begins war — as it is His Majesty's enemy, it will likewise be Sunashshura's — they will fight side by side.

§23 (A ii 29–30) Sunashshura will take the movable property, civilian captives, and troops of a city which he conquers. No one may challenge him.

§24 (A ii 31–33) And His Majesty will take the movable property, civilian captives, and troops of a city which he conquers. No one may challenge him. The city, however, will remain the territory of His Majesty.

§25 (A ii 34–36) And if some city in the land of Sunashshura begins war — as it is Sunashshura's enemy, it will likewise be His Majesty's — they will fight side by side.

§26 (A ii 37–38) Sunashshura will take the movable property, civilian captives, and troops of a city which he conquers. No one may challenge him.

§27 (A ii 39–41) And His Majesty will take the movable property, civilian captives, and troops of a city which he conquers. No one may challenge him. The city, however, will remain the territory of Sunashshura.

§28 (A ii 42–45) If some land begins war against His Majesty, that land is covered by Sunashshura's oath. His Majesty will request military assistance from Sunashshura, and Sunashshura must provide it to him.

§29 (A ii 46–48) If Sunashshura provides troops and says: "Lead them out against the enemy," His Majesty may lead them out. If he does not say this, they will remain on guard in his land.

§30 (A ii 49–50) If he leads the troops out against the enemy, the troops of His Majesty will take the civilian captives which they conquer. The troops of Sunashshura will take the civilian captives which they conquer.

§31 (A ii 52–55) If some land begins war against Sunashshura, that land is covered by His Majesty's oath. Sunashshura will request military assistance from His Majesty, and His Majesty must provide it to him.

§32 (A ii 56–58) And if His Majesty provides troops and says: "Lead them out against the enemy," Sunashshura may lead them out. If he does not say this, they will remain on guard in his land.

§33 (A ii 59–62) If he leads the troops out against the enemy, the troops of Sunashshura will take the civilian captives which they conquer. The troops of His Majesty will take the civilian captives which they conquer.

§34 (A ii 63–69) If a serious threat arises against His Majesty, and the enemy enters his land in force — if the land of Sunashshura is spared, you, Sunashshura, come together with your military levies to my aid. If you are busy with some matter, send your son at the head of your military levies. Come to my aid!

§35 (A iii 2–6) [If] a serious threat [arises against] Sunashshura, and the enemy comes into his land in force — if the land of My Majesty is spared, I, My Majesty, will come together with my military levies to your aid. If My Majesty is busy with some matter, I will send a high nobleman at the head of my military levies.

§36 (A iii 7–10) Whoever begins war against My Majesty will certainly also be Sunashshura's enemy. Sunashshura will certainly be my support. We shall do battle with him.

§37 (A iii 11–13) Whoever begins war against Sunashshura will certainly also be your enemy, Your Majesty. Your Majesty will be my(!) support. We shall do battle with him.

§38 (A iii 14–15) I, Sunashshura, must seek out whoever incites revolt against Your Majesty.

§39 (A iii 16–17) And you, Your Majesty, must certainly seek out whoever incites revolt against Sunashshura.

§40 (A iii 18–19) In the future Hatti must certainly not incite any evil revolt against the land of Kizzuwatna.

§41 (A iii 20–21) And in the future the land of Kizzuwatna must certainly not incite any evil revolt against Hatti.

§42 (A iii 22–24) If a Hittite hears some information concerning Sunashshura from the mouth of some enemy, he must inform(?) Sunashshura.

§43 (A iii 25–27) And if a man of the land of Kizzuwatna hears some information concerning His Majesty from the mouth of some enemy, he must inform(?) His Majesty.

§44 (A iii 28–30) If His Majesty sends his messenger to Sunashshura, Sunashshura must not harm him in any way. He must not ensnare(?) him by means of a magical plant.

§45 (A iii 31–34) If Sunashshura <sends> either his son or his messenger before His Majesty — or if Sunashshura himself comes — His Majesty must not harm them in any way. He must not ensnare(?) them by means of a magical plant.

§46 (A iii 35–36) Hatti and the land of Kizzuwatna shall be united. They must certainly maintain friendly relations with one another.

Alliance against the Hurrians

§47 (A iii 37–39) Furthermore: If any cities of the land of Hurri interfere in the cities of Sunashshura, we will fight side by side against the ruler of Hurri, in any of his cities.

§48 (A iii 40–44) The troops of My Majesty shall take all the civilian captives which they conquer, and the troops of Sunashshura shall take all the civilian captives which they conquer. I, My Majesty, will give the territory of that city to Sunashshura. I, My Majesty, will truly extend his land.

§49 (A iii 45–49) And in regard to whatever cities of the land of Hurri we defeat — I, My Majesty, will take all that I, My Majesty, desire. And I(!) will give to Sunashshura all that he desires. In the future the land of Kizzuwatna must not ever again turn to the land of Hurri.

§50 (A iii 50–55) Furthermore: If the ruler of Hurri hears that Sunashshura has freed himself from his sphere and has turned to My Majesty — if on account of [Sunashshura] the King of Hurri prepares some diplomatic gift, for the sake of Sunashshura, I, [My Majesty], will not accept his gift.

§51 (A iii 56–59) [If] the King of Hurri renounces his claim(?) on Sunashshura, saying as follows: "The land of Kizzuwatna belongs to Your Majesty. I(!) will indeed have no illicit relations(?) [with] the land of Kizzuwatna," < . . . >

§52 (A iii 60–63) [If] the King of Hurri stipulates under oath as follows: "[Your Majesty] should prepare a diplomatic gift exchange with me, the King of Hurri," [and then] the King of Hurri does not renounce his claim(?) on Sunashshura, I, [My Majesty], will not accept his gift.

§53 (A iv 1–4) [Too fragmentary for translation.]

§54 (A iv 5–10) I will never later give back to the King of Hurri anything of the land of Hurri which was turned over to the possession of Sunashshura — [neither] merchants nor the population of the city of Urussa. [If] afterwards the ruler of Hurri asks for them ever so politely, I, My Majesty, will not agree. The ruler of Hurri shall take an oath about this.

§55 (A iv 11–13) If this enemy of mine, of My Majesty, is indeed my enemy, then he is also your enemy, Sunashshura. This enemy must always have to fight with both of us.

Military Obligations

§56 (A iv 14–18) And if Sunashshura says as follows: "Were the troops of Hatti really to come to my aid, terror of them would be cast over my land!"

— nonetheless, as much infantry and chariotry as I, My Majesty, provide to you, Sunashshura must provide to me exactly as much infantry and chariotry.

§57 (A iv 19–24) Furthermore: When I, My Majesty, go into battle against another land — either against [the land] of Hurri or against Arzawa — Sunashshura must provide 100 teams of chariotry and 1,000 infantrymen and march in the army in the company of My Majesty. You must provide them with the travel provisions which they will get until they arrive in the presence of My Majesty.

Future Relations with Ruler of Hurri

§58 (A iv 25–31) Furthermore: We will certainly erase the tablet of the oath which had been made previously. We will indeed discard the word of the ruler of Hurri. Moreover, Sunashshura is no longer [the subject] of the ruler of Hurri. We will make another tablet. In addition, Sunashshura must not send his messenger to the ruler of Hurri, and he must not allow the messenger of the land of Hurri into his land.

Trustworthiness of Envoy

§59 (A iv 32–39) Furthermore: In regard to a tablet which I, My Majesty, send you — a tablet upon which words have been set down — and the words <of> the messenger, which he speaks orally in response to you — if the words of the messenger are in agreement with the words of the tablet, trust that messenger, O Sunashshura. But if the words of the speech of the messenger are not in agreement with the words of the tablet, you, Sunashshura, shall certainly not trust the messenger and shall certainly not take to heart the evil content of that report of his.

Frontiers

§60 (A iv 40–42) In the direction of the sea the city of Lamiya belongs to His Majesty and the city of Bitura belongs to Sunashshura. The border district will be surveyed and divided between them. His Majesty may not fortify Lamiya.

§61 (A iv 43–51) The city of Aruna belongs to His Majesty. Toward Bitura the border district will be surveyed and divided between them. His Majesty shall not fortify Aruna. The city of Saliya belongs to His Majesty and the cities of Zinziluwa and Erimma belong to Sunashshura. The border district will be surveyed and divided between them. His Majesty may fortify Saliya. The city of Anamusta belongs to His Majesty and the mountain of the city of Zaparasna belongs to Sunashshura. The border district will be surveyed and divided between them. His Majesty may fortify Anamusta.

§62 (A iv 52–57) Since long ago the frontier between the two of them has been as follows: the Great King should hold that which is on the city of Turutna's side of the border, and Sunashshura should hold that which is on the land of Adaniya's side. In the direction of the city of Luwana the city of Turpina is the frontier of Sunashshura. The Great King should hold that which is on Hatti's side, and Sunashshura should hold that which is on Adaniya's side.

§63 (A iv 58–61) The city of Sirika belongs to His Majesty and the city of Luwana belongs to Sunashshura. The Samri River is its frontier. The Great King must not cross the Samri River to Adaniya's side, and Sunashshura shall not cross the Samri River to Hatti's side.

§64 (A iv 62–66) In the direction of the city of Zilapuna the Samri River is the frontier. In the direction [of . . .] the Samri River is indeed the frontier of Sunashshura. Sunashshura shall not cross the Samri River to Hatti's side, and the Great King [shall] not [cross the Samri River] to [Adaniya's] side.

Hittite Text[1]

Defensive Alliance against Revolt

§1 (A ii 1') [. . .] if he does [not . . .] him and bring him to His Majesty.

§2 (A ii 2'–4') If he goes himself via another land to the land of Kizzuwatna, Sunashshura must seize him and send him back to His Majesty.

§3 (A ii 5') The provision for Sunashshura is the same.

Defections

§4 (A ii 6'–10') But if some other land, or a city, or an army defects to His Majesty, and His Majesty writes a cordial letter for Sunashshura: "That one now belongs to me. Acknowledge it," you, Sunashshura, shall not cause it to fall away. He shall keep his eyes turned to His Majesty.[2]

Fugitives

§5 (A ii 11'–iii 5) If a fugitive from Hatti goes to [Kizzuwatna], Sunashshura shall seize him and give him back to His Majesty. But if someone hides a fugitive, and he is discovered in his house, he must pay twelve unfree persons. If he cannot come up with twelve unfree persons, he himself [must be killed].[3] If a slave hides a fugitive,[4] and if his master will not make restitution on his behalf — will not pay the twelve unfree persons —

§6 (A iii 6–7) if his master does not make restitution on his behalf, he must forfeit the slave himself.

§7 (A iii 8) And the provision for Sunashshura is the same.

§8 (A iii 9–12) [If] a fugitive from Hatti goes to another [land], and from the other land goes back to Kizzuwatna, Sunashshura must seize him and [give] him back to His Majesty.

§9 (A iii 13) And the provision for Sunashshura is the same.

§10 (A iii 14–18) [If] a fugitive comes from another land, [*Remainder of Text A is too fragmentary for translation.*]

[*Gap of uncertain length.*]

Stance against Mittanni

§11 (B rev.! 1'–6') [If the King of the land of Mittanni] begins [war against the King of Hatti], and to him [. . . , His Majesty] will write [to Sunashshura: [" . . . and] recognize him/it!" Sunashshura shall [not] do any evil . . . [. . .] to him. But if he does not become an ally of His Majesty, I will defend my land in the face of [. . .] But he will write to His Majesty, and infantry and chariotry will not come [. . .] If for the sake of the infantry and chariotry < . . . >

§12 (B rev.! 7'–10') [If the King of the land of] Mittanni begins war against the King of Hatti, Sunashshura must not give [. . .] to him. He must not allow him to pass through his land, but must defend his land. He must not come [in a hostile manner(?) (against Hatti) together with] infantry and chariotry. If it suits Sunashshura, he will [come to the aid] of His Majesty. But if it does not suit him, he will not come.

§13 (B rev.! 11'–12') [If the King of the land] of Mittanni begins war against the land of Kizzuwatna, [if it suits] His Majesty, he will go to the aid of Sunashshura. But if it does not suit him, he will not go.

§14 (B rev.! 13'–15') [If someone] undertakes evil [against the King] of Hatti — either [the land] of Mittanni [or another land] — and Sunashshura hears(!) of it, it is a matter which must be reported [to His Majesty].

[*Text breaks off.*]

No. 3
Treaty between Suppiluliuma I of Hatti
and Huqqana of Hayasa

The land of Hayasa, of which Azzi (see §29) was a part, was situated somewhere in northeastern Anatolia, probably in the region that would later become Armenia. It stood at a lower stage of political development than Hatti, being ruled in the time of Suppiluliuma I by a number of tribal chiefs, paramount among whom was Huqqana. Note that this treaty partner is never referred to here as "king" of his land, and that it is foreseen that he must exert his powers of persuasion on another potentate of Hayasa rather than simply command him (§30).

The primary manuscript presents both the agreement with Huqqana (columns i–iii) and the text of an earlier accord with the worthies of Hayasa as a kind of appendix (column iv). The second manuscript seems not to have included the older document (see Carruba 1988).

The basic concern of the Suppiluliuma–Huqqana treaty is the loyalty of the subordinate to the Hittite king in the face of both internal and external threats to his rule. In addition, since Huqqana has entered the intimate circle of Suppiluliuma's court through marriage to his sister, the Hittite monarch issues several injunctions concerning the personal behavior of the vassal. Huqqana must not divulge any information he might learn about the affairs of the court (§§24–25), and he must observe the sexual customs of Hatti, even though they are stricter than those of his native region (§§25–28).

In order to underline the seriousness of these latter constraints, Suppiluliuma — or his scribe — has included in the text an admonitory anecdote concerning a certain Mariya, who was killed after being caught out in misconduct with a palace woman (§28). This man may be identical with the individual of the same name mentioned in the earlier treaty (§34), but is obviously not the man from whom Huqqana is ordered to divorce his daughter (§29). Perhaps the latter was a descendant of the first Mariya.

Introduction

§1 (A i 1–5) Thus says My Majesty, Suppiluliuma, King of Hatti: I have now elevated you, Huqqana, a lowly dog, and have treated you well. In Hattusa I have distinguished you among the men of Hayasa and have given you my sister in marriage.

Loyalty to Hittite Dynasty

§2 (A i 6–11) All of Hatti, the land of Hayasa, and the outlying and central lands have heard of you. Now you, Huqqana, recognize only My Majesty as overlord. And recognize my son whom I, My Majesty, designate: "Everyone shall recognize this one," and thus distinguish among <his brothers(?)>.

§3 (A i 12–21) Furthermore, benevolently recognize my sons — his brothers — and [my] brothers in brotherhood and comradeship. But beyond that you shall not recognize any other nobleman, whoever he might be, behind the back of My Majesty. Recognize [only] My Majesty and protect My Majesty! And as I, My Majesty, have treated you, Huqqana, [well] — if you, Huqqana, do not in the future benevolently protect My Majesty, and if the person of My Majesty is not as dear to you as your own person is dear to you, and the concerns of My Majesty have not taken precedence for you, you will transgress the oath.

§4 (A i 22–30) And if you are not well-disposed to the person of My Majesty, the soul of My Majesty, and the body of My Majesty, and do not hold me in a protective embrace in the same way as you are well-disposed to your own person, soul, and body, and hold yourself in a protective embrace, and if the concerns of My Majesty have not taken precedence for you — or if you ever hear evil concerning My Majesty from someone and conceal it from me, and do not speak of it to me, and do not point out that person but even hide him, you will transgress the oath.

Mutual Loyalty

§5 (A i 31–34) You, Huqqana, benevolently protect My Majesty, and stand behind only My Majesty. You shall not recognize anyone else beyond that. And I, My Majesty, will benevolently protect you. Later, I will protect your sons, and my son will protect your sons.

§6 (A i 35–40) And if you always behave well and benevolently protect My Majesty, then I, My Majesty, will later act favorably in regard to your sons, and my son will benevolently protect your sons. I, My Majesty, will protect you. I have now placed these words under oath for you, and we have now summoned the Thousand Gods to assembly in this matter.

Divine Witnesses

§7 (A i 41–47) The Sun-god of Heaven, the Sun-goddess of Arinna, the Storm-god of Heaven, the Storm-god of Hatti, the Storm-god of Aleppo, the Storm-god of Arinna, the Storm-god of Zippalanda, the Storm-god of Sapinuwa, the Storm-god of Nerik, the Storm-god of Hisashapa, the Storm-god of Sahpina, the Storm-god of the Army, the Storm-god of the Market(?), the Storm-god of Uda, the Storm-god of Kizzuwatna, the Storm-god of Pittiyarik, the Storm-god of Samuha, [the Storm-god] of Sarissa, the Storm-god of Hurma, the Storm-god of Lihzina, the Storm-god of the Ruin Mound, the Storm-god [of . . .], the Storm-god of Hulasa, Hebat of Uda, Hebat of Kizzuwatna,

§8 (A i 48–59) the Tutelary Deity, the Tutelary Deity of Hatti, Zithariya,

Karzi, Hapantaliya, the Tutelary Deity of Karahna, the Tutelary Deity [of the Countryside], the Tutelary Deity of the Hunting Bag, Aya, Ishtar, Ishtar of the Countryside, Ishtar of Nineveh, [Ishtar] of Hattarina, Ishtar, Queen of Heaven, Ninatta, Kulitta, the War-god, the War-god of Illaya, the War-god [of Arziya], all the deities of the army, Marduk, Allatu, [the Sun-goddess] of the Earth, Huwassanna of Hupisna, Ayabara of Samuha, Hantitassu [of Hurma], Katahha of Ankuwa, [Ammamma] of Tahurpa, the Queen of Katapa, Hallara of Dunna, the [mountain-dweller] gods, the [mercenary] gods, all the deities of Hatti, the deities [. . .] of the land, the deities of heaven, the deities of the earth, the mountains, [the rivers, the springs, the clouds], heaven, the earth, the great sea — they [shall be witnesses]. [*After the ends of three lines there is a gap of about thirty lines at the close of column i of Text A.*]

Curse

§9 (A ii 1) [. . .] and if you do not tell me about him, but even [hide] him,

§10 (A ii 2–9) or go over to him, abandoning My Majesty — if you act thus, these oath deities will not leave you alone, nor on your account will they leave alone that man to whom you go over. They shall destroy him. And the oath gods shall not neglect this matter in regard to both of you, and they shall not make it permissible for both of you. They shall destroy both of you together and thereby fulfill the wishes of My Majesty.

Blessing

§11 (A ii 10–13) But if you, Huqqana, protect only My Majesty and take a stand only behind My Majesty, then these oath gods shall benevolently protect you, and you shall thrive in the hand of My Majesty.

Alliance

§12 (A ii 14–21)[5] And when I, My Majesty, am with the army — if I go in battle to the aid of [. . .], you [must go on campaign] with me. [If I go on campaign] against either an enemy land or an enemy city, you must be with me. And if you are then my [border guard] and watchman, and if you look upon My Majesty as upon your own person, and if you think as follows: "Let whatever happens affect Huqqana, but let every good thing happen to His Majesty," you will uphold the oath.

§13 (A ii 22–25) Protect me from everything! Whoever is evil to [My Majesty] shall be evil to you. If he is My Majesty's enemy, he shall be your enemy. [If] a land or a city is My Majesty's enemy, it shall be your enemy.

§14 (A ii 26–31) [If] some enemy presents himself for My Majesty, or if someone [initiates] a revolt, and I write to you, if you do not come to me immediately with infantry and chariotry, but even prefer him — or if you hear about it yourself and do not then come to me immediately, these oath gods shall destroy you.

Alliance against Revolt

§15 (A ii 32–38) Or further, if some Hittite undertakes evil against me, whatever sort of person he might be — if you hear about him and do not tell me about him at that moment, but even cover up for him, thinking as follows: "Although I am bound by oath, I won't say anything or [do] anything. Let that man do as he will.

§16 (A ii 39–44) Furthermore [. . .]" And if [you think] such [a thought and] do not report the evil person [to My Majesty immediately], but you [even . . .] proceed to go over to his side, [these] oath gods shall destroy [you, Huqqana]. They shall not make it [permissible] for you.

§17 (A ii 45–51) Or if you do [something] like this: You undertake [something] against me, or [do not actually undertake it yourself], but someone else [does — if] you do something like that, [these oath] gods shall destroy [you, Huqqana. They shall not make] it permissible for you, and shall not forgive you for it.

§18 (A ii 52–59) Or whatsoever [evil] matter you hear of — [if] you conceal it from me and do not report it to me, [or] conceal that person [from me] and do [not report] him to me, but even hide him — we [have placed] such matters as these under oath for you. If you do not observe it but transgress it, then these oath gods shall destroy you.

§19 (A ii 60–69) But because people <are treacherous . . . > — And [if] because we do not find [your] obligation, if it is not set down on [that] tablet of the oath, [*Six lines too fragmentary for translation.*] [Then these oath gods shall not] forgive [you for this matter, and these oath gods shall destroy you]. [*The next three lines in Text A are too fragmentary for translation. Text B begins with §19, and four fragmentary lines follow a short gap.*]

§20 (B obv. 1'–7') [. . . Or] when I send [. . .] to the army, [and] you hear of [an evil deed] — if you do [not] write to me about it, but you [conceal it and] do not come [to me immediately], you will transgress the oath.

§21 (B obv. 8'–12') Or if it concerns(?) [the land] of Hayasa — if [you hear of] an evil deed, whatever sort of deed, and if [you do not come] to me [immediately] — or if I write [. . .] to you: "Now [this] evil deed has now occurred," and you do not [come] to me immediately, then [these] oath gods shall destroy you.

§22 (B obv. 13'–16') If you benevolently protect My Majesty, and [stand] behind My Majesty, then [these] oath gods shall benevolently protect [you. And they shall benevolently protect] the land of Hayasa which [I gave to you].

[*The next portion of the treaty, represented by the badly damaged upper part of column iii of Text A and the fragmentary close of the obverse of Text B, cannot be translated.*]

Secrecy

§23 (A iii 18'–22') [In respect to the fact that] they now bring you up to my palace, and that [you hear about(?)] the customs of the palace — it is important! You shall not [divulge] outside the palace what [you . . .] or what you hear.

§24 (A iii 23'–39') Or if I, My Majesty, [impart] to you [my] innermost thoughts and [reveal] my concerns to you — if I have [singled out] some person for favor, saying: "This person behaves well, so I, My Majesty, will treat him well" — if you go and repeat this matter to him — (it shall be placed under oath for you). Or if I have singled out a person for harsh treatment saying: "This person is evil, so I, My Majesty, will treat him harshly" — if you go and repeat this matter to him — (it shall be placed under oath for you). [Or] if I have singled out some land or city for favor, saying: "It behaves well, so I, My Majesty, will treat it well" — if you repeat it to that land or city — (it shall be placed under oath for you). Or if I have singled out that land or city for favor or for harsh treatment, and you go and repeat it to them — it shall be placed under oath for you.

Sexual Conduct

§25 (A iii 40'–49') Furthermore, this sister whom I, My Majesty, have given to you as your wife has many sisters from her own family as well as from her extended family. They belong to your extended family because you have taken their sister. But for Hatti it is an important custom that a brother does not take his sister or female cousin (sexually). It is not permitted. In Hatti whoever commits such an act does not remain alive but is put to death here. Because your land is barbaric, it is in conflict(?). (There) one quite regularly takes his sister or female cousin. But in Hatti it is not permitted.

§26 (A iii 50'–58') And if on occasion a sister of your wife, or the wife of a brother, or a female cousin comes to you, give her something to eat and drink. Both of you eat, drink, and make merry! But you shall not desire to take her (sexually). It is not permitted, and people are put to death as a result of that act. You shall not initiate it of your own accord, and if someone else leads you astray to such an act, you shall not listen to him or her. You shall not do it. It shall be placed under oath for you.

§27 (A iii 59'–67') Beware of a woman of the palace. Whatever sort of palace woman she might be, whether a free woman or a lady's maid, you shall not approach her, and you shall not go near her. You shall not speak a word to her. Your slave or your slave girl shall not go near her. Beware of her. When you see a palace woman, jump far out of the way and leave her a broad path. Beware of this matter of a palace woman.

§28 (A iii 68'–73') Who was Mariya, and for what reason did he die? Did not a lady's maid walk by and he look at her? But the father of My Majesty himself looked out the window and caught him in his offense, saying: "You — why did you look at her?" So he died for that reason. The man perished just for looking from afar. So you beware.

Miscellaneous Demands

§29 (A iii 74'–83') When you go to the land of Hayasa, you shall no longer take (sexually) the wives of your brother, that is, your sisters. In Hatti it is not permitted. When you come up here to the palace, [that] matter is not permitted. Hereafter you shall not take a woman from the land of Azzi as (an additional) wife. Divorce the one whom you have already taken. She shall legitimately be your concubine, but you shall not make her your wife. And take your daughter away from Mariya and give her to (his?) brother. Turn over the civilian captives of Hatti who have crossed over to Hayasa. Return the border districts of Hatti.

§30 (A iii 84'–86') You, Huqqana, seize and argue with whoever does not turn over civilian captives of Hatti, but conceals them within your borders saying: "Why don't you give them back?" Let him become angry with you.

[*In the approximately eighteen lines that have been lost at the beginning of column iv of Text A the treaty with Huqqana comes to an end and the earlier agreement with Mariya and the men of Hayasa begins. The first fifteen lines of column iv are too fragmentary for connected translation, but we may observe that they deal with the loyalty of a group of men, addressed in the second person plural, to the Hittite dynasty. Note:* "I have now put you [. . .] under oath." (*A iv 4'f.*) *and* "[If you] do not in the future benevolently [protect] My Majesty, and do not protect my sons, my grandsons, offspring of the first [and second generations] . . . " (*A iv 8'–11'*)]

Loyalty to Hittite King

§31 (A iv 16'–25') [And if some person seeks] evil [. . .] against [My Majesty, whatever sort] of person [it might be] — if [it is . . . , if it] is a . . . of the king or a brother of the king, [if it is . . .], if it is infantry or [chariotry, if it is] some male or female subject, [if it is] some [. . .], if it is some army, [if it is some . . .], if it is some land, [if it is some city(?)], if it is any [sort] of person —

§32 (A iv 26'–33') [if I write] to you, [and you do not come to me] immediately with infantry and chariotry, [but even] allow [him] to make his escape(?), thinking: "How will we follow [. . .], or will we go?," you will transgress the oath. [If] you [men] of Hayasa favor a Hittite (pretender), and abandon me [and] go over [to him], these oath gods shall destroy whoever of you commits this act, together with your wives, your sons, your households, and your land.

§33 (A iv 34'–40') If you do not always listen to me, whatever I write to you, or if you do not come to me immediately when I write to you for infantry and chariotry, or if some other enemy comes in battle against me, and I write to you, and you do not come immediately to [my] aid, but even allow him to make his escape(?), you will transgress the oath.

Blessing

§34 (A iv 41'–44') And [if] in the future you men of Hayasa benevolently protect me, I will benevolently protect you men of Hayasa, Mariya, and your male relatives in Hayasa. I will also benevolently protect the land of Hayasa itself.

§35 (A iv 45'–46') And if you behave well and benevolently protect My Majesty and Hatti, I, My Majesty, will behave well toward you.

Curse

§36 (A iv 47'–49') But if you in any way do evil, then I, My Majesty, will treat you badly. I, My Majesty, shall be free from this oath before the gods.

§37 (A iv 50'–59') And if [you men] of Hayasa and Mariya do not observe these words which I have now placed under oath for you, then these oath gods <shall> thoroughly <eradicate> your persons, together with your wives, [your] sons, your [brothers], your sisters, your families, your households, your fields, [your cities(?)], your vineyards, your threshing floors, your cattle, your sheep, [and your other possessions]. They shall also eradicate them from the Dark Netherworld below. I [myself] will not do any harm to the men of Hayasa, Mariya, or <the land> of Hayasa.

Colophons

Text A: Complete.

Text B: Second tablet of the oath [of Huqqana], . . .

No. 4
Treaty between Suppiluliuma I of Hatti
and Niqmaddu II of Ugarit

Although early in his initial campaign in Syria Suppiluliuma had written
to Niqmaddu inviting him to throw in his lot with Hatti (see No. 19), several of the latter's anti-Hittite neighbors urged him to join in resisting the
advance of the Anatolian (see No. 28A, §2). It seems as if the king of
Ugarit avoided taking a stand until his own territory had been invaded by
the armies of these other Syrian rulers, at which time he appealed to Suppiluliuma for aid (see §§1–2 here).

Hittite assistance indeed repulsed the intruders, but its acceptance
meant that Ugarit became a Hittite vassal, a status marked by the issuance
of the present treaty. Nonetheless, Suppiluluma sought to preserve the dignity of his new subordinate by refraining from entering Niqmaddu's territory, receiving his submission in the city of Alalah in the land of Mukish to
the north.

The text is not complete, but relatively little has been lost. It appears that
only three topics were included among the stipulations: the right of Niqmaddu to retain fugitives from the forces of his local enemies (§3), the
boundaries of Ugarit (§§4–5), and an alliance between Ugarit and Hatti,
stated in very general terms (§6). However, we learn from other documents
(Nos. 28 and 31B) that a rather large tribute was imposed on Ugarit.

Text A bears the impression of a stamp seal of Suppiluliuma and his
queen Tawananna (Schaeffer et al. 1956: 6, fig. 6), but the sealing of Text B
has been broken away.

Historical Introduction

§1 (A obv. 1–8) Thus says His Majesty, Suppiluliuma, Great King, King
of Hatti, Hero: When Itur–Addu, king of the land of Mukish; Addu-nirari,
king of the land of Nuhashshi; and Aki-Teshshup, king of Niya were hostile
to the authority of His Majesty, the Great King, their lord; assembled their
troops; captured cities in the interior of the land of Ugarit; oppressed(?) the
land of Ugarit; carried off subjects of Niqmaddu, king of the land of
Ugarit, as civilian captives; and devastated the land of Ugarit;

§2 (A obv. 9–28; B obv. 1'–2') Niqmaddu, king of the land of Ugarit, turned to Suppiluliuma, Great King, writing: "May Your Majesty, Great King, my lord, save me from the hand of my enemy! I am the subject of Your Majesty, Great King, my lord. To my lord's enemy I am hostile, [and] with my lord's friend I am at peace. The kings are oppressing(?) me." The Great King heard these words of Niqmaddu, and Suppiluliuma, Great King, dispatched princes and noblemen with infantry [and chariotry] to the land of Ugarit. And they chased the enemy troops [out of] the land of Ugarit. [And] they gave [to] Niqmaddu [all of] their civilian captives whom they took (from the enemy). [And Niqmaddu, king of the land] of Ugarit [. . .] honored the princes and noblemen very much. He gave them silver, gold, bronze, [and . . .] He arrived [. . .] in the city of Alalah before His Majesty, Great King, his lord, and [spoke as follows] to His Majesty, Great King, his lord: "[. . .] with words of hostility [. . .] Niqmaddu is [not] involved [. . .]" [*The following four lines on the obverse are too fragmentary for translation. After a gap of uncertain length, Text B resumes.*] And [Suppiluliuma, Great King], witnessed [the loyalty] of Niqmaddu.

Fugitives

§3 (B obv. 3'–20') Now Suppiluliuma, Great King, King of Hatti, has made the following treaty with Niqmaddu, king of the land of Ugarit, saying: If in the future fugitives of the land of Nuhashshi, or of the land of Mukish, or of other lands, leave those lands and enter the land of Ugarit and the service of the king of Ugarit, no other king of another land shall take them from the control of Niqmaddu, king of the land of Ugarit, nor from the control of his sons or grandsons, forever. My Majesty, Great King, has made a treaty to this effect.

§4 (B obv. 21'–23') Furthermore, all of the land of Ugarit, together with its border districts, together with [its] mountains, together with its fields, together with [. . .] [*Text B breaks off here. After a gap the treaty concludes with the reverse of Text A.*]

Frontiers

§5 (A rev. 1'–7') [*The first three lines are too fragmentary for translation.*] [. . . up to Mount] Igari-ayali, together with Mount Hadamgi, [. . .]itki-tiya, Panishtai, Nakhati, Halpi and Mount Nana, Shalma, Gulbata, Zamirti, Sulada, Maraili, and Himulli.

Alliance

§6 (A rev. 8'–15') [Now] Suppiluliuma, Great King, King of Hatti, Hero, has deeded by means of a sealed document these [border districts], cities, and mountains to Niqmaddu, [king] of the land of Ugarit, and to his sons and grandsons forever. Now Niqmaddu is hostile to my enemy and at peace with my friend. He has put himself out greatly for My Majesty, Great King, his lord, and has observed the treaty and state of peace with Hatti. Now My Majesty, Great King, has witnessed the loyalty of Niqmaddu.

Divine Witnesses

§7 (A rev. 16'–21') And whoever alters the words of this treaty tablet will transgress the oath. The Thousand Gods shall be aware (of the perpetrator, beginning with) the Storm-god of Heaven, the Sun-god of Heaven, the Storm-god of Hatti, the Sun-goddess of Arinna, Hebat of Kizzuwatna, Ishtar of Alalah, Nikkal of Nubanni, and the Storm-god of Mount Hazzi.

No. 5
Treaty between Suppiluliuma I of Hatti
and Aziru of Amurru

In the middle of the fourteenth century B.C.E. there emerged in the northern coastal region of what is today Lebanon the political entity known as Amurru. Founders of this state were Abdi-Ashirta and his sons, foremost among whom was Aziru. These men were originally minor vassals of the Egyptian pharaoh, but they exploited the unsettled situation attendant upon Hittite expansion to extend their domination over their neighbors and to incorporate much of their territory into Amurru. Although he initially sought to play off the Egyptians and Hittites against one another, Aziru was eventually forced to enter into the Hittite imperial system by accepting this vassal treaty from Suppiluliuma. (On the career of Aziru, see Klengel 1964a; Liverani 1983; and Singer 1991a: 148–58).

Alliance and the treatment of fugitives are the chief interests of this document, which displays many similarities with agreements concluded with other Syrian vassals of Hatti, especially Nos. 7, 8, 9, and 16. Indeed, since the paragraphs containing stipulations, divine witnesses, curses, and blessings in these treaties have been largely constructed from the same basic blocks of text, modified only slightly in each instance to fit the context, it is possible to restore many broken passages through mutual comparison (see del Monte 1986). For further treaties between Hatti and Amurru see Nos. 8, 16, and 17.

The Akkadian-language version of this text has come down to us in at least three copies, but only a single manuscript of the Hittite-language composition has been found. The present translation is based primarily on the Hittite text, but many restorations have been drawn from the Akkadian.

Preamble; Relations of Subordinate to Great King; Tribute

§1 (i 1–13) [Thus says My Majesty, Suppiluliuma, Great King, King of Hatti], Hero, Beloved [of the Storm-god: I], My Majesty, [have taken you, Aziru, as] my [subject, and I have placed] you upon [the throne of your father. And] if you, [Aziru, in the future do not protect] the King of Hatti, [your lord, and Hatti], you will transgress the oath. As your [soul, your person, your wives], your [sons], and your land [are dear] to you, [may the soul of the King, the person] of the King, the body of the King, and [Hatti likewise be dear to you]. In the future observe [the treaty of the King of Hatti, of his sons and grandsons], and of Hatti. 300 shekels [of refined gold], first-class and good, shall be your tribute [each year for the King] of Hatti. [It] shall be weighed out [with the weights] of the merchants [of Hatti. You], Aziru, [must come] yearly to My Majesty, [your lord], in Hatti.

Historical Introduction

§2 (i 14–26) Previously [. . .] the King of Egypt, the King of the land of Hurri, the king of the land [of Ashtata(?)], the king of the land of Nuhashshi, the king of the land of Niya, the king of the land [of Kinza(?), the king of the land of Mukish], the king of the land of Aleppo, and the king of the land of Carchemish — all of these kings — suddenly became hostile [to My Majesty]. But Aziru, king of the land [of Amurru], came up from the gate of Egyptian territory and became a vassal [of] My Majesty, [King] of Hatti. And I, My Majesty, Great King, [accordingly rejoiced] very much. Did not I, My Majesty, Great King, accordingly rejoice very much? As I to Aziru [. . .] Because Aziru [knelt down] at the feet [of My Majesty, and] came from the gate of Egyptian territory, and knelt [down at the feet of My Majesty], I, My Majesty, Great King, [took up] Aziru and ranked him (as king) among his brothers.

[*The remainder of column i, as far as it is preserved, and the beginning of column ii are too fragmentary for translation. The first portion of this damaged section seems to present the speech delivered by Aziru to Suppiluliuma at the time he was accepted into vassalage.*]

Offensive Alliance

§3 (ii 9'–24') Whoever is My Majesty's [friend shall be] your friend. [Whoever] is My Majesty's enemy [shall be your] enemy. If the King [of

Hatti] goes against the land [of Hurri], or Egypt, or Babylonia, [or the land of Ashtata], or [the land] of Alshi — [whatever foreign lands] located near your borders are hostile [to My Majesty], or whatever friendly lands — [that is, friendly to My Majesty] — located near [your borders — the land of Mukish(?), the land of Kinza, the land] of Nuhashshi — turn [and] become [hostile to the King of Hatti — when the King of Hatti goes to attack] this enemy, if you, Aziru, do [not] mobilize wholeheartedly [with infantry] and chariotry, and do not fight him wholeheartedly, you will have transgressed the oath.

§4 (ii 25'-39') [And] if I, My Majesty, send to you, Aziru, [to your aid], a prince or a high-ranking nobleman, [together with infantry] and chariotry, or if I send (forces) [to attack] another land — [if] you, Aziru, do not mobilize wholeheartedly [with infantry] and chariotry, [and] do not attack [this] enemy, you will have transgressed the oath. [And if] you commit some [misdeed, thinking as follows]: "Although I am under oath, [either let him defeat the enemy], or let the enemy defeat him. [I don't want] to know anything about it." — you will have transgressed the oath. [Or if] you write to [that] enemy, saying: "[The infantry and chariotry] of Hatti [are now coming to attack]. Be on guard!" — [you] will [have] transgressed the oath.

Ransom of Prisoners(?)

§5 (ii 40'-46') [And if] infantry and chariotry of Hatti [. . . , then . . .] shall [not] seize a single person [of] Hatti. [If you do not ransom(?) him] with alacrity, and [do not] send him [back] to the King of Hatti, you will [have] transgressed the oath.

Defensive Alliance

§6 (ii 47'-iii 3') [And if some] other [enemy] rises up against the King of Hatti, and [attacks Hatti], or if someone carries out a revolt [against the King] of Hatti, [and you], Aziru, hear of it, [and] do not wholeheartedly come to the aid [of My Majesty with infantry and chariotry], you will have transgressed the oath. [But if] it is not [possible] for you, Aziru, to come, [send your son] or your brother, together with infantry [and chariotry], to the aid [of the King] of Hatti. [Or] if [someone oppresses(?) you, either . . . , or anyone at all, and you send to the King of Hatti: "Come to my aid," then I, the King, will come to your aid, and I, My Majesty, will send] infantry and chariotry [to your aid, and they will defeat] that enemy [for you].

Relations of Subordinate to Agents of Great King

§7 (iii 4'–16') [Now], because Aziru turned [to] My Majesty for vassalage of his own free will, I, My Majesty, [will send] noblemen of Hatti, and infantry [and chariotry, to him from] Hatti to the land of Amurru. [Because] they will go up to your cities, protect [them]. Treat them in a gracious(?) manner. They shall walk like brothers before [you]. Protect [the King] of Hatti. [If] some Hittite seeks evil against [you], Aziru — if he seeks to carry off the spoils of a city or your(!) land, [then] he will have transgressed the oath.

Fugitives

§8 (iii 17'–28') And whatever [civilian captives] of that land [His Majesty] has carried off — civilian captives of the land of Hurri, [civilian captives] of the land of Kinza, civilian captives of the land of Niya, [or] civilian captives of the land of Nuhashshi — if [some] man or woman among them flees from Hatti and enters your land, you must not think as follows: ["Although I] am subject to the treaty and under oath, I don't want to know anything about this. They will be . . . in my land." [You], Aziru, must rather seize [them]. Send [them] off [to the King] of Hatti.

§9 (iii 29'–34') [If] someone speaks about [evil matters concerning] My Majesty before you, Aziru, whether [a Hittite] or your own subject, and you, [Aziru], do not seize him and send him to the [King] of Hatti, you will have transgressed the oath.

§10 (iii 35'–44') Whatever citizens of Amurru are living in Hatti, whether a nobleman or a slave of the land of Aziru — if you [seek] him from the King of Hatti — if the King of Hatti [gives] him back to you, then take him. But if the King [of Hatti] does not give him back to you, and he flees and comes [to you, if] you, Aziru, accept [him, you will have transgressed the oath].

§11 (Akkadian F 1'–3'; Hittite iv 1'–5') [And if] some [population sets out and comes to the land of Aziru, and you, Aziru, speak unfavorable words before them and direct them] to the mountains [or to another land, you will have transgressed the oath. You, Aziru, seize them and turn them over] to the King of Hatti. [If] you, [Aziru, do not seize] them [and turn them over] to the King of Hatti, [you will] have [transgressed the oath].

§12 (iv 6'–11') If a Hittite comes as a fugitive [from Hatti] and turns to you, [you, Aziru, seize] him [and] send him to the King [of Hatti]. But [if you do not send him, then you will have] transgressed [the oath].

§13 (Akkadian F 8'–9'; Hittite iv 12"–14") [If a fugitive flees] from the land of Amurru [and comes to Hatti, the King of Hatti will not seize him and return] him. [It is not permitted for the King of Hatti to return] a fugitive. [If a fugitive comes to the land of Amurru from . . . , you], Aziru, [shall not detain him, but] shall release him [to] Hatti. [If you detain him], you [will] have [transgressed the oath].

§14 (iv 15"–18") And if you, [Aziru, want something, request it] from the King of Hatti, and take [whatever the King of Hatti gives to you]. You shall not take what [the King of Hatti does not give to you].

Loyalty of Subordinate

§15 (iv 19"–26") You, Aziru [. . .] And you [. . .] And if you, [Aziru, do not seek . . .] the prosperity [afforded by Hatti] and the protection of Suppiluliuma, [Great King, King of Hatti], but rather seek the prosperity afforded by another [land — by the land of Hurri] or by Egypt [. . . And if you seek] another [protector, then you will] have [transgressed the oath].

[*Three lines too fragmentary for translation.*]

Divine Witnesses

§16 (iv 30"–32") I have now summoned [the Thousand Gods to assembly for this oath, and I have called them to witness]. They [shall be] witnesses. [*The Hittite text ends here, but copy A of the Akkadian version presents a long enumeration of the gods and goddesses guaranteeing the oath, and adds two further paragraphs:*]

§16 (*continued*) (A rev. 1'–10') [. . . Huwassana of] Hupisna, [Tapisuwa of Ishupitta, the Lady of Landa], Kuniyawanni [of Landa, NIN.PÌSAN.PÌSAN of] Kinza, Mount Lebanon, [Mount Shariyana, Mount Pishaisha], the mountain-dweller [gods], the mercenary gods, [Ereshkigal, all the male] deities [and female deities of Hatti], all the male [and female] deities [of the land of Kizzuwatna], all [the male and] female [deities] of Amurru, [all the primeval deities] — Nara, Namsara, Minki, [Tuhusi, Ammunki, Ammizzadu], Alalu, Antu, [Anu, Apantu, Enlil, Ninlil] — the mountains, the rivers, the springs, [the great sea, heaven and earth, the winds, and the clouds]. They shall be witnesses [to this] treaty [and oath].

Curse

§17 (A rev. 12'–16') [All the words of the treaty and of the oath which are written] on this tablet — [if Aziru does not observe these words of] the treaty and of the oath, [but transgresses the oath, then] these oath gods shall destroy Aziru, [together with his person, his wives, his sons, his grandsons, his household], his city, his land, and [his possessions].

Blessing

§18 (A rev. 17'–20') [But if Aziru observes these words of the treaty] and of the oath which [are written] on [this tablet], then these oath gods shall protect [Aziru], together with [his person, his wives, his sons, his grand-sons], his household, his city, his land, [and his possessions].

No. 6
Treaties between Suppiluliuma I of Hatti and Shattiwaza[6] of Mittanni

These two documents, which together constitute a single diplomatic agreement, are presented as if they were the words of Suppiluliuma I, on the one hand, and of Shattiwaza, on the other. However, similarities of language and content leave no doubt that both treaties were composed by the Hittite chancellery on behalf of the Great King. So dependent is No. 6B upon No. 6A that we can restore large damaged sections of the former from the latter without hesitation. Both were written in Hittite as well as Akkadian, but the Akkadian versions preserve by far the more complete text in each instance and form the basis for my translations.

This composition is a major source for the history of the expansion of Hatti into northern Syria in the mid-fourteenth century, during the course of which Suppiluliuma destroyed the state of Mittanni. Suppiluliuma's early efforts toward this end included the undermining of Tushratta, king of Mittanni, through the cultivation of a rival line of Hurrian rulers: Artatama II, who was styled "king of Hurri," and his son Shuttarna III. When Tushratta was murdered in a palace coup, one of his sons, Shattiwaza, fled to Hatti, where Suppiluliuma offered him protection as well as the hand of one of his daughters in marriage. When Shuttarna later proved himself to be a creature of Assyria, the Great King abandoned him in favor of his own protegé, Shattiwaza.

Although the details of many events and the relationship of the office of "king of Mittanni" to that of "king of Hurri" remain obscure (see Wilhelm 1982: 40–41, 49–53; Harrak 1987: 15–24), it is clear that Mittanni was eliminated as a major power and replaced with rump states under the control of Hatti and Assyria.

In order to preserve the fiction of Mittannian independence, No. 6B was written as an act of Shattiwaza. It differs from No. 6A chiefly in omitting almost all provisions. It consists only of historical prologue, god lists, and curses and blessings. The narrative portion is patently tendentious (see

Klengel 1969: 9–10; Beckman 1993), condemning the cooperation of
Artatama II and Shuttarna III with Assyria, while justifying the conduct of
Shattiwaza in casting his lot with Hatti.

Of particular religious and historical interest is the appearance of the
Indic deities Mitra, Varuna, Indra, and the Nasatyas among the divine witnesses of Mittanni (No. 6A §14, No. 6B §11 — see Thieme 1960).

No. 6A
Treaty between Suppiluliuma I of Hatti
and Shattiwaza of Mittanni

Historical Introduction

§1 (A obv. 1–16) When My Majesty, Suppiluliuma, Great King, Hero,
King of Hatti, Beloved of the Storm-god, and Artatama, king of the land of
Hurri, made a treaty with one another, at that time Tushratta, king of the
land of Mittanni, called for attention from the Great King, King of Hatti,
Hero. And I, Great King, Hero, King of Hatti, turned my attention to
Tushratta, king of the land of Mittanni: I plundered the lands of the west
bank of the River (Euphrates), and I annexed Mount Lebanon. A second
time King Tushratta was presumptuous to me, and spoke as follows: "Why
are you plundering on the west bank of the Euphrates?" — thus King
Tushratta — "If you plunder the lands of the west bank of the Euphrates,
then I too will plunder the lands of the west bank of the Euphrates." King
Tushratta desired to bring it under control(?): "If you plunder them, what
will I do to them? If a lamb, or if a kid of my land is . . . , I will cross over
from the east bank of the Euphrates." I, Great King, King of Hatti, main-
tained my pride before him. In the time of the father of the King of Hatti,
the land of Isuwa became hostile, so that the troops of Hatti entered the
land of Isuwa. In the time of my father, the troops of the city of Kurtalissa,
the troops of the city of Arawanna, the land of Zazisa, the land of Kalasma,
the land of Timana, Mount Haliwa, Mount Karna, the troops of the city of
Turmitta, the land of Alha, the land of Hurma, Mount Harana, half of the
land of Tegarama, the troops of the city of Tepurziya, the troops of the city
of Hazka, and the troops of the city of Armatana became hostile. But My
Majesty, Suppiluliuma, Great King, Hero, King of Hatti, Beloved of the
Storm-god, defeated them. Now the troops which had escaped from me
had entered the land of Isuwa, and all these troops and these lands which
had become hostile in the time of my father were dwelling beyond the land
of Isuwa among the enemy.

§2 (A obv. 17–24) And I, My Majesty, Suppiluliuma, Great King, King of Hatti, Hero, Beloved of the Storm-god, set out against the presumptuousness of King Tushratta. I crossed the Euphrates and went to the land of Isuwa. For the second time I overpowered the land of Isuwa and for the second time I made them my subjects. The troops and lands which in the time of my father entered the land of Isuwa: the troops of the city of Kurtalissa, the troops of the city of Arawanna, the land of Zazisa, the land of Kalasma(!), the land of Timana, Mount Haliwa, Mount Karna, the troops of the city of Turmitta, the land of Alha, the land of Hurma, Mount Harana, half of the land of Tegarama, the troops of the city of Tepurziya, the troops of the city of Hazka, and the troops of the city of Armatana — these troops and those lands I overpowered and returned to Hatti. I freed the lands which I captured; they dwelt in their places. All the people whom I released rejoined their peoples, and Hatti incorporated their territories.

§3 (A obv. 25–29) And I, My Majesty, Suppiluliuma, Great King, King of Hatti, Hero, Beloved of the Storm-god, reached the land of Alshi and the district of Kutmar, and I overpowered them. I gave it as a gift to Antaratli of the land of Alshi. I penetrated to the district of Shuta and plundered the district of Shuta. I reached the city of Washshukkanni in search of plunder. I brought to Hatti the cattle, sheep, and horses of the district of Shuta, along with its possessions and its civilian captives. But King Tushratta fled. He did not come against me for battle.

§4 (A obv. 30–37) I crossed the Euphrates again and overpowered the land of Aleppo and the land of Mukish. Takuwa, king of Niya, came before me for peace terms in the land of Mukish. But behind the back of Takuwa, his brother Aki-Teshshup, brought(!) the land of Niya, and the city of Niya to hostility. And this Aki-Teshshup united the chariot warriors. Heshmiya, Asiri, Zulkiya, Habahi, Birriya, and Niruwabi, along with their chariotry and their infantry, made common cause with Akiya, king of Arahati. They seized the city of Arahati and began war, thinking: "<Let> us fight with the Great King, King of Hatti." I, Great King, King of Hatti, overpowered the city of Arahati. I captured Akiya, king of Arahati; Aki-Teshshup, brother of Takuwa; and all of their chariot warriors, together with their possessions, and brought them to Hatti. I also brought the city of Qatna, together with its belongings and possessions, to Hatti.

§5 (A obv. 38–47) When I went to the land of Nuhashshi, I captured all of its territory. (Its king) Sharrupshi alone escaped, but I captured his mother, his brothers, and his children, and I brought them to Hatti. I installed Takip-sharri, subject of Sharrupshi, in kingship over the city of Ukulzat. I went to the land of Apina, but I did not seek to attack the land of

Kinza. But (its king) Shutatarra, together with his son Aitaqqama and his chariotry, came against me for battle. I drove him off, and they entered the city of Abzuya. I invested Abzuya, and I captured Shutatarra, together with his children, his chariot warriors, his brothers, and [his possessions], and I brought them to Hatti. I went to the land of Apina, and Ariwana, king of the land of Apina, and his noblemen Wambadura, Akparu, and Artaya, came against me for battle. I brought all of these, together with their land and their possessions, to Hatti. Because of the presumptuousness of King Tushratta, I plundered all of these lands in one year and brought them to Hatti. From Mount Lebanon and from the far bank of the Euphrates I made them my territory.

§6 (A obv. 48–58) When his son conspired with his subjects, he killed his father, King Tushratta. And with the death of King Tushratta the Storm-god decided the legal case of Artatama. His son brought the dead Artatama[7] back to life. The entire land of Mittanni went to ruin, and the land of Assyria and the land of Alshi divided it between them. Until now I, Great King, Hero, King of Hatti, have not crossed to the east bank, and have not taken even a blade of straw or a splinter of wood of the land of Mittanni. When I, Great King, King of Hatti, heard about the poverty of the land of Mittanni, I, King of Hatti, had the palace officials bring them cattle, sheep, and horses. But there was confusion among the Hurrians, and Shutatarra,[8] together with the chariot warriors, sought to kill Prince Shattiwaza. However, he escaped and came into the presence of My Majesty, Suppiluliuma, King of Hatti, Hero, Beloved of the Storm-god. I, Great King, spoke thus: "The Storm-god has decided his legal case. As I have taken up Shattiwaza, son of King Tushratta, in my hand, I will seat him upon the throne of his father, so that the land of Mittanni, the great land, does not go to ruin. I, Great King, King of Hatti, have given life to the land of Mittanni for the sake of my(!) daughter. I took up Shattiwaza, son of Tushratta, in my hand, and I gave him a daughter in marriage."

Succession

§7 (A obv. 59–67) Prince Shattiwaza shall be king in the land of Mittanni, and the daughter of the King of Hatti shall be queen in the land of Mittanni. Concubines will be allowed for you, Shattiwaza, but no other woman shall be greater than my daughter. You shall allow no other woman to be her equal, and no one shall sit as an equal beside her. You shall not degrade my daughter to second rank. In the land of Mittanni she shall exercise queenship. The sons of Shattiwaza and the sons of my daughter —

their sons and grandsons — [shall] in the future be equals in the land of Mittanni. In the future the Mittannians shall indeed not plan rebellion against Prince Shattiwaza, against my daughter, the queen, [against his sons], or against his grandsons. In the future Prince Shattiwaza shall be a brother and equal [to my sons], and the sons of Prince Shattiwaza — his(!) sons and grandsons [. . .] — shall be brothers and equals to my grandsons.

Friendship and Alliance

§8 (A obv. 68–73) In the future the Hittites and the Mittannians [shall not look upon one another] with a malevolent eye. The Hittites shall not do evil to the Mittannians; [the Mittannians] shall not do evil to the Hittites. When the King of Hatti goes to war, the king of [the land] of Mittanni [shall attack] any enemy of [Hatti]. As someone is the enemy of the land of Mittanni, [he shall be] the enemy [of Hatti. The friend] of the King of Hatti [shall be] the friend of the king of the land [of Mittanni].

[*The lower portion of Text A has been lost, and it is impossible to recover a translatable text from the other manuscripts. Fragmentary lines A rev. 1–8 suggest that the missing portion of the treaty continued the discussion of military obligations.*]

Fugitives

§9 (A rev. 9–13) If a fugitive flees from Hatti [and goes to the land of Mittanni, the Mittannians shall seize and] return [him]. If a fugitive of the land of Mittanni [flees and goes to Hatti], the King of Hatti will not seize him and return him. It is not permitted. [The . . .] of the Sun-goddess of Arinna [is . . .] The household which Prince Shattiwaza is establishing in Hatti [shall take charge of(?)] the fugitive. Shattiwaza shall settle him in the city (that is, Hattusa?). [He] will belong to Hatti.

Frontiers

§10 (A rev. 14–21) I, Great King, King of Hatti, captured the lands of Mittanni. I did not capture them in the time of Prince [Shattiwaza]; I captured them in the time of Tushratta. The Euphrates [is my frontier(?)]. In my rear I established Mount Lebanon as my frontier. And all the cities of [the land of Carchemish — the cities of Carchemish], Murmurik, Shipri, Mazuwati, and Shurun — these fortified cities of [the land of Carchemish] I gave [to Piyassili], my son. All the cities which are situated in the land of Ashtata, on the west bank (of the Euphrates) of the land of Mittanni —

Ekalte, [. . .], Ahuna, and Terqa — these cities belong to the land of Ashtata. Since Prince Piyassili crossed the Euphrates with [Prince] Shattiwaza
and penetrated to the city of Irrite, all the cities on the west bank which
Piyassili, [my son], holds — these belong to Piyassili.

Mutual Relations of Subordinates

§11 (A rev. 22–27) And I, Great King, King of Hatti, will revive the dead
land of Mittanni, and I will restore it to its place. You shall not again act
independently, nor transgress your treaty, nor shall you seek further territories for yourselves. Prince Piyassili and Prince Shattiwaza — their territories [will be . . .] for one another. If a city of Prince Piyassili writes secretly
to Shattiwaza, then Shattiwaza must reveal its secret communication. He
must seize its messenger and send him to Piyassili, his brother. Nor will
Shattiwaza write in a furtive(?) manner to a city of Piyassili. Piyassili and
Shattiwaza are bound to one another in brotherhood.

§12 (A rev. 28–34) If Shattiwaza summons Piyassili to the city of Irrite
[or] to Taite for consultation(?), Shattiwaza shall not plan any evil against
Piyassili, his brother, and he may not cause another man to undertake evil
against Piyassili. And the cities which Shattiwaza has given up to Piyassili
shall not plan any evil. No one shall plan any evil matter or maliciousness
against Piyassili. If Piyassili summons Shattiwaza to Carchemish for con-
sultation(?), Piyassili shall not plan any evil matter or maliciousness against
Shattiwaza. Whatever cities [of] Shattiwaza are situated on the banks of
the Euphrates shall be retained, but he shall not seize another city on the
bank of the Euphrates.

Deposition of Treaty; Divine Witnesses of Hatti

§13 (A rev. 35–53) A duplicate of this tablet is deposited before the Sun-
goddess of Arinna, since the Sun-goddess of Arinna governs kingship and
queenship. And in the land of Mittanni a duplicate is deposited before the
Storm-god, Lord of the *kurinnu* of Kahat. It shall be read repeatedly, for
ever and ever, before the king of the land of Mittanni and before the Hurrians. Whoever, before the Storm-god, Lord of the *kurinnu* of Kahat, alters
this tablet, or sets it in a secret location — if he breaks it, if he changes the
words of the text of the tablet — in regard to this treaty we have summoned
the gods of secrets and the gods who are guarantors of the oath. They shall
stand and listen and be witnesses: The Sun-goddess of Arinna, who governs

kingship and queenship in Hatti, the Sun-god, Lord of Heaven, the Storm-god, Lord of Hatti, Sheri, Hurri, Mount Nanni, Mount Hazzi, the Storm-god, Lord of the Market(?), the Storm-god, Lord of the Army, the Storm-god, Lord of Help, the Storm-god of Pittiyarik, the Storm-god of Nerik, the Storm-god, Lord of the Ruin Mounds(?), the Storm-god of Aleppo, the Storm-god of Lihzina, the Storm-god of Samuha, the Storm-god of Hurma, the Storm-god of Sarissa, the Storm-god of Sapinuwa, the Storm-god of Hisashapa, the Storm-god of Tahaya, the Storm-god of [. . .], the Storm-god of Kizzuwatna, the Storm-god of Uda, the Tutelary Deity of Hatti, the Tutelary Deity of Karahna, Zithariya, Karzi, Hapantaliya, the Tutelary Deity of the Countryside, the Tutelary Deity of the Hunting Bag, Lelwani, Ea, Damkina, Telipinu of Tawiniya, Telipinu of Turmitta, Telipinu of Hanhana, the Proud Ishtar,[9] Askasepa, the Grain-deity, the Moon-god, Lord of the Oath, Ishhara, Queen of the Oath, Hebat, Queen of Heaven, Hebat of Aleppo, Hebat of Uda, Hebat of Kizzuwatna, the War-god, the War-god of Hatti, the War-god of Illaya, the War-god of Arziya, Yarri, Zappana, Hasamili, Hantitassu of Hurma, Abara of Samuha, Katahha of Ankuwa, the Queen of Katapa, Ammamma of Tahurpa, Hallara of Dunna, Huwassanna of Hupisna, the Lady of Landa, Kuniyawanni of Landa, the mountain-dweller gods, the mercenary gods, all the male deities and female deities of Hatti, the male deities and female deities of the land of Kizzuwatna, the deities of the Netherworld — Nara, Namsara, Minki, Ammunki, Tuhusi, Ammizzadu, Alalu, Anu, Antu — Enlil, Ninlil, Belet-ekalli, the mountains, the rivers, the sea, the Euphrates, heaven and earth, the winds, the clouds,

Divine Witnesses of Mittanni

§14 (A rev. 54–58) the Storm-god, Lord of Heaven and Earth, the Moon-god and the Sun-god, the Moon-god of Harran, heaven and earth, the Storm-god, Lord of the *kurinnu* of Kahat, the Deity of Herds of Kurta, the Storm-god, Lord of Uhushuman, Ea-sharri, Lord of Wisdom, Anu, Antu, Enlil, Ninlil, the Mitra-gods, the Varuna-gods, Indra, the Nasatya-gods, the underground watercourse(?), Shamanminuhi, the Storm-god, Lord of Washshukkanni, the Storm-god, Lord of the Temple Platform(?) of Irrite, Partahi of Shuta, Nabarbi, Shuruhi, Ishtar, Evening Star,[10] Shala, Belet-ekalli, Damkina, Ishhara, the mountains and rivers, the deities of heaven, and the deities of earth.

Curses

§15 (A rev. 58–69) They shall stand and listen and be witnesses to these words of the treaty. If you, Prince Shattiwaza, and you Hurrians do not observe the words of this treaty, the gods, lords of the oath, shall destroy you [and] you Hurrians, together with your land, your wives, and your possessions. They will draw you out like malt from its husk. As one does not get a plant from the midst of . . . , so you, together with any other wife whom you might take (in place of my daughter), and you Hurrians, together with your wives, your sons, and your land, shall thus have no progeny. And these gods, who are lords of the oath, shall allot you poverty and destitution. And you, Shattiwaza — they shall overthrow your throne. And you, Shattiwaza — these oath gods shall snap you off like a reed, together with your land. Your name and your progeny by another wife whom you might take shall be eradicated from the earth. And you, Shattiwaza, together with your land, because of not delivering goodness and recovery(?) among the Hurrians — you(!) shall be eradicated. The ground shall be ice, so that you will slip. The ground of your land shall be a marsh of . . . , so that you will certainly sink and be unable to cross. You, Shattiwaza, and the Hurrians shall be the enemies of the Thousand Gods. They shall defeat you.

Blessings

§16 (A rev. 70–75) If you, Prince Shattiwaza, and you Hurrians observe this treaty and oath, these gods shall protect you, Shattiwaza, together with your wife, [daughter of the King] of Hatti, her sons and grandsons, and you Hurrians, together with your wives and your sons, and [together with your land]. And the land of Mittanni [shall return] to its former state. It shall prosper and expand. And you, Shattiwaza, your sons and grandsons by the daughter of the [Great] King, [King of Hatti] — the Hurrians shall accept you(!) for kingship for eternity. [Prolong the life] of the throne of [your father]; prolong the life of the land of Mittanni.

No. 6B
Treaty between Shattiwaza of Mittanni and Suppiluliuma I of Hatti

Historical Introduction

§1 (obv. 1–7) [Thus says] Shattiwaza, son of Tushratta, king of [the land] of Mittanni: Before Shuttarna, son of Artatama, [King of Hurri], altered the [. . .] of the land of Mittanni, King Artatama, his father, did wrong. He used up the palace of the kings, together with its treasures. He exhausted them in payment to the land of Assyria and to the land of Alshi. King Tushratta, my father, built a palace and filled it with riches, but Shuttarna destroyed it, and it became impoverished. And he broke the [. . .] of the kings, of silver and gold, and the caldrons of silver from the bath house. And [from the wealth(?)] of his father and his brother he did not give anyone (in Mittanni) anything, but he threw himself down before the Assyrian, the subject of his father, who no longer pays tribute, and gave him his riches as a gift.

§2 (obv. 8–20) Thus says Shattiwaza, son of King Tushratta: The door of silver and gold which King Saushtatar, my (great-)great-grandfather, took by force from the land of Assyria as a token of his glory and set up in his palace in the city of Washshukkanni — to his shame Shuttarna has now returned it to the land of Assyria. All the utensils of the storehouse of gifts(?) of silver and gold he gave to the land of Alshi. He exhausted the house of the king of the land of Mittanni, together with its treasures and its riches. He filled it with dirt. He destroyed the palace and exhausted the households of the Hurrians. He had the noblemen brought and extradited to the land of Assyria and the land of Alshi. They were turned over and impaled in the city of Taite. Thus he brought an end to the Hurrians. But Aki-Teshshup fled before him and entered Babylonia. Two hundred chariots fled with him, and the King of Babylonia took away for himself the two hundred chariots and all the possessions of Aki-Teshshup. He made Aki-Teshshup assume the same rank as his chariot warriors. He conspired(?) to kill him. He would have killed me, Shattiwaza, son of King Tushratta, too, but I escaped from his hands and called upon the gods of His Majesty, Suppiluliuma, Great King, King of Hatti, Hero, Beloved of the Storm-god. They led me on a road without [. . .] The gods of the King of Hatti and the gods of the king of Mittanni caused me to reach His Majesty, Suppiluliuma, Great King, King of Hatti, Hero, Beloved of the Storm-god.

§3 (obv. 21–30) At the Marassantiya River I fell at the feet of His Majesty, Suppiluliuma, Great King, King of Hatti, Hero, Beloved of the Storm-god. [The Great King] took me by the hand and rejoiced over me and questioned me at length concerning all the customs of the land of Mittanni. [And when] he had heard exhaustively [about the customs] of the land of Mittanni, the Great King and Hero spoke as follows: "If I conquer Shuttarna and [the troops of] the land of Mittanni, I will not reject you but will adopt you as my son. I will stand by you and place you on the throne of your father. And the gods know My Majesty, Suppiluliuma, Great King,

King of Hatti, Hero, Beloved of the Storm-god. He never goes back on the words which issue from his mouth." Thus says Shattiwaza, son of Tushratta: I rejoiced at the words of the King, my lord, which I heard. I, Prince Shattiwaza, spoke to the Great King, my lord: "If you, my lord, will give me life, and the gods will stand by me, then the Great King, King of Hatti, Hero, Beloved of the Storm-god, shall certainly not remove king Artatama from his royal throne. Let me stand as his designated successor, and let me rule the land of Mittanni. Shuttarna treated the lands badly, but I will never do anything for ill."

§4 (obv. 31–40) And when I, Prince Shattiwaza, came before the Great King, I had only three chariots, two Hurrians, two other attendants, who set out with me(!), and a single outfit of clothes — which I was wearing — and nothing else. And the Great King took pity on me and gave me chariots mounted with gold, chariot horses with armor, [. . .], a tent of linen, servants of the . . . -house, two vessels of [silver] and gold, together with their cups of silver and gold, silver utensils of the bath house, a silver wash basin, festive garments of the wool-worker — all this and everything <of> the craftsman. He . . . me to Piyassili, [his son], and the King entrusted me to the hand of Piyassili, to his chariotry, [and] to his troops. From the city of Carchemish where we arrived, we sent a messenger to the people of the city of Irrite, but Shuttarna had influenced the Hurrians with the riches of Tushratta and had united them. We sent to them in Irrite, and these Hurrians sent back to Piyassili: "Why are you coming? If you are coming for battle, come, but you shall not return to the land of the Great King!" When we had heard the words of the people of Irrite, we — Prince Piyassili and Prince Shattiwaza — crossed the Euphrates and arrived at Irrite ready for battle.

§5 (obv. 41–47) And the gods of the Great King, King of Hatti, protected us, and the Hurrians whom Shuttarna had sent as protection to Irrite, as well as the chariotry and troops of the district of Irrite, gathered in wait for us. We reached Irrite, and the troops and chariotry which had sat within the city came out before us. We captured and destroyed all the . . . [which . . .] When the people of Irrite . . . them [. . .] they assembled. In Irrite and all the districts of Irrite they came before us for peace. [. . .] The people of the city of Harran and [the districts] of Harran assembled and came to us. [. . . in] Harran we will establish them.

§6 (Akkadian obv. 48–65; Hittite lines 1'–20') [The Assyrian . . .] sent him/it to besiege [Washshukkanni] and gave them a single chariot warrior as leader. [But] when he [came] to the city [of Washshukkanni, the people of] Washshukkanni refused to make peace. But when the infantry and char-

iotry [of Assyria] besieged Washshukkanni, Prince Piyassili and I, Prince
Shattiwaza, [were] in Irrite. A messenger came to us from Washshukkanni
[and] spoke [as follows]: "The infantry and chariotry of Assyria are coming
for battle [against the infantry and chariotry] of Hatti." [Then(?) . . .] we
marched out, [and] their(?) [. . .] came to meet [us], saying: "[. . . And] in
the [presence] of the scribe [of] the gate of the city of [. . .] And the
infantry and chariotry of Assyria [. . . " . . .] he took away. But when to us
[. . .], we went up [to Washshukkanni. But] the city of Pakarripa [. . .]
turned. And when [the people of Pakarripa] heard that [Prince] Piyassili
and [Prince] Shattiwaza, and both the infantry and the chariotry of Hatti
were going up to Washshukkanni,

§6 (continued) (Hittite lines 21'–29') the people of Pakarripa deserted
and became allies [of Hatti]. And we [went] out from Washshukkanni and
went to Pakarripa. Word was brought to us: "The Assyrian is coming
against you in battle." The environs of Pakarripa were desolate, and hunger
caught up with the troops. The Assyrians, however, were not to be seen
again. They did not come against us in battle, and we went after the Assyrians to the city of Nilapshini. But the Assyrians did not come against us in
battle there either.

§7 (Akkadian rev 1–6; Hittite lines 30'–38') [*This section, where the final
defeat of Shuttarna by the army of Piyassili and Shattiwaza is seemingly nar-
rated, is too fragmentary for translation.*]

Deposition of Treaty; Divine Witnesses of Hatti

§8 (Akkadian rev. 7–24) [A duplicate of this tablet is deposited] in the
land [of Mittanni before the Storm-god, Lord of the *kurinnu* of Kahat. It
shall be read repeatedly, for ever and ever], before the king of the land [of
Mittanni and before the Hurrians. Whoever, before the Storm-god, Lord of
the *kurinnu* of Kahat, alters] this tablet, [or sets it in a secret location — if
he breaks it, if he changes the words of the text of the tablet] — in regard to
[this treaty we have summoned the gods of secrets and the gods who are
guarantors of the oath. They shall stand] together [and listen and be witnesses: The Sun-goddess of Arinna, who] governs [kingship and queenship
in Hatti, the Sun-god, Lord of Heaven, the Storm-god, Lord of Hatti,
Sheri, Hurri, Mount Nanni, Mount Hazzi, the Storm-god, Lord of the
Market(?)], the Storm-god, Lord of the Army, [the Storm-god, Lord of
Help, the Storm-god of Pittiyarik, the Storm-god of Nerik, the Storm-god,
Lord of the Ruin Mounds(?), the Storm-god of Aleppo, the Storm-god of
Lihzina], the Storm-god of Samuha, [the Storm-god of Hurma, the Storm-

god of Sarissa, the Storm-god of Sapinuwa, the Storm-god of Hisashapa, the Storm-god of Tahaya, the Storm-god of . . . , the Storm-god of Kizzuwatna], the Storm-god of Uda, [the Tutelary Deity of Hatti, the Tutelary Deity of Karahna, Zithariya, Karzi, Hapantaliya, the Tutelary Deity of the Countryside], the Tutelary Deity of the Hunting Bag, [Lelwani, Ea, Damkina, Telipinu of Tawiniya], Telipinu [of Turmitta, Telipinu of Hanhana, the Proud Ishtar, Askasepa, the Grain-deity, the Moon-god, Lord of the Oath, Ishhara, Queen of the Oath, Hebat, Queen of Heaven, Hebat of Aleppo, Hebat of Uda, Hebat] of Kizzuwatna, [the War-god, the War-god] of Hatti, [the War-god of Illaya, the War-god of Arziya, Yarri], Lord of the Bow, [Zappana, Hasamili], Hantitassu [of Hurma, Abara of Samuha, Katahha of Ankuwa], the Queen of Katapa, [Ammamma] of Tahurpa, [Hallara of] Dunna, Huwassanna [of Hupisna, the Lady of Landa], Kuniyawanni [of Landa], the mountain-dweller gods, the mercenary [gods], the male deities [and female deities of Hatti, the male deities and female deities] of the land of Kizzuwatna, Ereshkigal, the primeval [deities] — Nara, [Namsara, Minki, Ammunki, Tuhusi], Ammizzadu, Alalu, Anu, [Antu — Enlil], Ninlil, Belet-ekalli, [the mountains, the rivers, the Tigris and the Euphrates, heaven] and earth, the winds, and the clouds,

Curses

§9 (rev. 25–34) [They shall stand and listen and be] witnesses [to] these words of the treaty. If [you], Shattiwaza, and you Hurrians [do not observe] the words of this treaty, these gods of the oath [shall destroy you, Shattiwaza, and] you Hurrians, together with your land, together with your wives, together with [your sons], and together with your possessions. They will draw you out [like malt] from its husk. As one does not get a plant from . . . — if you, Shattiwaza, [. . .] — so [you] together with [any other] wife whom you might take (in place of my daughter), and you Hurrians, together with their wives and their sons, shall thus [have no progeny]. And these gods, lords of the oath, shall allot you poverty and destitution. And they shall overthrow your [throne], Shattiwaza. And you, Shattiwaza — these oath gods shall snap you off like a reed, together with your land. Your name and your progeny by another wife whom you might take shall be eradicated from [the earth]. And you, Shattiwaza, together with your land, because of not delivering goodness and recovery(?) among the Hurrians — [you(!) shall be eradicated. The ground shall] be ice, so that you will slip. The ground of your land shall be a marsh of . . . , so that you will certainly sink and be unable to cross. [You], Shattiwaza, and you Hurrians shall be the enemies of the Thousand Gods. They shall defeat you.

Blessings

§10 (rev. 35–39) If you, Shattiwaza, and you Hurrians observe this treaty and oath, these gods shall protect you, Shattiwaza, together with the daughter of the Great King of Hatti, her sons and grandsons, and you Hurrians, together with your wives and your sons, and together with your land. And the land of Mittanni shall return to its previous state. It shall prosper and expand. And you(!), Shattiwaza, your sons and grandsons by the daughter of the Great King, King of Hatti — they shall accept you(!) for kingship for eternity. Prolong the life of the throne of your father; prolong the life of the land of Mittanni.

Divine Witnesses of Mittanni; Curses and Blessings

§11 (rev. 40–62) The Storm-god of Heaven and Earth, the Moon-god and the Sun-god, the Moon-god of Harran, heaven and earth, the Storm-god, Lord of the *kurinnu* of Kahat, the Storm-god, Lord of Uhushuman, Ea, Lord of Wisdom, the Deity of Herds of Kurta, Anu and Antu, Enlil and Ninlil, the Mitra-gods, the Varuna-gods, Indra, the Nasatya-gods, the underground watercourse(?), Shamanminuhi, the Storm-god, Lord of Washshukkanni, the Storm-god of the Temple Platform(?) of Irrite, Nabarbi, Shuruhi, Ishtar, Ishtar, Star, Shala, Belet-ekalli, the Lady of the *ayakki*-shrine, Ishhara, Partahi of Shuta, the mountains, the rivers, and the springs, the deities of heaven and earth. If I, Prince Shattiwaza, and the Hurrians do not observe the words of this treaty and of the oath, let me, Shattiwaza, together with my other wife, and us Hurrians, together with our wives, together with our sons, and together with our land — as a fir tree when it is felled has no more shoots, like this fir tree let me, Shattiwaza, together with any other wife whom I might take, and us Hurrians, together with our lands, together with our wives, and together with our sons, like the fir tree have no progeny. As the water of a drainpipe never returns to its place, let us, like the water of a drainpipe not return to our place. Let me, Shattiwaza, together with another wife whom I might take, and us Hurrians, together with our possessions, ascend to heaven like smoke. As salt has no seed, let me, Shattiwaza, together with any other wife whom I might take, and the Hurrians, together with our lands, our wives, and our sons, like salt indeed have no progeny. Like a (dissolved) lump of salt let us not return to our place. I, Shattiwaza — if any other wife whom I might take < . . . >, my throne shall be overthrown. If we do not observe this treaty and oath, the gods, lords of the oath, shall destroy us. Thus says Prince Shattiwaza and indeed also the Hurrians: If we observe this treaty and oath of

His Majesty, Suppiluliuma, Great King, King of Hatti, Hero, Beloved of the Storm-god, the gods whose names we have invoked shall go with us, exalt us, protect us, and be good to us. Let our(!) lord Shattiwaza go in front, and let us enjoy a bountiful harvest in his protection. Let us experience goodness and peace. The Storm-god, Canal Inspector of Heaven and Earth, shall be our helper for eternity. Let Shattiwaza, us Hurrians, and the land of Mittanni experience joy of heart and peace of mind for eternity. As His Majesty, Suppiluliuma, Great King, Hero, King of Hatti, Beloved of the Storm-god, loves his lands, his troops, his sons and his grandsons like his table (companions?), he shall love us — me Shattiwaza, us Hurrians, and the land of Mittanni, together with our lands and together with our possessions, like these.

Colophon

One tablet of Kili-Teshshup, of his treaty and his oath, complete.

No. 7
Treaty between Suppiluliuma I of Hatti and Tette of Nuhashshi

In the fourteenth century B.C.E., Nuhashshi was a complex of small states located to the south of the territory controlled by the city of Aleppo and to the southeast of that belonging to Ugarit. Most prominent among these states in the period in which the Hittite empire was established was that ruled by Sharrupshi, who was induced — or forced — to abandon his earlier allegiance to Mittanni and accept vassalage to Hatti.

The loss of the better part of the historical introduction to the present text prevents us from following developments in detail, but somehow rule in this Nuhashshi land passed to Sharrupshi's grandson Tette, with whom Suppiluliuma concluded this treaty. Despite the oath of loyalty imposed upon him, however, Tette joined in the revolts against Hatti during the first decade of the reign of Mursili II (see No. 30) and was killed, or at least removed from his throne. (On the career of Tette, see Bryce 1988; Klengel 1992: 154–55.)

This treaty belongs to the "Syrian group" discussed above in the introduction to No. 5.

Preamble; Historical Introduction

§1 (A i 1–11) Thus says My Majesty, Suppiluliuma, Great King, King of Hatti, Hero: When the king of the land of Mittanni sought to kill Sharrupshi, and the king of the land of Mittanni entered the land of Nuhashshi together with his infantry levies and his chariotry, and when he oppressed(?) him, Sharrupshi sent his messenger to the King of Hatti, saying: "I am the subject of the King of Hatti. Save me!" And I, My Majesty, sent infantry and chariotry to his aid, and they drove the king of the land of Mittanni, together with his troops and his chariotry out of the land of Nuhashshi.

§2 (A i 12–22) And I, Great King, was not silent in regard to that matter, but I went to the aid of Sharrupshi. And because at that time the land of Isuwa had become hostile to the King of Hatti, [I, King] of Hatti, [went] to the land of Isuwa. When I had destroyed the land of Isuwa, then [I went] to [the aid] of Sharrupshi against the land of Mittanni. When [I reached] the region of Mount Kashiyara, [Antaratli], king of the land of Alshi, [attacked(?)] My Majesty [. . . Mount] Kashiyara [. . .] as [. . .] I destroyed.

[*The ends of eleven lines follow, after which the lower half of the column has been totally lost. Somewhere in this section Tette's replacement of Sharrupshi as ruler of Nuhashshi, under whatever circumstances, must have been related. The text picks up in the middle of a paragraph.*]

Tribute

§3 (A ii 1–5) [. . . shekels of gold(?)] shall be his yearly tribute. It shall be weighed out with the weights of the merchants of Hatti. Tette shall come yearly to My Majesty, his lord, in Hatti.

Offensive Alliance

§4 (A ii 6–32) He shall be at peace with my friend and hostile to my enemy. If the King of Hatti goes against the land of Hurri, or Egypt, or Babylonia, or the land of Ashtata, or the land of Alshi — whatever foreign lands are located near your borders and are hostile to the King of Hatti, or whatever lands located near your borders which are at peace with the King of Hatti — the land of Mukish, the land of Aleppo, the land of Kinza — and which should turn and become hostile to the King of Hatti — when I, the King of Hatti, go forth to attack, if Tette does not mobilize <whole>heartedly, or if he does not fight wholeheartedly, he will transgress the oath. Or if I [send] a prince or a high-ranking nobleman, together with his infantry and his chariotry, to the aid of Tette, or else to attack another land — if Tette does not mobilize wholeheartedly with [his] infantry and his

chariotry, and does not fight with the enemy, he will transgress the oath. Or
if he commits some misdeed, thinking as follows: "Although I am under
oath and subject to the treaty, either let the enemy defeat him, or let him
defeat the enemy. I don't want to know anything about it." — he will transgress the oath. Or if he should write to that enemy, saying: "The troops of
Hatti are now coming to attack. Be on guard!" — he will transgress the
oath.

[*There follow an uninscribed space sufficient to accommodate about seven lines,
and then a damaged section mentioning the lands of Hurri, Ashtata, and Upa.*]

Defensive Alliance

§5 (A ii 48–56) [If] some other enemy rises up [against] the King of
Hatti, [and] attacks [Hatti], or if someone carries out [a revolt] against the
King of Hatti, and Tette hears of it, [then] he must come [immediately
with] his infantry and his chariotry to the aid of the Prince.[11] But if it is not
possible for Tette [to come], either his son, [or] his [brother], or his (high-
est-ranking) military nobleman shall come immediately [with] infantry and
chariotry to the aid of the King of Hatti.

§6 (A iii 1–18) [Or if] someone oppresses(?) [Tette, either . . . , or anyone
at all], and [he sends] to the King of Hatti: "Come [to my aid]," then the
King will come [to his aid]. And he will send either a . . . , [or a . . . , or] a
prince, or a high-ranking nobleman, [together with infantry and chariotry,
and they will defeat] that enemy. [And now] Tette has turned to [the King
of Hatti for vassalage because of] his security(?) and his concern for him-
self(?). And [if I send noblemen of Hatti, together with] infantry and chariotry to [the land of Nuhashshi, they will enter] his cities, [and he must
protect] and provision them. [. . . They shall walk] like [brothers] before
[him. He must protect] the King of Hatti. And [furthermore, whatever
Hittite seeks evil] against [Tette] — if [he seeks to carry off the booty of his
city or his land, he will transgress the oath].

Fugitives

§7 (A iii 19–28) And [whatever civilian captives] the King [of Hatti has
carried off from the land of Nuhashshi — civilian captives of the land of
Hurri], civilian captives [of the land of Kinza, civilian captives of the land]
of Niya, or civilian captives [of the land of Mukish — if some] man or
woman among them [flees] from [Hatti] and enters [your land, you shall
not think as follows]: "Although I am subject [to the treaty and under oath,

I] don't want [to know anything about this. Let them stay] in [my land]."
Tette shall rather seize [them and] return them [to the King of Hatti].

§8 (A iii 29–32) If someone incites Tette to evil [matters], whether [a Hittite or] his own subject, and Tette [does not seize him] and send him [to the King] of Hatti, he will transgress [the oath].

§9 (A iii 33–40) Whatever citizens of Nuhashshi are living in Hatti — [whether a nobleman] or a slave, a woman or a slave girl — [if Tette seeks him from] the King of Hatti — [if the King of Hatti] gives him to him, he shall take him. [But if the King of Hatti] does not give him, [and he flees and comes] to [Tette, if] Tette steals him back, [he will transgress the oath].

§10 (A iii 41–52) And if [some population sets out and comes] to the land [of Tette, and Tette speaks unfavorable words before them and directs them to the mountains, or to] another [land, he will transgress the oath. Rather, speak favorable words before them and direct them on the road to] Hatti. [If] a fugitive [from the land of Hurri or from] another [land comes to the land of Nuhashshi, Tette shall not detain him, but] he shall release him [to Hatti. If he does detain him], he will transgress [the oath].

§11 (A iii 53–56) [And whatever Tette] wants, he shall request [from the King of Hatti]. He shall take whatever [the Prince gives him]. He shall not take whatever the Prince [does not give him].

Loyalty of Subordinate

§12 (A iii 57–58) [And as I] have treated Tette well, [restoring him to life] when dead, and returning him to his land, [. . .] [*The first eight lines or so of column iv have been lost. They certainly included the summoning to assembly of the gods and goddesses who follow here:*]

Divine Witnesses

§13 (A iv 9'–18') [The Sun-god of Heaven, the Sun-goddess of Arinna, the Storm-god of Heaven, the Storm-god] of Hatti, [Sheri, Hurri, Mount Nanni, Mount] Hazzi, [the Storm-god of the Market(?), the Storm-god of the Army, the Storm-god of . . . , the Storm-god of Aleppo, the Storm-god of Zippalanda, the Storm-god of Nerik, the Storm-god of Lihzina], the Storm-god [of the Ruin Mound, the Storm-god] of Hisashapa, [the Storm-god of] Sahpina, the Storm-god [of Sapinuwa, the Storm-god of] Pittiyarik, the Storm-god [of Samuha, the Storm-god of Hurma], the Storm-god of Sarissa, [the Storm-god] of Help, the Storm-god of Uda, [the Storm-god of Kizzuwatna, the Storm-god] of Ishupitta, the Storm-god of Nuhashshi,

§14 (A iv 19'–24') [the Tutelary Deity], the Tutelary Deity of Hatti, Zithariya, [Karzi], Hapantaliya, the Tutelary Deity of Karahna, [the Tutelary Deity of the Countryside, the Tutelary Deity] of the Hunting Bag, Ea, Allatu, [Telipinu of] Turmitta, Telipinu [of Tawiniya], Telipinu of Hanhana, [Pirwa], Askasepa,

§15 (A iv 25'–29') [the Moon-god], Lord of the Oath, Ishhara, Queen of the Oath, Hebat, [Queen] of Heaven, Ishtar, Ishtar of the Countryside, Ishtar of Nineveh, Ishtar of Hattarina, Ninatta, Kulitta, the War-god, the War-god of Hatti, the War-god of Illaya, the War-god of Arziya, Yarri, Zappana,

§16 (A iv 30'–43') Hantitassu of Hurma, Abara of Samuha, Katahha of Ankuwa, the Queen of Katapa, Ammamma of Tahurpa, Hallara of Dunna, Huwassanna of Hupisna, Tapisuwa of Ishupitta, the Lady of Landa, Kuniyawanni of Landa, NIN.PÌSAN.PÌSAN of Kinza, Mount Lebanon, Mount Shariyana, Mount Pishaisha, the mountain-dweller gods, the mercenary gods, Ereshkigal, all the male deities and female deities of Hatti, all the male deities and female deities of the land of Kizzuwatna, all the male deities and female deities of the land of Nuhashshi, all the primeval deities — Nara, Namsara, Minki, Tuhusi, Ammunki, Ammizzadu, Alalu, Antu, Anu, Apantu, Enlil, Ninlil,

Divine Witnesses (coninued); Curse and Blessing

§17 (A iv 44'–57') the mountains, the rivers, the springs, the great sea, heaven and earth, the winds, and the clouds. They shall be witnesses to this treaty and oath. All the words of the treaty and oath which are written on this tablet — if Tette does not observe these words of the treaty and oath, but transgresses the oath, then these oath gods shall destroy Tette, [together with his person], his wives, his sons, his grandsons, his household, his city, his land, and together with his possessions. But if Tette observes [these] words [of the treaty] and oath which [are written] on [this tablet, these oath gods shall protect] Tette, together with his person, his wives, [his sons, his grandsons], his family, [his household], his city, his land, [and together with his possessions].

Colophon

Text A: This tablet [. . .] and of [. . .]

No. 8
Treaty between Mursili II of Hatti
and Tuppi-Teshshup of Amurru

After the death of Aziru (see No. 5), Amurru was ruled for a short time by his son Ari-Teshshup, who was in turn succeeded by his own son Tuppi-Teshshup. Mursili confirmed the latter in office, despite his poor health, because of the express wish of his father (§4). Reflecting the resurgence of Egyptian influence in Syro-Palestine under the first pharaohs of the Nineteenth Dynasty, we find here significant variation from the standard provisions of the "Syrian group" of treaties (see introduction to No. 5) in the warning against the resumption of tribute payments to Egypt (§5), and against diplomatic relations with the land of the Nile (§6). Nonetheless, there is no evidence that Tuppi-Teshshup betrayed his Hittite masters. (On his reign, see Singer 1991a: 162–63; Klengel 1992: 167–68.)

This text is preserved in both Hittite- and Akkadian-language versions. I have used the former as the basis of my translation.

Preamble

§1 (B i 1–2) [Thus says] My Majesty, Mursili, [Great King, King of Hatti], Hero, Beloved of the Storm-god; [son of] Suppiluliuma, [Great King, King of Hatti, Hero]:

Historical Introduction

§2 (B i 3–12) Aziru, your [grandfather, Tuppi-Teshshup], became the subject of my father.[12] When it came about that the kings of the land of Nuhashshi [and the king of the land of Kinza became hostile (to my father)], Aziru did not become hostile.[13] [When my father made war on his enemies], Aziru likewise made war. And Aziru protected only my father, and my father protected [Aziru], together with his land. [He did not seek] to harm him in any way. [And Aziru] did not anger [my father] in any way. He always paid him[14] [the 300 shekels of refined, first-class gold which] he had imposed [as tribute].[15] My father died, and I [took my seat] upon the throne [of my father]. But [as] Aziru had been in [the time of my father], so he was in my time.

§3 (B i 13–19) Then it happened that [the kings of the land of Nuhashshi and the king of the land of Kinza] became hostile to [me],[16] but [your grandfather] Aziru [and your father Ari-Teshshup . . .] them. They sup-

ported me alone as overlord. [And when Aziru became an old man] and
was no longer able to go on military campaign as he had always gone to war
[with infantry] and chariotry, [then] Ari-Teshshup [likewise went to war
with the infantry and chariotry of the land of Amurru]. And My Majesty
destroyed those [enemies . . .]

[*An undetermined number of lines have been lost.*]

§4 (A i 11'–18') But when your father died, according to [the request of
your father], I did not cast you off. Because your father had spoken your
name before me during his lifetime(?), I therefore took care of you. But you
were sick and ailing. [And] although you were an invalid, I nonetheless
installed you [in] place of your father. I made your [. . .] brothers and the
land of Amurru swear an oath to you.

Mutual Loyalty; Tribute

§5 (A i 19'–34') And as I took care of you according to the request of
your father, and installed you in place of your father, I have now made you
swear an oath to the King of Hatti and the land of Hatti, and to my sons
and grandsons. Observe the oath and the authority of the King. I, My
Majesty, will protect you, Tuppi-Teshshup. And when you take a wife and
produce a son, he shall later be king in the land of Amurru. And as you protect My Majesty, I will likewise protect your son. You, Tuppi-Teshshup, in
the future protect the King of Hatti, the land of Hatti, my sons, and my
grandsons. The tribute which was imposed upon your grandfather and
upon your father shall be imposed upon you: They paid 300 shekels of
refined gold by the weights of Hatti, first-class and good. You shall pay it
likewise. You shall not turn your eyes to another. Your ancestors paid tribute to Egypt, [but] you [shall not pay it . . .] [*About seven lines have been
badly damaged or lost entirely.*]

Loyalty against Egypt

§6 (B ii 4'–9') [If] you commit [. . .], and while the King of Egypt [is
hostile to My Majesty you] secretly [send] your messenger to him, [or you
become hostile] to the King of Hatti [and cast] off the authority of the
King of Hatti, becoming a subject of the King of Egypt, you, Tuppi-
Teshshup, will transgress the oath.

Offensive Alliance

§7 (B ii 10'–17'; A ii 1'–12') [Whoever] is [My Majesty's] enemy shall be your enemy. [Whoever is My Majesty's friend] shall be your friend. And if [any] of the lands which are "protectorates" [of the King of Hatti should become hostile] to the King of Hatti, and if I, My Majesty, come against that [land for attack], and you do not mobilize wholeheartedly with [infantry and chariotry, and do] not [make war wholeheartedly] and without hesitation on the enemy, you will transgress the oath. [And if you commit some misdeed], or to [. . .], and you [think] as follows: ["Although I am under oath, either] let them defeat [the enemy, or let] the enemy [defeat] them. <I don't want to know anything about it.>" — you will transgress the oath. [Or if] you send a man [off] to that [enemy] to warn [him as follows]: "The infantry and chariotry of [Hatti] are now coming. Be on guard!" — [you] will transgress the oath.

Defensive Alliance

§8 (A ii 13'–24') As I, My Majesty, protect you, Tuppi-Teshshup, be an auxiliary army for My Majesty and [for Hatti]. And if some [evil] matter arises in Hatti, and [someone] revolts against My Majesty, and you hear [of it], lend assistance [together with] your [infantry] and your chariotry. Take a stand immediately to help [Hatti]. But if it is not possible for you to lend assistance (personally), send aid to the King of Hatti either by your son [or] your brother, together with your infantry and your [chariotry]. If you do not send aid to the King of Hatti [by your son] or your brother, together with your infantry and your chariotry, you will transgress the oath.

§9 (A ii 25'–29') If some matter oppresses you, Tuppi-Teshshup, or someone revolts against you, and you write to the King of Hatti, then the King of Hatti will send infantry and chariotry to your aid. [At this point the scribe of Text A, the only manuscript which covers this portion of the treaty, has apparently committed an error in copying from an older tablet, for the final line of the paragraph incongruously reads: "you will transgress the oath."]

Relations of Subordinate to Agents of Great King

§10 (A ii 30'–37') If Hittites bring you, Tuppi-Teshshup, infantry and chariotry — because they will go up to your cities, Tuppi-Teshshup must regularly provide them with food and drink. And if any Hittite undertakes an evil matter against Tuppi-Teshshup, such as the plunder of his land or of his cities, or the removal of Tuppi-Teshshup from kingship in the land of Amurru, he will transgress the oath.

Fugitives

§11 (A ii 38'–45') Whatever civilian captives of the land of Nuhashshi and the land of Kinza my father carried off, or I carried off — if one of these civilian captives flees from me and comes to you, and you do not seize him and give him back to the King of Hatti, you will transgress the oath. And if you should even think as follows (concerning a fugitive): "[Come] or go! Wherever you go, I don't want to know about you." — you will transgress the oath.

Appeal of Royal Command

§12 (A ii 46'–iii 11) If someone should bring up before you, Tuppi-Teshshup, evil matters against the King or against Hatti, you shall not conceal him from the King. Or if My Majesty speaks confidentially of some matters to you: "Perform these deeds or that deed," then make an appeal right there at that moment concerning whatever among(!) those deeds you do not want to perform: "I cannot do this deed. I will not perform it." And when the King again commands, and you do not perform a deed of which you are capable, but rebuff(?) the King, or if you do not observe the matter of which the King speaks to you confidentially, you will transgress the oath.

Fugitives (continued)

§13 (A iii 12–22) If some population or fugitive sets out, travels toward Hatti, and passes through your land, set them well on their way and point out the road to Hatti. Speak favorable words to them. You shall not direct them to anyone else. If you do not set them on their way and do not show them the road to Hatti, but direct them to the mountains — or if you speak evil words before them, you will transgress the oath.

§14 (A iii 23–29) Or if the King of Hatti beleaguers some country through battle, and it flees before him, and comes into your country — if you [want] to take anything, ask the King of Hatti for it. You shall not take [it on your own initiative]. If you take [anything] on your own initiative and conceal it, you will transgress the oath.

§15 (A iii 30–31) Furthermore, if a fugitive comes [into your land in flight], seize him and [turn] him [over]. [*A break of uncertain length intervenes here.*]

Divine Witnesses

§16 (B iii 5'–6') [. . . The Thousand Gods shall now stand] for this [oath]. They shall observe [and listen].

§17 (B iii 7'–17') [The Sun-god of Heaven, the Sun-goddess] of Arinna, the Storm-god of Heaven, the Storm-god of Hatti, [Sheri], Hurri, Mount Nanni, Mount Hazzi, [the Storm-god of the Market(?), the Storm-god] of the Army, the Storm-god of Aleppo, the Storm-god of Zippalanda, [the Storm-god] of Nerik, the Storm-god of Lihzina, the Storm-god of the Ruin Mound, [the Storm-god of Hisashapa], the Storm-god of Sahpina, the Storm-god of Sapinuwa, [the Storm-god of Pittiyarik], the Storm-god of Samuha, the Storm-god of Hurma, [the Storm-god of Sarissa], the Storm-god of Help, the Storm-god of Uda, [the Storm-god of Kizzuwatna], the Storm-god of Ishupitta, [the Storm-god of . . .], the Storm-god of Arkata, the Storm-god of Tunip, [the Storm-god of Aleppo] resident in Tunip, Milku [of the land of Amurru],

§18 (B iii 18'–23') [the Tutelary Deity, the Tutelary Deity] of Hatti, Zithariya, Karzi, [Hapantaliya], the Tutelary Deity of Karahna, the Tutelary Deity of the Countryside, [the Tutelary Deity of the Hunting Bag], Ea, Allatu, [Telipinu] of Turmitta, [Telipinu] of Tawiniya, Telipinu [of Hanhana], Bunene, Askasepa,

§19 (B iii 24'; A iv 1–3) [the Moon-god, Lord of the Oath, Ishhara], Queen of the Oath, [Hebat, Queen of Heaven, Ishtar, Ishtar of the Countryside, Ishtar of Nineveh, Ishtar of Hattarina, Ninatta], Kulitta, the War-god of Hatti, the War-god of Illaya, the War-god of Arziya, Yarri, Zappana,

§20 (A iv 4–20) Hantitassu of Hurma, Abara of Samuha, Katahha of Ankuwa, [the Queen] of Katapa, Ammamma of Tahurpa, Hallara of Dunna, Huwassanna of Hupisna, Tapisuwa of [Ishupitta], the Lady of Landa, Kuniyawanni of Landa, NIN.PÌSAN.PÌSAN of Kinza, [Mount] Lebanon, Mount Shariyana, Mount Pishaisha, the mountain-dweller gods, the mercenary gods, [Ereshkigal], the male deities and female deities of Hatti, [the male deities] and female deities of Amurru, [all] the primeval deities — Nara, Namsara, [Minki], Tuhusi, Ammunki, Ammizzadu, Alalu, Antu, Anu, Apantu, Enlil, Ninlil — the mountains, the rivers, the springs, the great sea, heaven and earth, the winds, and the clouds. They shall be witnesses to this treaty [and] to the oath.

Curse

§21 (A iv 21–26) All the words of the treaty and oath [which] are written [on] this tablet — if Tuppi-Teshshup [does not observe these words] of the treaty and of the oath, then these oath gods shall destroy Tuppi-Teshshup, [together with his person], his [wife], his son, his grandsons, his household, his city, his land, and together with his possessions.

Blessing

§22 (A iv 27–32) But if Tuppi-Teshshup [observes] these [words of the treaty and of the oath] which [are written] on this tablet, [then] these oath gods [shall protect] Tuppi-Teshshup, together with his person, his wife, his son, his grandsons, [his city, his land], his(!) household, his subjects, [and together with his possessions].

Colophon

Text C: [First tablet of Tuppi-Teshshup(?), of the treaty], complete.

No. 9
Treaty between Mursili II of Hatti
and Niqmepa of Ugarit

Although the three copies of this Akkadian-language treaty with the second successor of Niqmaddu II do not in themselves preserve the complete text, it may nonetheless be largely restored through comparison with other members of the "Syrian group" (see introduction to No. 5). The line numbers here are those given in the edition of del Monte (1986).

This composition is marked by extensive confusion of grammatical person: The Hittite Great King refers to himself in both the first and third persons, and to his junior partner in both the second and third persons. Despite this, the sense of the document is generally clear enough, and I have therefore in most cases retained the phraseology of the original in order to give the reader a sense of the clumsiness often apparent in Akkadian texts composed by Hittite scribes.

The greater portion of this treaty is given over to the problem of fugitives, a reflection of the concern of the Hittite ruler to secure an adequate supply of manpower, a concern also evident in No. 33.

Preamble; Relations of Subordinate to Great King

§1 (lines 1–12) Thus says My Majesty, Mursili, [Great King], King of Hatti: I [. . . with] your brothers, Niqmepa, and I, the King, placed you upon the throne of your father and returned the land of your father to you. You, Niqmepa, together with your land, are my subject. And [if] you, Niqmepa, from this day on into the future do not protect the King of Hatti, [your] lord, [and] Hatti, you will transgress the oath. As you yourself, Niqmepa, your person, your wives, your sons, and your land are dear to you, the body [of the King], the person of the King, the sons of the King, and Hatti shall forever be dear [to you]. In the future observe the peace treaty of the King of Hatti, of the sons of the King, of the grandsons [of the King], and of Hatti. Now you, Niqmepa, come before the King! But if it is ever impossible for you to come — perhaps some matter will arise before you — it shall be exempted from the oath.

Offensive Alliance

§2 (lines 13–21) You shall be at peace with my friend and hostile to my enemy. If the King of Hatti goes against the land of Hanigalbat, or Egypt, or Babylonia, or the land of Alshi — whatever [foreign] lands located near the borders of [your] land are hostile to the King of Hatti, [or] whatever lands [located near the borders of your land] and friendly to the King of Hatti — [the land of Mukish, the land] of Aleppo, the land of [Nuhashshi] — turn and become hostile to the King [of Hatti — when the King] of Hatti goes out to attack them, [if you, Niqmepa], do not mobilize wholeheartedly with [your] infantry [and your chariotry], and if you do not fight [wholeheartedly], you will transgress the oath.

§3 (lines 22–29) And if [I send] to your aid, Niqmepa, [a high-ranking nobleman, together with] his [infantry and his] chariotry, or [if I send troops] to attack another [land], and you, [Niqmepa, do not mobilize wholeheartedly with your infantry and your chariotry], and [do not fight] with the enemy, [but rather] commit [a misdeed], thinking as follows: "[Although I am under oath and subject to the treaty], either let the enemy defeat them, [or let them defeat the enemy]. I don't want to know anything about it." — you will transgress the oath. Of if you [send] to that enemy, saying: "[The troops of Hatti] are [now] coming to attack. [Be on guard!" — you will transgress the oath].

Defensive Alliance

§4 (lines 30–34) And if [some other enemy rises up] against the King of Hatti, [and attacks Hatti], or if [he carries out a revolt] against the King [of Hatti, and you, Niqmepa, hear of it, then you must immediately come to the aid of the Great King], together with your [infantry] and your chariotry. But if it is not possible [for] Niqmepa to come, [either his son or his brother shall immediately come to] the aid of the King [of Hatti, together with infantry and chariotry].

§5 (lines 35–38) And if someone oppresses(?) you, [Niqmepa, either . . .], or anyone at all, and [you send] to the King [of Hatti: "Come to my aid]," then the King [will come] to [your aid]. He will send [either a prince or a high-ranking nobleman, together with infantry and chariotry, and they will defeat that] enemy [for you].

Relations of Subordinate to Agents of Great King

§6 (lines 39–44) [I], King [of Hatti, have now taken you], Niqmepa, [into my service. If I send noblemen], together with the infantry and chariotry of [Hatti to the land of Ugarit], and [they enter] your cities, [Niqmepa must take care of them and provision them]. They shall [walk] like brothers before him. [And you must protect the King of Hatti]. And [furthermore], if any Hittite seeks [evil against Niqmepa, or undertakes] to [conquer] one of his cities or his land, [he will transgress the oath].

Fugitives

§7 (lines 45–50) And whatever civilian captives [the Great King has carried off] from your land, or civilian captives of Hanigalbat, civilian captives [of Kinza, civilian captives of Niya], or civilian captives of Nuhashshi [and Mukish — if some man or woman from among] these [civilian captives] flees [and enters] your land, [you shall not think as follows: "Although I] am subject to the treaty and under oath, I don't want to know anything about this]. Let them stay [in my land]." Niqmepa shall rather seize [them and return them to the King of Hatti].

§8 (lines 51–53) If [someone incites] you, Niqmepa, to [evil] matters, whether a Hittite or a citizen of [Ugarit, and you, Niqmepa do not seize him and send him] to the King of Hatti, [you will transgress the oath].

§9 (lines 54–57) Whatever citizen of Ugarit [living in Hatti, whether a nobleman, or a male or] female slave — if Niqmepa seeks [him] from the King [of Hatti — if he turns him over, he shall take him]. But if the King [of

Hatti] does not turn [him] over, [and he flees and comes to you], and if Niqmepa thus steals him, [he will transgress the oath].

Confidentiality of Communications of Great King

§10 (lines 58–60) [And whatever] matters I, the King [of Hatti, tell you] in confidence [. . .], conversely I will tell you. But if [you, Niqmepa, do not hold these matters in confidence], you will transgress the oath.

Fugitives (continued)

§11 (lines 61–69) [And if] some [population] sets out [and comes] to [your land], and you, Niqmepa, [speak] unfavorable words before them [and direct them] to the mountains or to another land, you will transgress the oath. Speak favorable words before them! Show them [to] the road (to Hatti)! Give [them] beer and provisions. [And if] the population of some foreign [land] oppressed(?) by battle [sets out] and enters the land of Ugarit, Niqmepa [shall seize them] and turn them over [to the King] of Hatti. If Niqmepa does not seize [them] and turn them over [to the King of Hatti, you will transgress] the oath.

§12 (lines 70–72) If a fugitive [flees] from Hatti [and comes to the land of Ugarit], Niqmepa shall seize him [and return him] to Hatti. [If you do not return him, you will transgress] the oath.

§13 (lines 73–78) If a fugitive [flees] from the land [of Ugarit] and comes [to Hatti], the King of Hatti [will] not [seize him and return him. It is not permitted] for the King of Hatti to [return a fugitive. If a fugitive] comes [to the land of Ugarit] from Hanigalbat [or from another land], Niqmepa shall not [detain him, but shall allow him to go to Hatti]. If you detain him, [you will transgress the oath].

§14 (lines 79–80) And whatever Niqmepa [wants, he shall request from the King of Hatti, and he shall take whatever] the King of Hatti [gives him. He shall not take whatever the King of Hatti does not give him].

Loyalty of Subordinate

§15 (lines 81–86) And as I have [. . .] Niqmepa and treated him well — if [you, Niqmepa, . . . , do not seek the prosperity afforded by Hatti] and the protection of Mursili, Great King, [King of Hatti, but rather seek the prosperity afforded by] another land — by Hanigalbat, [or by Egypt] — if [you seek] the protection of [another] Great King, [you will transgress the oath]. And [the Thousand Gods] shall gather in assembly [for this treaty. They shall listen and be witnesses].

Divine Witnesses

§16 (lines 87–92) [The Sun-god of Heaven, the Sun-goddess] of Arinna, [the Storm-god of Heaven, the Storm-god of Hatti, Sheri, Hurri, Mount Nanni, Mount Hazzi, the Storm-god of the Market(?), the Storm-god of the Army, the Storm-god of Aleppo, the Storm-god of Zippalanda, the Storm-god of Nerik, the Storm-god of Lihzina, the Storm-god of the Ruin Mound, the Storm-god of Hisashapa], the Storm-god of Sahpina, [the Storm-god of Sapinuwa, the Storm-god of Pittiyarik], the Storm-god of Samuha, [the Storm-god of Hurma], the Storm-god of Sarissa, the Storm-god [of Help, the Storm-god of Uda], the Storm-god of [Kizzuwatna, the Storm-god] of Ishupitta, the Storm-god [of Ugarit],

§17 (lines 93–96) the Tutelary Deity, the Tutelary Deity of Hatti, Zithariya, [Karzi], Hapantaliya, the Tutelary Deity of Karahna, the Tutelary Deity of the Countryside, [the Tutelary Deity] of the Hunting Bag, Ea, Allatu, Telipinu [of] Turmitta, Telipinu of [Tawiniya], Telipinu [of] Hanhana, [Bunene], Pirwa, Askasepa,

§18 (lines 97–100) the Moon-god, Lord [of the Oath], Ishhara, Queen of the Oath, [Hebat, Queen of Heaven, Ishtar], Ishtar of the Countryside, Ishtar of Nineveh, [Ishtar of Hattarina, Ninatta, Kulitta], the War-god, the War-god of Hatti, [the War-god of Illaya, the War-god of Arziya], Yarri, Zappana,

§19 (lines 101–111) Hantitassu of Hurma, [Abara of Samuha, Katahha] of Ankuwa, the Queen [of Katapa, Ammamma of Tahurpa], Hallara of Dunna, [Huwassanna of Hupisna], Tapisuwa of Ishupitta, the Lady [of Landa], Kuniyawanni [of Landa, NIN.PÌSAN.PÌSAN] of Kinza, Mount Lebanon, Mount [Shariyana, Mount Pishaisha], the mountain-dweller [gods], the mercenary gods, [Ereshkigal, all the male deities and] female [deities of Hatti, all] the male deities [and female deities] of the land of Ugarit, all the primeval deities] — Nara, Namsara, Minki, [Tuhusi, Ammunki, Ammizzadu], Anu, Alalu, Antu, [Apantu, Enlil, Ninlil — the mountains], the rivers, the springs, the great sea, heaven and [earth, the winds], and the clouds. [They shall be witnesses] to this treaty and [oath].

Curse

§20 (lines 112–115) All the words of [the treaty and of the oath which] are written [on] this [tablet] — if Niqmepa does not observe these words

[of] the treaty and of the oath, then these oath [gods] shall destroy Niqmepa, together with [his person], his wives, his sons, his grandsons, his [household], his city, his land, and his possessions.

Blessing

§21 (lines 116–119) But if Niqmepa observes [these] words [of the treaty] and of the oath which [are written] on this tablet, [these oath gods] shall protect [Niqmepa], together with his person, his wives, his sons, [his grandsons, his household, his city, his land], and together with his possessions.

No. 10
Treaty between Mursili II of Hatti
and Targasnalli of Hapalla

This treaty forms part of a group along with Nos. 11, 12, and 13, all of which reflect the new political organization imposed on western Anatolia by Mursili II after his defeat of Uhha-ziti of Arzawa in the fourth year of his reign (cf. No. 12, §§3–4 and Götze 1933: 36–77). In order that Hatti need never again face a power as strong as Arzawa in this region, the Hittite king divided his former adversary into its component parts, including Hapalla, Mira-Kuwaliya, Seha River-Appawiya, Wilusa, and the rump state of Arzawa Minor, and concluded treaties with vassal kings he himself had installed.

These treaties are all very similar to one another (see Heinhold-Krahmer 1977: 130–35), often displaying word-for-word correspondences. Although not all portions are preserved in each text, each of these compositions originally had a historical introduction, provisions focusing primarily on support for Hatti against internal and external enemies, a section detailing the relationship of the western vassals to one another, a list of divine witnesses, and a curse and blessing.

[*The upper portion of the only tablet known for this composition has been lost, along with the preamble and the historical introduction.*]

Defensive Alliance

§1 (obv. 5'–9') [If some] person quarrels [with My Majesty] and insults My Majesty, [whether it is a brother of the King(?)], a prince, a high-ranking nobleman, a trusted official(?), a palace servant, a unit of the infantry or

chariotry — whatever sort of person it might be, and he comes to you, and
you do not seize him and turn him over, but even turn to him [and] go over
to him, or if you conceal him from My Majesty, you will have [transgressed]
the oath.

§2 (obv. 10'–17') [Furthermore], if some evil plan to revolt arises even in
Hatti, and you hear of it, take a stand immediately to aid My Majesty. [If]
it is not [possible] for you to come, send [infantry] and chariotry to the aid
of My Majesty. Let a nobleman lead them. [But if] you [somehow] ignore
the evil and think as follows: "Let this evil take place," [then] you will have
[thereby] transgressed the oath. And if [you hear] in advance of some evil
plan to revolt, [and] either some [Hittite] or some [man of Arzawa is at
fault] — these [which] are now independent of you (that is, the rulers of
the other Arzawa lands) — and you do [not] quickly write in advance to My
Majesty, but ignore [these men], and think as follows: "Let this evil take
place," then you [will] have [transgressed the oath].

§3 (obv. 18'–23') [Or] if some matter of hostilities comes up for Hatti, in
that an enemy [arises] against [My Majesty, and] I write [to you]: "Take
charge of infantry and chariotry and [take a stand] immediately to aid My
Majesty," [then] take charge of infantry and chariotry and take a stand
immediately to aid My Majesty. [If] it is not possible for you, then write to
My Majesty, [but] put [the infantry] and chariotry in the charge of one of
your noblemen. [Bring] them to the aid of My Majesty. If you do not bring
infantry and chariotry to my aid, you will thereby have transgressed [the
oath].

Hittite Garrisons

§4 (obv. 24'–27') Furthermore, have regard for the garrison troops which
I, My Majesty, have left behind for you as you have regard for your[self],
your household, and your servants. Sustain them and treat them well. You
shall not mistreat [them in any way]. If you do mistreat them in any way,
you will thereby have transgressed the oath.

Rumors

§5 (obv. 28'–34') Furthermore, because people are treacherous, if
rumors circulate, and someone comes and whispers before you: "His
Majesty is undertaking such and such against you," write . . . about this
matter to My Majesty. And if the matter is true, when I, My Majesty, write
back [to you], you shall not act rashly, nor [do] . . . [And] you shall not

commit evil [against] My Majesty. But if you do act rashly and commit evil against My Majesty, [then] you will thereby have transgressed the oath. Furthermore, whoever is My Majesty's enemy shall be [your] enemy, and whoever is your enemy is My Majesty's enemy.

Fugitives

§6 (obv. 35'–40') [The matter of] fugitives shall likewise be placed under oath: If a fugitive comes in flight from [Hatti], arrest him and turn him over to me. If [a civilian captive] under a service obligation(?) or a free man comes from the land of [Hapalla] as a fugitive to Hatti, I will not give [him] back to you. It is not permitted to give a fugitive back from Hatti. But [if] he is a cultivator, or a weaver, a carpenter, or a leatherworker — whatever sort of craftsman, and he does not [deliver] his assigned work, [but] runs off and comes to Hatti, I will arrest him and give him back to you.

Security of Subordinate

§7 (obv. 41'–rev. 1) But [if] someone seeks to kill you, Targasnalli, or your son, but [then] escapes and comes to Hatti — as he is your enemy, he is likewise [My Majesty's] enemy. I will arrest him and give him back to you. In regard to the land which [I], My Majesty, [have given] to you — if you, Targasnalli, protect My Majesty, but the population somehow refuses [to remain] as your subjects, and they become hostile to you, saying as follows: "[We desire] another [lord]," I, My Majesty, will absolutely refuse. I will by no means give [the land] of Hapalla to another. Only you [shall be] its lord.

Relations among Subordinates

§8 (rev. 2–8) [Furthermore], within my realm there are now three free men: you, Targasnalli, Mashuiluwa, and [Manapa-Tarhunta]. One shall not quarrel with another, nor shall one go to another [in flight] as a subject. If he does go to someone, he shall [expel] him. [And one] shall not quarrel with [another], nor shall one seek to kill another, nor shall he arrest [him]. And if you, Targasnalli, [harm] them, I will back them. You shall be my enemy. But if they harm [you], I will back you. They [shall be] my enemies.

§9 (rev. 9–15) [And] because I have given [you] a single oath, you shall be united as you have a single oath. [None of you] shall be hostile to [another]. As for the free men who surround you (that is, other regional rulers) — [they] shall not be hostile to any one of you, while at peace with another. They shall be hostile to all [of you], and you shall all continually make war in common on them. [They shall not be] at peace with any one of you. None of you shall secretly try to kill another. I, My Majesty, will be hostile to [whoever] does this, and he shall be my enemy. I will continually make war on [him] like an enemy. This matter too shall be placed under oath.

§10 (rev. 16–24) [Or] if you have some legal dispute, you shall not act rashly, nor do . . . , [nor] be angry. If you yourselves have a resolvable dispute(?), then set out and come before My Majesty, so that I, My Majesty, can set you on the proper path by means of a judgment. But if you do not have a resolvable dispute(?), then send noblemen to My Majesty. I, My Majesty, [will investigate] for you the legal dispute which you have, so that I can set you on the proper path by means of a judgment. You shall not act rashly, nor do . . . , nor be angry.

Relations of Subordinate to Agents of Great King

But if an [enemy] arises against you, Targasnalli, and you write to me: "Send me infantry and chariotry," and I send you infantry and chariotry, but you do not take them out [against] the enemy, but somehow betray them [to] the enemy, you will thereby have transgressed the oath.

§11 (rev. 25–32) Or if you request infantry and chariotry from My Majesty, [or] you request infantry and chariotry from a Hittite border commander who is in your vicinity, or you summon him yourself and speak as follows: "An enemy has arisen against me. Help me make war on him," so that either I, My Majesty, send you [infantry] and chariotry, or the border commander of my land helps you and [goes] against that enemy — if it does not somehow completely engage you, and you do not make war without hesitation on that enemy with your infantry, your chariotry, and your land, but you think as follows: "Let either the enemy defeat them, or let them defeat the enemy." — you will have transgressed the oath. Or if you abandon the infantry and chariotry somewhere in [your own(?)] times, then this too shall be placed under oath.

§12 (rev. 33–49) [Furthermore], in regard to the troops which I provide for you in garrison and send to your assistance — if someone [of them] flees in your land, or [. . .] with someone, [. . .] but you do [not . . .] after him, you will have transgressed the oath. Turn him over! But [if] you somehow(?) do not know about him, [it] shall be exempted [from the oath]. [And if] wholeheartedly . . . If any Hittite at all [flees], and you track him down — hand him over! Or if infantry and chariotry march through [your land], and someone falls asleep, or becomes ill, [or . . .] seizes him, or someone [kidnaps] a man — an Arzawan — from the army, [and] enslaves

[him], or he is sold, and the commander of the army says to you: "One of my men [is missing(?)]" — [if] it does not somehow completely engage you, so that you search for him, and [turn] him over, [then] you will [have] transgressed the oath. Furthermore, the land which I, My Majesty, have given to you and [which] constitutes [the border districts] of Hatti — if some enemy mobilizes and goes to [attack] those border districts, and you get word but do not [write] in advance to the commander in the land, [and] do not lend assistance, but ignore the evil, you will have transgressed the oath. Or if the enemy has [. . .], but you do not promptly aid him (the Hittite commander), and do not fight the enemy, you will transgress the oath. [Or] if the enemy marches through your land, and you do not fight him, but even say [as follows to him]: "Go attack, and carry off plunder! I don't [want to know] anything about it." — [then] you will thereby have transgressed the oath.

Civilian Captives

§13 (rev. 50–54) [Furthermore], because I, My Majesty, conquered the land of Arzawa, I have made the civilian captives whom I carried off (to Hatti) [subject] to the service obligation. And if [someone of] the civilian captives whom my father carried off — either a man of Arzawa [or a Hittite] — flees and comes to your land, [and you do not seize him] and turn him over to me, but [even hide] him from me, [then] you will thereby [have transgressed] the oath.

Divine Witnesses

§14 (rev. 55–57) [Now we have summoned] the Thousand Gods to assembly [in regard to this] oath. [They shall listen and] be [witnesses]: The Sun-god of Heaven, the Sun-goddess [of Arinna, . . . the Storm-god] of Lihzina, [. . .]

[*The remainder of the reverse has been lost, and along with it the greater part of the list of deities. On the left edge is preserved a fragment of a blessing.*]

Blessing

§15 (left edge 3'–4') [If you observe these words, the gods shall benevolently protect you, together with your wife, your sons, your grandsons], your [cities], your threshing floor, [your vineyard, your field, your oxen, your sheep, and together with all your possessions]. You shall thrive [in the hand of My Majesty, and you shall live to an old age in the hand of My Majesty].

No. 11
Treaty between Mursili II of Hatti
and Kupanta-Kurunta of Mira-Kuwaliya

This treaty of the "Arzawa group" (see introduction to No. 10) was concluded by Mursili II with the king of the closely associated lands of Mira
and Kuwaliya. Bearing the same name as an earlier adversary of Hatti in
the west (see No. 27, §§8–10), this Kupanta-Kurunta seems to have been a
loyal vassal. The historical introduction to his agreement with Mursili, however, centers on the perfidy of his adoptive father and predecessor
Mashuiluwa, whose bad example Kupanta-Kurunta is enjoined not to follow (see del Monte 1974).

Preamble

§1 (B i 1–2) [Thus says] My Majesty, Mursili, Great King, King of Hatti,
Hero; [son of] Suppiluliuma, Great King, King of Hatti, Hero:

Historical Introduction

§2 (B i 3–10) [Formerly] his brothers beleaguered Mashuiluwa, defeated
him, and forced him to flee from the land. Then he came to my father, and
my father did not turn him out, but took him up and gave him his daughter,
my sister Muwatti, in marriage. She was your (adopted) mother, Kupanta-
Kurunta. But my father was (occupied) in another land and was not able to
back him.

§3 (B i 11–21) But when my father died, and I, My Majesty, had seated
myself upon the throne of my father, I backed him. I supported him, and
the gods of my father protected me. I defeated the enemy for him and conquered the entire land of Arzawa. That which I, My Majesty, took as booty
I brought back to Hattusa for myself. But I established the borders of the
lands which I left in place. I gave the land of the Seha River to Manapa-
Tarhunta. I gave the land of Hapalla to Targasnalli. And I gave the land of
Mira and the land of Kuwaliya [back] to Mashuiluwa. I gave the house of
his father and the throne of his father back to him. Finally, I made him lord
in the land of Mira.

§4 (B i 22–29; D i 30–33) Formerly, when I installed Mashuiluwa for
lordship in the land of Mira, Mashuiluwa said to me as follows: "I have no
son. The population grumbles(?) against us: 'Tomorrow will it be this way or
that way?' Because I have no son, while Kupanta-Kurunta is the son of my
brother, give him to me, my lord, as son. Let him be my son. And in the

future [let him be] lord in the land." [I gave] you, Kupanta-Kurunta, to Mashuiluwa as son. Then I caused the land of Mira and the land of Kuwaliya to swear an oath to Mashuiluwa, Muwatti, and you, Kupanta-Kurunta. Moreover, I, My Majesty, protected Mashuiluwa, and in no way mistreated him. But Mashuiluwa quarreled with me, stirred up the land of Pitassa and the Hittites, my own subjects, against me, and would have [begun war] against me.

§5 (D i 34–43) But when I, My Majesty, heard about this matter, then in no way did I, My Majesty, seek to harm Mashuiluwa. [Nor] had I previously mistreated him [in any way]. I said as follows: "I will go and settle this matter." Then I set out and went to settle this matter. And when I arrived at the city of Sallapa, I wrote to Mashuiluwa: "Come here to me!" But because Mashuiluwa saw his offense, he accordingly refused me, [My Majesty], fled before me, and went over to the land [of Masa]. I, My Majesty, went and attacked the land of Masa and destroyed it.

§6 (D i 44–49; C i 6'–11') Then I, My Majesty, sent a man to the other men of the land of Masa to whom Mashuiluwa had gone over. I wrote to them as follows: "Mashuiluwa was my sworn ally, but he quarreled with me, stirred up my subjects against me, and would have begun war against me. Now he has fled before me and has just come to you. Seize him and turn him over to me! If you do not seize him and turn him over to me, I will come and destroy you, together with your land." And when the men of the land of Masa heard this, they became frightened and seized Mashuiluwa, and turned him over to me. I took him by the hand, and [because] he had offended [against me, My Majesty], I took him to Hattusa.

§7 (C i 12'–22') Because Mashuiluwa formerly had no son, and took you, Kupanta-Kurunta, the son of his brother, as his son — Are you, Kupanta-Kurunta, not aware that if in Hatti someone commits the offense of revolt, the son of whatever father commits the offense is an offender too? And that they take the house of his father away from him, and either give it to someone else or take it for the palace? Now, because your father, Mashuiluwa, committed an offense, and because you, Kupanta-Kurunta, were Mashuiluwa's son, even if you were in no way an offender, could they not have taken the house of your father and your land away from you and given it to someone else? I could have made someone else lord in the land.

§8 (C i 23'–28') Now I, My Majesty, have not mistreated you, Kupanta-Kurunta, in any way. I have not turned you out. I have not taken the house of your father or the land away from you. I have given the house of your father and your land back to *you*, and I have installed *you* in lordship for the land. I have given you the land of Mira and the land of Kuwaliya. The borders shall be the same for you as they were in the time of Mashuiluwa.

Frontiers

§9 (C i 29'–35') On this side, in the direction of the city of Maddunassa, the fortified camp of Tudhaliya shall be your frontier. And on the other side, the sinkhole of the city of Wiyanawanda shall be your frontier. You shall not cross over beyond the city of Aura. On this side, in the direction of the Astarpa River, the land of Kuwaliya shall be your frontier. This land shall be yours, protect it! You shall not found a single city in the direction of the Astarpa River, or in that of the Siyanta River. If you do found even a single city, you will have transgressed the oath, and I will come as an enemy and attack it.

§10 (C i 36'–38'; A i 27–34) But if some settlement establishes itself, it shall be your enemy in the same way as it is My Majesty's enemy. Attack it! A single sacred city belonging to Mashuiluwa himself is situated on the Siyanta River, and it shall be exempted from the oath. Protect for yourself this land which I, My Majesty, have given to you. Furthermore, you shall not desire any border district of Hatti, [and] you shall not take for yourself any border district of Hatti. Or if because I, My Majesty, did not give you anything on this side, in the direction of the Astarpa River and the Siyanta River, you cross the frontier and take something for yourself, you will have offended against the oath, and have transgressed the oath. The oath gods shall pursue you unrelentingly.

Loyalty to Hittite Dynasty

§11 (A i 35–47) And when your father Mashuiluwa offended against My Majesty, were not you, Kupanta-Kurunta, a son(?) to Mashuiluwa? Although you were in no way an offender, <could you not have been punished?> I did not take the house of your father or the land away from you. I did not make someone else lord. I gave the house of your father and the land back to *you*, and I installed *you* in lordship for the land. And as I, My Majesty, have not in the past mistreated you in any way, Kupanta-Kurunta, in the future, Kupanta-Kurunta, [protect] me, My Majesty, as overlord. And further in the future protect the descendants of My Majesty, to the first and second generation, [as] overlords. You shall not seek to harm them, and you shall not [become implicated] in any evil. You shall not desire any other power (over you). [In the future] protect My Majesty as overlord.

[*Gap of significant length.*]

Defensive Alliance

§12 (C ii 3'–10') [If someone quarrels with My Majesty], whether it is a prince, [a high-ranking nobleman, a palace servant], a unit of the infantry or chariotry — whatever sort [of person it might be], you shall not [defect] from My Majesty and shall not become implicated with him. You shall not go over to him. [As] you have stood on the side of My Majesty, you shall continue to stand only on the side of My Majesty. Be an effective and strong helper for My Majesty. And later be an effective and strong helper for the descendants of My Majesty.

§13 (C ii 11'–12') And later your descendants, Kupanta-Kurunta, to the first and second generation, shall be effective and strong helpers.

§14 (C ii 13'–25') But if in the future, you, Kupanta-Kurunta, do not protect My Majesty and the descendants of My Majesty as overlords, but defect from them, and are not an effective and strong helper for them, and desire [someone] else as overlord, you will have transgressed the oath. Or if someone plots a matter of revolt against My Majesty, and he flees before me and comes to you, and you do not seize him and turn him over to me, but either go over to him or help him escape, saying as follows: "Go, save yourself somehow!" — then you, Kupanta-Kurunta, will have committed an offense before the oath gods and will have transgressed the oath. The oath gods shall pursue you unrelentingly.

§15 (C ii 26'–iii 11) Furthermore, if some evil plan to revolt arises in Hatti, in that some foreign land begins war against My Majesty, but everything is well with My Majesty, wait for word from My Majesty. And when I, My Majesty, write to you, respond accordingly. But if domestically someone carries out a revolt against My Majesty, whether a nobleman, a unit of the infantry or chariotry — or whatever sort of person it might be, if I, My Majesty, put things right, then I will capture that person or that unit of the infantry or chariotry. But if I, My Majesty, write to you: "Take charge of infantry and chariotry. Send them to my aid immediately," then take charge of infantry and chariotry. Send them to My Majesty immediately. But if I write to you alone: "Drive here alone," then drive here alone. But if I, My Majesty, do not write to you about this matter of revolt, but you hear about it in advance, you shall not ignore it. If it is possible for you, take charge of infantry and chariotry. Send them to the aid of My Majesty immediately. If it is not possible for you, wait for word from My Majesty. And when I, My Majesty, write to you, respond accordingly.

§16 (C iii 12–21) But if someone revolts against My Majesty and beleaguers me(!) — or later someone revolts against the descendants of My Majesty and beleaguers them — and I write to you, then send infantry and chariotry to my aid immediately. But if the messenger is unable to come, and you hear about the matter in advance (of his arrival), do not wait for word from My Majesty. You shall not first take a bird oracle about it. Take charge of infantry and chariotry and be of assistance. And if you do not observe these stipulations, then you will transgress the oath. The oath gods shall pursue you unrelentingly.

§17 (C iii 22–28; D iii 47–66; B iii 27'–30') And if you hear in advance about some evil plan to revolt, and either some Hittite or some man of Arzawa carries out the revolt — these which are now independent of you (that is, the rulers of the other Arzawa lands) — but you do not quickly send word in advance to My Majesty, but somehow ignore (the actions of) these men, and think as follows: "Let this evil take place," you will have transgressed the oath. Or how did Mashuiluwa recently act? He promptly sent me word about É.GAL.PAP: "É.GAL.PAP is fomenting revolt." Then afterwards he became silent about the matter and did not write me anything further. Then he even did an about-face and let himself be enlisted by É.GAL.PAP. He swore an oath to him, and they joined forces. He made my subjects take oaths against me and he revolted against me. You, Kupanta-Kurunta, shall not act like Mashuiluwa. If someone is fomenting evil against My Majesty, when you hear word of it, send word in advance accurately and without hesitation. When you hear of such a matter and write about it to My Majesty, you shall not thereafter become silent about the matter. And you shall not do an about-face, [and] shall not let yourself be enlisted by that person. Whatever person should [do] such a thing — as he is My Majesty's enemy, he shall likewise be your enemy. But if you, Kupanta-Kurunta, in any way hear of such a matter and then are silent about the matter, and do not write to My Majesty about it, [but] let yourself be enlisted by that person, [then] you, Kupanta-Kurunta, will thereby have [offended] before [the gods and] have transgressed the oath. The oath gods shall pursue you unrelentingly.

§18 (A iii 3–12) [Or] if some matter of hostilities comes up for Hatti, in that an enemy arises against My Majesty, and I write to you, Kupanta-Kurunta: "Take charge of infantry and chariotry [and] take a stand immediately to aid My Majesty," then take charge of infantry and chariotry and take a stand immediately [to aid] My Majesty. If it is not possible for you, then write to My Majesty, but put the infantry and chariotry in the charge of one of your noblemen. Bring them immediately to the aid of My Majesty. But if you do not bring infantry and chariotry immediately to my aid, then you will have offended before [the gods, and] have transgressed the oath. The oath gods shall pursue you unrelentingly.

Hittite Garrisons

§19 (D iv 12'–18') Furthermore, have regard for the garrison troops which I, My Majesty, have left behind for you, as you, Kupanta-Kurunta, treat yourself, your household, and your servants. Sustain them and treat them well. You shall not mistreat them in any way. But if you do mistreat them in any way, then you will thereby have offended before the gods and have transgressed the oath. The oath gods shall pursue you unrelentingly.

Rumors

§20 (D iv 19'–34') Furthermore, because people are treacherous, if rumors circulate and someone comes and whispers before you: "His Majesty is undertaking such and such to your disadvantage, and will take either the house of your father or the land away from you, or he will mistreat you in some way," write about this matter to My Majesty. And if the matter is true, when I, My Majesty, write to you, you shall not act rashly, nor do . . . And you shall not commit evil against My Majesty. This matter shall be taken to your heart. Take it to your heart today! Because your father Mashuiluwa offended against My Majesty, and you, Kupanta-Kurunta, were Mashuiluwa's son, even if you were in no way an offender — could not I, My Majesty, have deposed you right then, if My Majesty had been disposed to disfavor? I could even now have taken the house of your father and the land away from you and have given [it] to someone else. I could have made someone else lord in the land.

§21 (E iv 14'–33') Because My Majesty was not now disposed to disfavor, I did not depose you. [I did not take] the house of your father and the land away from you, [and] I did not give [them] to someone else. I did [not] make [someone else lord] in the land. [I gave] the house of your father and the land [back] to *you*, and I installed *you* in lordship [for the land. And if] someone speaks an evil word concerning My Majesty to you, Kupanta-Kurunta: "His Majesty is undertaking [such] and such to your disadvantage" — [this matter] shall be taken to your heart as a regulation. Take this [matter] to your heart today! [You shall not] act rashly, nor do . . . [And] you shall not commit evil [against My Majesty. As you have stood] on the side of My Majesty, continue to stand only on the side of My Majesty. [If] someone speaks [an evil] word concerning My Majesty before you, Kupanta-Kurunta, and you [conceal] it from My Majesty, [and] act rashly, and [commit some] evil against My Majesty, you, Kupanta-Kurunta, will offend [before the gods] and transgress the oath. [The oath gods] shall pursue [you] unrelentingly.

Fugitives

§22 (E iv 34'–45') [The matter of a fugitive shall be placed] under oath as follows: [If a fugitive] from Hatti comes [in flight to your land, arrest] him [and turn him over to me. If a civilian captive under a service obligation(?)] or some free man [comes as a fugitive to Hatti, I will not give him back to you. It is not] permitted [to give back a fugitive from Hatti]. But if he is a cultivator, or a weaver, [a carpenter, a leatherworker — whatever] sort of craftsman, and if he does not deliver [(his assigned) work in Mira], but runs off and [comes] to Hatti, I will arrest him and give him back to you.

§23 (F i 8'–22') [If] someone revolts against [you], Kupanta-Kurunta, [and . . .], but you [hear] about the matter in advance, [so that that] person takes fright, [and] flees [from your land], and comes to Hatti — as [you, Kupanta-Kurunta], are a subject of My Majesty [and] protect [My Majesty as overlord], concerning that [person who] revolts against you — I, My Majesty, [will not be silent in] that matter. As he is your enemy, [he is likewise My Majesty's enemy]. But if you, Kupanta-Kurunta, defect from [My Majesty . . . as overlord, offend against My Majesty in some way], and [defect from] him [. . .] Then I, [My Majesty, will not back] you [in this matter. It shall be exempted] from the oath. [*A gap of uncertain length follows.*]

§24 (A iv 1–19) [*The initial lines here are too fragmentary for connected translation. An enemy apparently threatens* "some [city] or some fortress" *of Kupanta-Kurunta.*] . . . I, My Majesty, will [not] be silent [in] that matter. As they are your enemies, they are likewise [My Majesty's] enemies. But if you, Kupanta-Kurunta, offend against My Majesty in some way, and attempt to harm My Majesty, you will forfeit my support. How did Mashuiluwa act? He offended against My Majesty and then defected from him. [But his own subjects] took the side of My Majesty, saying as follows: "You have offended [against] His Majesty, but we are the subjects of His Majesty alone." And if you, Kupanta-Kurunta, act like this, your subjects will defect from you and take the side of My Majesty. I will not back you in this matter. It shall be exempted from the oath.

Relations among Subordinates

§25 (A iv 20–37) Furthermore, it is you who are the three free men: you, Kupanta-Kurunta, Manapa-Tarhunta, and Targasnalli. [Because] I have given [you a single oath], be united. [None of you] shall be hostile [to another], nor shall one [try to kill] another. As for the free men who [surround you] (that is, other regional rulers) — they shall not [be hostile] to any one of you, while at peace with another. They shall be hostile to all [of you], and [you shall] all [continuously make war] on them. None of you shall secretly try to kill another. . . . One shall not go to another in flight. If he does go to someone, he shall expel him. And if you, Kupanta-Kurunta, harm them, I will back them. You shall be my enemy. But them concerning [. . .] If some one of them, either Targasnalli or Manapa-Tarhunta, becomes hostile [to] My Majesty, and [does evil] against My Majesty . . . [*Eight fragmentary and untranslatable lines are followed by a gap.*]

Relations of Subordinates to Agents of Great King

§26 (G ii 1'–8') [. . . Or if the enemy marches through] your [land], and you do not fight him, but even [say] as follows to him: "Go attack, and [carry off plunder]! I don't want [to know anything (about it)." — then you, Kupanta-Kurunta], will thereby have transgressed the oath. [The oath gods shall] pursue [you unrelentingly].

Civilian Captives

§27 (G ii 9'–iii 10) [Furthermore], because [I], My Majesty, [conquered] the land [of Arzawa], I have made the civilian captives whom [I carried off to Hattusa] subject to the service obligation. [And] if someone of the civilian captives [whom my father carried] off — either a man of Arzawa or [a Hittite — flees and] comes to your land, and you do [not] seize [him] and turn him over, [but even] hide [him from me], you will have transgressed the oath. While Mashuiluwa was [with] you, if then [some] Hittite or man of [Arzawa] fled before Mashuiluwa, [. . .] [*Small gap.*]

Reading of Treaty Tablet

§28 (I iv 1'–8') [Furthermore, this tablet which] I have made [for you, Kupanta-Kurunta], shall be read out [before you three times yearly, and you, Kupanta-Kurunta], observe [these] words. [These words are by no means] reciprocal. [They] issue from [Hatti. Now] you, Kupanta-Kurunta, protect My Majesty [. . .] You must not [do] evil [against My Majesty. Hatti] will not prepare [evil] against you. [I have] now [summoned] the Thousand Gods to assembly [for this oath]. They shall [observe and] listen.

Divine Witnesses of Hatti

§29 (I iv 9'–15') The Sun-god of Heaven, [the Sun-goddess of Arinna], the Powerful Storm-god, the Storm-god of Heaven, Sheri, [Hurri], Mount

Nanni, Mount Hazzi, [. . .], the Storm-god of the Market(?), the Storm-god of the Army, [the Storm-god of Aleppo, the Storm-god of Zippalanda], the Storm-god of Nerik, the Storm-god of [. . .], the Storm-god of Uda, the Storm-god of [. . .], the Storm-god of Sapinuwa, the [Storm-god of . . .], the Proud Storm-god, the Storm-god of [. . . *Break of around ten lines.*]

§30 (J rev. 1'–9') [. . . , Abara of Samuha, . . . , Hallara] of Dunna, [. . .], Huwassanna [of Hupisna], the mountain-dweller gods, the [mercenary] gods, all the male deities and female deities [of Hatti], the Sun-goddess of the Earth, the primeval [deities — Nara], Namsara, Minki, [Tuhusi, Ammunki, Ammizzadu], Alalu, Kumarbi, Anu, [Antu, Apantu, Enlil], Ninlil — the mountains, the rivers, the springs, [the great sea, heaven and earth, the winds], and the clouds.

Divine Witnesses of Mira

§31 (J rev. 10'–11') All the [deities] of the land of Mira, [. . . , the male deities], the female deities, the mountains, the rivers, [. . . *Text breaks off.*]

No. 12
Treaty between Mursili II of Hatti
and Manapa-Tarhunta of the Land of the Seha River

Restorations to the historical introduction of this member of the "Arzawa group" of treaties (see introduction to No. 11) have been drawn from the similar account of events presented in the Annals of Mursili II (Götze 1933: 66–71).

Preamble; Historical Introduction

§1 (A i 1–13) Thus says My Majesty, Mursili, Great King, King [of Hatti, Hero]: Your father left you, Manapa-Tarhunta [behind . . .], and you were a child. Your brothers [. . .] and Ura-Tarhunta plotted to kill [you], and would [have killed] you, [but] you escaped. [They caused] you [to flee] from [the land of the Seha River], and [you went] over to the people of the city of Karkisa. [They took] your land and the house of your father [away] from you, and took them for themselves. [But I, My Majesty, commended you, Manapa-Tarhunta], to the men of Karkisa. [I repeatedly sent] gifts [to] the men of Karkisa. [My brother also] pleaded [with them on your behalf]. Because of our words the men [of Karkisa] protected you.

§2 (A i 14–18) [But] when Ura-Tarhunta proceeded [to transgress] the oath, [the oath] gods seized him, and the men [of the land of the Seha River] drove him [out]. But [because of our words] the men [of the land of the Seha River] received you (back), and because of [our] words they protected you.

§3 (A i 19–33) But [when] it happened that my brother [Arnuwanda died], and I, My Majesty, [seated myself] on the throne [of my father], then I, My Majesty, came and [backed] you. [I caused] the people of the land of the Seha River [to swear an oath] to you, and because of my [words they protected] you. [They . . .] you wholeheartedly. [*Four lines too fragmentary for translation.*] But [when it happened that Uhha-ziti, king of the land of Arzawa, began war against My Majesty], then [you, Manapa-Tarhunta, offended against My Majesty]. You backed [Uhha-ziti, my enemy, and made war] on My Majesty. You did not back [me].

Fugitives

§4 (A i 34–62) [But when I went on campaign] against Uhha-ziti and against [the people of Arzawa], because Uhha-ziti [had transgressed the oath] in regard to me, the oath gods seized [him, and I destroyed him]. And because you [had taken the side of Uhha-ziti], I [would] have destroyed you likewise. [But] you fell [down] at [my feet], and [you dispatched old] men [and old women] to me. [And] your messengers [fell] down at [my] feet. You sent [to me] as follows: "Spare me, my lord. [May my lord not] destroy [me]. Take me as a vassal and [. . .] my person. [I will turn] <over> from here(!) [all] the civilian captives of the land of Mira, [the civilian captives] of Hatti, [or] the civilian captives of Arzawa — whichever come [over] to me." Then I, My Majesty, had [compassion] for you, [and] because of that I acceded [to you and made] peace with you. And as I, My Majesty, had compassion for you and made peace with you, now seize and hand [over] to me all civilian captives of the land of Arzawa who come over to you — whoever [flees] before me — and whatever civilian captives of the land of Mira [or of] Hatti come [over] to you . . . You shall not leave a single man behind, nor shall you [allow] anyone out of your land, or allow him to cross into another land. Gather up the civilian captives and turn them [over] to me. If you carry out all these matters, [then] I will take [you] as a vassal. Be my ally. In the future this shall be [your] regulation. [Observe it]. It shall be placed under oath for you.

Frontiers

§5 (A i 63–67) I have now given you the land of the Seha River and the land of [Appawiya]. This shall be your land — protect [it]! You shall not hereafter desire a Hittite person or a border district of Hatti. [If] you do perversely desire a Hittite person or a border district of Hatti, you will have transgressed the oath.

[*It is not possible to draw connected sense from the scraps of text preserved in Texts A and B for the remainder of column i. Only traces of seven lines of column ii remain in Text B. The eight partial lines at the head of column iii in Text B are also badly damaged, but it can be recognized that they deal with the possibility of revolt, and with the relationship of Manapa-Tarhunta with Uhha-ziti.*]

Defensive Alliance

§6 (B iii 9–14) And now, if someone somehow [carries out] a revolt against [My Majesty, whether it is] some person or some unit of troops — [whoever it is] — and you, Manapa-Tarhunta, somehow [hear about him], become his partisan, and turn away [from My Majesty], that too [shall be placed] under oath.

Relations among Subordinates

§7 (B iii 15–19) Furthermore, [I], My Majesty, [have] now [given] you, [Manapa-Tarhunta], the land of the Seha River and the land of Appawiya. This shall be your land — protect it! [And I have given] the land of Mira and the land of Kuwaliya to Mashuiluwa. [And] I have given the land of Hapalla to Targasnalli. This shall be your territory — protect it!

§8 (B iii 20–23) Now you, Manapa-Tarhunta, shall not take anything away from Mashuiluwa, and Mashuiluwa shall not take [anything] away from you. You, Manapa-Tarhunta, shall not quarrel with Mashuiluwa, and Mashuiluwa [shall not] quarrel with [you].

§9 (B iii 24–27) [Now you shall be] favored [by Mashuiluwa], and Mashuiluwa shall be favored [by you]. If [some] legal dispute comes up, you shall place [it] before My Majesty, and I, [My Majesty], will decide it.

§10 (A iii 19'–29') [Furthermore, you], Manapa-Tarhunta, [shall not approach] Mashuiluwa as an enemy, and you shall not [kill] him. [Mashuiluwa] shall not approach [you] as an enemy, [and] he shall not kill you. But if Mashuiluwa does [quarrel] with you and approaches you as an enemy, and kills you, [then] Mashuiluwa will thereby be My Majesty's enemy. I, My Majesty, will continually make war on [Mashuiluwa]. But if you, Manapa-Tarhunta, quarrel [with Mashuiluwa], and approach Mashuiluwa [as an enemy], and kill him, then you, Manapa-Tarhunta, will be My Majesty's enemy. I will continually make war on you. And this matter too will be placed under oath.

§11 (A iii 30'–36') [A subject] of Mashuiluwa shall not [come] as a fugitive to your land, and a subject [of yours] shall not go as a fugitive [to] Mashuiluwa. You shall be favored by one another (in this regard). And if some person from among the civilian captives which the father of My Majesty carried off to Hatti flees from me, and you, Manapa-Tarhunta, do not give him back, this too will be placed under oath.

§12 (A iii 37'–47') Those subjects of mine who are in flight from me, My Majesty, shall be your enemies, just as they are Mashuiluwa's enemies. You shall continually make war on them, just as Mashuiluwa continually makes war on them. And [as] you, Manapa-Tarhunta, do not allow them [into your land], Mashuiluwa shall likewise not allow them in. They shall be [your] common enemies. [But if] they make peace, then they shall make peace with you in common. They shall [not be] at peace with any one of you, while hostile to another. And this matter too will be placed under [oath].

Divine Witnesses

§13 (A iii 48'–51') We have now summoned the Thousand Gods to assembly for this oath. They shall stand, observe, and listen. And they shall be [witnesses].

§14 (A iii 52'–54'; B iv 1–3) [The Sun-god of Heaven, the Sun-goddess of Arinna, the Storm-god] of Heaven, the Powerful Storm-god, [. . . , Sheri, Hurri], Mount Nanni, [Mount Hazzi, . . .], the Storm-god of the Market(?), the Storm-god of the Army, [the Storm-god of . . . , the Storm-god of Pittiyarik], the Storm-god of Nerik, the Storm-god of the Ruin Mound, [the Storm-god of . . . , the Storm-god of Aleppo], the Storm-god of Uda, the Storm-god of Kummanni,

§15 (B iv 4–6) [the Storm-god of . . . , the Storm-god of Hisashapa], the Storm-god of Samuha, the Storm-god of Sapinuwa, [the Storm-god of . . . , the Storm-god] of Sahpina, the Storm-god of Hurma, the Storm-god of Sarissa, the Storm-god [of . . .], the Storm-god of Help, the Storm-god of Zippalanda,

§16 (B iv 7–13) the Tutelary Deity, the Tutelary Deity of Hatti, Zithariya, Karzi, Hapantaliya, the Tutelary Deity of Karahna, the Tutelary Deity of the Countryside, the Tutelary Deity of the Hunting Bag, Allatu, Enki,

Telipinu, Pirwa, the Moon-god, <Lord> of the Oath, Hebat, Great Queen, [. . .], Ishtar, Ishtar of the Countryside, Ishtar of Nineveh, [Ishtar] of Hattarina, Ninatta, Kulitta, [Ishhara], Queen of the Oath,

§17 (B iv 14–20) [the War-god], the War-god of Hatti, the War-god of Illaya, the War-god of Arziya, Yarri, Zappana, Abara of Samuha, Hantitassu of Hurma, Katahha of Ankuwa, the Queen of Katapa, Ammamma of Tahurpa, Hallara of Dunna, Huwassanna of Hupisna, the mountain-dweller gods, all the mercenary gods of Hatti,

§18 (B iv 21–25) [the male deities] and the female deities of Hatti, the Sun-goddess of the Earth, all the primeval deities — Nara, Namsara, Minki, Ammunki, [Tuhusi], Ammizzadu, Alalu, Kumarbi, Anu, Antu, Enlil, Ninlil —

§19 (B i 26–27) [the mountains, the rivers], the springs, the great sea, [heaven and earth], the winds, the rivers, and the clouds.

[*A relatively short break intervenes.*]

Curse

§20 (A iv 29'–39') [And if] you, [Manapa-Tarhunta, together with the people of the land] of the Seha River [and] the land of Appawiya, do [not] observe [these words, and in the future, to the first and second generation, you turn] away, or you alter [these words] of the tablet — whatever [is contained] on this tablet, then these [oath gods] shall eradicate you, together with [your] person, your [wives], your sons, your [grandsons], your household, [your land], your infantry, your horses, [your chariots(?)], and together with your [possessions], from the Dark Earth.

Blessing

§21 (A iv 40'–46') [But if] you, Manapa-Tarhunta, observe these [words] of the tablet, and in the future you do not [turn] away from the [King] of Hatti, together with [my sons, and from the word of the oath, then] these oath gods shall [benevolently] protect you. And [your sons] shall thrive [in the hand of My Majesty].

Colophon

Text A: Single tablet of the treaty of [Manapa-Tarhunta].

No. 13
Treaty between Muwattalli II of Hatti
and Alaksandu of Wilusa

A generation later than the other "Arzawa treaties" (see introduction to No. 11), this text has the best-preserved list of divine witnesses among the group. Wilusa was the northwesternmost of the Arzawa lands and has been identified by many authorities with the later Ilios, an alternative name for Troy in classical Greek sources (Güterbock 1986; Watkins 1986).

Preamble

§1 (B i 1–2) Thus says My Majesty, Muwattalli, Great King, [King] of Hatti, Beloved of the Storm-god of Lightning; son of Mursili, Great King, Hero:

Historical Introduction

§2 (B i 2–14) Formerly, when my forefather Labarna had conquered all the lands of Arzawa and the land of Wilusa, thereafter the land of Arzawa began war, and the land of Wilusa defected from Hatti — but because the matter is long past, I do not know from which King. [And] when the land of Wilusa [defected] from Hatti, its people were indeed at peace with the Kings of Hatti from afar, [and] they regularly sent [them messengers]. But when Tudhaliya came [. . .] against the land of Arzawa, he did not enter [the land of Wilusa. It was] at peace [with him] and regularly sent [him messengers. . . .] and Tudhaliya [. . .] forefathers in the land [of . . .]

§3 (B i 15–20) The king of the land of Wilusa [was] at peace with him, [and] he regularly sent [messengers to him], so that he did not [enter] the land against him. [And when] the land [of Arzawa began war once more], and my grandfather Suppiluliuma came and [attacked the land of Arzawa], Kukkunni, king of the land [of Wilusa, was at peace] with him. And he did not come against him, [but regularly sent] messengers [to my grandfather Suppiluliuma].

[*The remainder of column i in Text B has been lost. The following twenty or so lines in Text A are too fragmentary for translation. We can recognize, however, an account of the reorganizational activities of Mursili II in the west:* "[He gave] the land of Arzawa [to Piyama-Kurunta. He gave] the land of Kuwaliya [to Mashuiluwa. He gave the land of the Seha River and] the land of Appawiya [to Manapa-Tarhunta. He gave] the land of Hapalla [to Targasnalli]."]

§4 (A i 43'–56') But when my father died, I seated [myself on the throne] of my father. [And] you indeed protected [me . . . as overlord]. But [when] it happened [that the men of the land of Arzawa] began war against me, and they entered [. . . your land(?)], then you called on me for help. I came [to your aid], and I destroyed the land of Masa. [And] I destroyed [the land of . . .] The civilian captives, cattle(?), and sheep(?) [. . .] them to Mount Kupta[(-) . . .] I took(?), but for you, [Alaksandu, . . .] I destroyed those lands [. . .] and [I brought] them back to Hattusa [. . . to] your father [. . .] Alaksandu [. . .]

Defensive Alliance; Succession

§5 (A i 57'-79') [*The first five lines of this paragraph are too fragmentary for translation.*] . . . no [one] in the land of Wilusa concerning kingship [. . .] Because the population grumbles(?), [. . . When your] day of death[17] arrives, Alaksandu, then [. . .] In regard to the [son] of yours whom you designate for kingship — [whether he is by] your wife or by your concubine, and even if he is still a child — if the population of the land refuses him and says as follows: "He is the progeny [. . .]" — I, My Majesty, will not agree. Later my son and my grandson, to the first and second generation, will protect that one alone. You, Alaksandu, benevolently protect My Majesty. And later protect my son and my grandson, to the first and second generation. And as I, My Majesty, protected you, Alaksandu, in good will because of the word of your father, and came to your aid, and killed your enemy for you, later in the future my sons and my grandsons will certainly protect your descendant for you, to the first and second generation. If some enemy arises for you, I will not abandon you, just as I have not now abandoned you. I will kill your enemy for you. But if your brother or someone of your family revolts against you, Alaksandu,

§6 (B ii 5-20) or later someone revolts against your son or your grandsons, and they seek the kingship of the land of Wilusa, I, My Majesty, will absolutely not depose you, Alaksandu. I will not take that one into my service. As he is your enemy, in exactly the same way he is My Majesty's enemy. [And] I, [My Majesty], will recognize only you, Alaksandu. [I will not recognize] that one. I will destroy his land. Now you, [Alaksandu], protect My Majesty. And later, your descendants, to the first [and second] generation, shall protect [the descendants of My Majesty] as overlords, to the first and second generation. They shall not plot evil [against them], nor shall they defect from them. And as I, My Majesty, have now made a treaty tablet for Alaksandu, you, Alaksandu, [and your descendants to the first] and second generation, act thus according to the treaty tablet. [And your descendants] shall protect only the sons of My Majesty [as overlords], to the first and second generation. You shall [not] plot [evil against] them, [nor defect from them].

[*The next forty lines or so, which are for the most part represented only by the ends of lines in Text A, are too fragmentary for translation.*]

§7 (A ii 58–74) [Furthermore, if some evil] plan to revolt [arises in Hatti, in that some foreign land] begins war [against My Majesty, but everything is well with My Majesty, wait for word from My Majesty. And] when [I, My Majesty, write] to you, respond accordingly. [But if someone carries out a revolt] against My Majesty, [whether a nobleman, a unit of the infantry or chariotry] — whatever sort of person [carries out] a revolt against <My Majesty> — if I, My Majesty, put things right, then [I will capture] that person or [that unit of the infantry or chariotry]. But if I write to you, Alaksandu: "Take charge of infantry and chariotry. Send(!) them to [my] aid immediately," then [send] them to me immediately. But if [I write] to you, Alaksandu, alone: "Drive here alone," then drive here alone. But if I, My Majesty, do not write [to you], but you [hear] in advance, you shall not ignore it. If it is [possible] for you, take charge of infantry and chariotry. Send(!) them [to my aid] immediately. You shall not first take a bird oracle.

§8 (A ii 75–81) And if you hear in advance about some evil plan to revolt, and either some man of the land of the Seha River or [some] man of the land [of Arzawa carries out the revolt] — these which are now independent of you (that is, the rulers of the other Arzawa lands) — and you know in advance about the matter, but do not write about it to My Majesty, but somehow ignore (the actions of) these men, and think as follows: "Let this evil take place," you will transgress the oath. When you hear about this matter, write about it in advance without hesitation to My Majesty.

§9 (A ii 82–85) The moment you hear of such a matter, you shall not be quiet about the matter. You shall not do an about-face, and you shall not let yourself be enlisted by such a person. As he is My Majesty's enemy, he shall likewise be your enemy.

§10 (A ii 86–iii 2) But if you, Alaksandu, do hear of such a matter, and [then] are quiet about the matter, and let yourself be enlisted by [that] person, then you, Alaksandu, will have offended before the oath gods. The oath gods shall pursue you unrelentingly.

Offensive Alliance

§11 (A iii 3–15) Your regulation concerning the army and chariotry shall be established as follows: If I, My Majesty, go on campaign from that land

— either from the city of Karkisa, the city of Masa,[18] the city of Lukka, or the city of Warsiyalla, then you too must go on campaign with me, together with infantry and chariotry. Or if I send some nobleman to go on campaign from this land,[19] then you must go on campaign with him also. But from Hatti, these are the military obligations for you: The Kings who are the equals of My Majesty — the King of Egypt, the King of Babylonia, the King of Hanigalbat, or the King of Assyria — if [someone] in this group comes in battle, or if domestically someone carries out a revolt against My Majesty, and I, My Majesty, write to you for infantry and chariotry, then send <infantry and> chariotry to my aid immediately.

Rumors

§12 (A iii 16–25) Furthermore, because people are treacherous, if rumors circulate, and someone comes and whispers before you: "His Majesty is undertaking such and such to your disadvantage, and will take the land away from you, or will mistreat you in some way," write about this matter to My Majesty. And if the matter is true, when I, My Majesty, write back to you, you shall not act rashly, nor do . . . And you shall not commit evil against My Majesty. As you have stood on the side of My Majesty, continue to stand only on the side of My Majesty.

§13 (A iii 26–30) If someone speaks an evil word concerning My Majesty before you, Alaksandu, and you conceal it from My Majesty, and act rashly and commit some evil against My Majesty, then you, Alaksandu, will have offended before the oath gods. The oath gods shall pursue you unrelentingly.

Relations among Subordinates; Relations of Subordinate to Agents of Great King

§14 (A iii 31–60) Furthermore, it is you who are the four kings in the lands of Arzawa: you, Alaksandu, Manapa-Kurunta,[20] Kupanta-Kurunta, and Ura-Hattusa. Now in the male line Kupanta-Kurunta is a descendant of the king of the land of Arzawa, but in the female line he is a descendant of the King of Hatti. He is the son of the sister of my father Mursili, Great King, King of Hatti, and the cousin of My Majesty. Those who are his subjects and the men of Arzawa are treacherous. If someone plots evil against Kupanta-Kurunta, you, Alaksandu, be an effective and strong helper for Kupanta-Kurunta, and protect him. And he shall protect you. If some subject of his revolts against Kupanta-Kurunta, and he comes to you, arrest him and give him back to Kupanta-Kurunta. One shall be an effective and strong helper for the other. One shall protect the other. Furthermore, the lands which I, My Majesty, have given to you, and which constitute the border districts of Hatti — if some enemy mobilizes and goes to attack those border districts, and you hear about it and do not write in advance to the one who is commander in the land, and do not lend assistance, but ignore the evil, you will transgress the oath. Or if the enemy attacks and holds (forces?) ready, but you do not lend assistance in advance, and do not fight the enemy, you will transgress the oath. Or if the enemy marches through your land, and you do not fight him, but say as follows to him: "Go attack, and carry off plunder! I don't want to know anything about it." — this too shall be placed under oath. The oath gods shall pursue you unrelentingly. Or if you request infantry and chariotry from My Majesty and will attack some enemy, and My Majesty gives you infantry and chariotry, but at the first opportunity you betray them to the enemy, this matter shall be under oath. The oath gods shall pursue you, Alaksandu, unrelentingly.

Fugitives

§15 (A iii 61–72)[21] I have established the matter of fugitives under oath as follows: If a fugitive comes [in flight] from your land to Hatti, [he will] not [be given] back. It is not permitted [to give] a fugitive back from Hatti. [But] if [some] craftsman flees, [. . .], and he does not deliver his assigned work, [he will be arrested and] turned over to you. [If some fugitive] from the land of an enemy is captured, [and he flees from Hatti], and [goes] away through your lands, [and you do not seize him] and send him on to me, [but] give [him] back [to] the enemy, this too shall be placed under oath.

Reading of Treaty Tablet

§16 (A iii 73–83) Furthermore, this tablet which I have made for you, Alaksandu, shall be read out before you three times yearly, and you, Alaksandu, shall know it. These words are by no means reciprocal. They issue from Hatti. Now you, Alaksandu, must not do evil against My Majesty. Hatti must not prepare [evil] against you. I, Labarna, Great King, Beloved of the Storm-god of Lightning, have now summoned [the Thousand Gods] in this [matter] and have invoked them as witnesses. They shall listen.

Divine Witnesses

§17 (A iv 1–9) [The Sun-god] of Heaven, King of the Lands, Shepherd of Humankind, the Sun-goddess of Arinna, [Queen] of the Lands, the personal Storm-god of Lightning of My Majesty, the Powerful Storm-god, [King of the Lands, the Storm-god of Hatti], King of the Lands, the Storm-god of Lightning, the Storm-god of Zippalanda, [the Storm-god of Nerik], the Storm-god of Aleppo, the Storm-god of the Market(?), [the Storm-god of . . .], the Storm-god of Arinna, the Storm-god of Hisashapa, the Storm-god of [Sapinuwa], the Storm-god of Samuha, the Storm-god of Hurma, the Storm-god of Sarissa, the Storm-god of Lihzina, the Storm-god of Uda, the Storm-god of Sahpina, the Storm-god of Help, Sheri, Hurri, Mount Nanni, Mount Hazzi, Hebat, Queen of Heaven,

§18 (A iv 10–16) the Tutelary Deity, the Tutelary Deity of Hatti, Karzi, Hapantaliya, the Tutelary Deity of Karahna, the Tutelary Deity of the Hunting Bag, Allatu, the Moon-god, Lord of the Oath, Ishtar, Ishtar of the Countryside, Ishtar of Nineveh, Ishtar of Hattarina, Ninatta, Kulitta, Ishhara, Queen of the Oath, the War-god, the War-god of Hatti, the War-god of Illaya, the War-god of Arziya, Yarri, Zappana,

§19 (A iv 17–23) Abara of Samuha, Hantitassu of Hurma, Katahha of Ankuwa, the Queen of Katapa, Ammamma of Tahurpa, Hallara of Dunna, Huwassanna of Hupisna, the mountain-dweller gods, the mercenary gods, all the male and female deities, <all the primeval deities> — Nara, Namsara, Ammunki, Tuhusi, Minki, Ammizzadu, Alalu, Kumarbi, Enlil, Ninlil —

§20 (A iv 24–30) Mount Hulla, Mount Zaliyanu, Mount Taha, the mountains, the rivers, and the springs of Hatti, the great sea, heaven and earth, the winds, the clouds, all [the deities] of the land of Wilusa: the Storm-god of the Army, [. . .]appaliuna, the male deities, the female deities, the mountains, [the rivers, the springs], and the underground watercourse(?) of the land of Wilusa. I, My Majesty, [Great] King, Beloved of the Storm-god of Lightning, have summoned them to assembly in witness.

Curse and Blessing

§21 (A iv 31–46) If you, Alaksandu, transgress these words of the tablet which stand on this tablet, then these Thousand Gods shall eradicate you, together with your person, your wife, your sons, your lands, your cities, your vineyard, your threshing floor, your field, your cattle, your sheep, and together with your possessions. They shall eradicate your progeny from the Dark Earth. But if you do observe these words, then these Thousand Gods whom I, My Majesty, Labarna, Muwattalli, Great King, have summoned to assembly — the deities of Hatti, the deities of Wilusa, and the personal Storm-god of Lightning of My Majesty — shall benevolently protect you, together with your wife, your sons, your grandsons, your cities, your thresh-ing floor, your vineyard, your field, your cattle, your sheep, and together with your possessions. You shall thrive in the hand of My Majesty, and you shall live to an old age in the hand of My Majesty.

Colophons

Text A: [Single] tablet of Alaksandu.
Text B: Tablet of the treaty of Alaksandu.
Text C: Second tablet [of] the treaty of [Alaksandu].

No. 14
Treaty between Muwattalli II of Hatti
and Talmi-Sharrumma of Aleppo

As indicated in §§ 1–2, the present text is the replacement edition of a treaty originally issued in the previous reign, a document that had in the meantime gone astray. This composition is important primarily because of its historical introduction, which provides a number of details concerning the relations of Hatti with northern Syria in the obscure Middle Hittite period of the fifteenth century B.C.E. In particular, there is related the maneuvering of the minor polities of Ashtata and Nuhashshi between Hatti and Mittanni (also referred to here as Hanigalbat) — and against their neighbor Aleppo (§§ 7–10, 12).

Preamble

§ 1 (A obv. 1–2) [Thus says] Tabarna, Muwattalli, Great King, King of Hatti, Hero; [son of Mursili, Great King, King of Hatti], Hero; grandson of Suppiluliuma, Great King, [King of Hatti, Hero]:

§ 2 (A obv. 3–8) My father Mursili made a treaty tablet for Talmi-Shar-rumma, King of Aleppo, but the tablet has been stolen. I, the Great King, have written another tablet [for him], have sealed it with my seal, and have given it to him. In the future no one shall alter a word of the text of this [tablet]. The word of Tabarna, Great King, is not something to be cast aside or something to break. Whoever alters it must die. The treaty tablet which my father Mursili made for him was written as follows:

§ 3 (A obv. 9–10) Thus says His Majesty, Mursili, Great King, King of Hatti; son of Suppiluliuma, Great King, King of Hatti, Hero:

Historical Introduction

§ 4 (A obv. 11–14) Formerly the kings of Aleppo possessed a Great King-ship, but Hattusili, Great King, King of Hatti, brought their kingship to fullness. After Hattusili, King of Hatti, Mursili, Great King, grandson of Hattusili, Great King, destroyed the kingship of Aleppo and the land of Aleppo.

§ 5 (A obv. 15–18) When Tudhaliya, Great King, ascended to the throne [of kingship], the king of Aleppo made peace with him. But the king of Aleppo turned around and settled with the king of Hanigalbat. Then because of this matter he destroyed them — the king of Hanigalbat and the king of Aleppo, [together with their lands(?)]. And he dismantled the city of Aleppo.

§ 6 (A obv. 19–20) The king of Aleppo committed an offense [against] the king of Hanigalbat, but he also committed an offense against Hattusili, [King] of Hatti.

§ 7 (A obv. 21–22) The people of Ashtata and [the people] of Nuhashshi requested [cities] and border districts of the land of Aleppo [from] the king [of Mittanni].

§ 8 (A obv. 23–24) And the king of Mittanni [came] and gave [these] cities and border districts [to the people] of Ashtata and the people of Nuhashshi [as] a benefaction for the sake of friendly relations.

§ 9 (A obv. 25–27) And he wrote tablets for them <concerning> [these] cities and concerning these border districts, and he sealed them with his seal. The people of Aleppo thus committed an offense against Hattusili, [King] of Hatti.

§ 10 (A obv. 28–32) [When the people of Ashtata] and [the people of] Nuhashshi [came] to Hattusili, King of Hatti, they requested the cities [and] the border districts of the land of Aleppo, [and the king of Hatti] came, and he gave the cities and the border districts of the land of Aleppo [. . . to the people of Ashtata] and the people of Nuhashshi as a benefaction. [He wrote tablets concerning these cities and border districts], and he sealed them [with] his seal. They still have them in their possession.

§ 11 (A obv. 33–36) [When Suppiluliuma, Great King], King of Hatti, my father, [ascended] to the throne of kingship, [he went against the King of Mittanni and took] the land of Carchemish, the land of Aleppo, and the lands of Nuhashshi, [but the land of Kinza and the land of Amurru] he took [from the possession] of the King [of Egypt. . . . and] he established Mount Lebanon [as his border].

§ 12 (A obv. 37–39) [And the cities and the border districts of the land of Aleppo] which [Hattusili, Great King], King of Hatti, gave to the [people] of Ashtata and the people of Nuhashshi [as a benefaction, . . .] the cities [and the border districts] of the land of Aleppo . . . [*The remaining seven preserved lines of the obverse and the first two preserved lines of the reverse are too fragmentary for translation. It is also unclear just how many lines have been lost along with the lower portion of the tablet. The text in the first portion of this gap probably related the actions of Suppiluliuma in returning to Aleppo her lost territories and in installing his son Telipinu, "the Priest," as ruler of the city.*]

Mutual Loyalty

§ 13 (A rev. 3–10) . . . The progeny of Talmi-Sharrumma shall protect the progeny of My Majesty, Mursili, [King of] Hatti, and the progeny of My Majesty, Great King, shall not depose the progeny of Talmi-Sharrumma. My Majesty, Great King, shall be the helper of Talmi-Sharrumma, king of Aleppo, and Talmi-Sharrumma, king of Aleppo, shall be the helper of My Majesty, Great King, King of Hatti. The progeny of My Majesty, Mursili, King of Hatti, shall be the helpers of the progeny of Talmi-Sharrumma, and the progeny of Talmi-Sharrumma shall be the helpers of the progeny of My Majesty. For we are all the progeny of Suppiluliuma, Great King. So let our house be one. The gods of Hatti and the gods of Aleppo shall be witnesses in this matter.

§ 14 (A rev. 11–16) In the future, the kingship of Aleppo shall not surpass the King of Hatti. Talmi-Sharrumma, king of Aleppo, shall protect My Majesty, Mursili, Great King, King of Hatti, and My Majesty, Mursili, Great King, shall protect Talmi-Sharrumma, king of Aleppo. No one shall take anything away from the possession of Talmi-Sharrumma or the possession of his son or his grandson. The son and the grandson of Talmi-Sharrumma, king of Aleppo, shall hold the kingship of Aleppo.

Witnesses

§ 15 (A rev. 17–22) [. . .], the scribe, wrote this tablet in Hattusa in the presence of [. . .]libbi, chief of the equerries; Sahurunuwa, king of Carchemish; [. . .]ya, chief of the equerries; Gassu, chief of the priests; Du[. . .], [. . .]; [. . .]li, *uriyanni*; Aranhapilizzi, commander of the troops [of the right; . . . , commander of the] troops of the left; Lupakki, chief of the palace servants; Mittana-muwa, chief of the scribes; and LAMMA-piya, *antuwasalli* of the King and scribe.

No. 15
Treaty between Hattusili III of Hatti
and Ramses II of Egypt

In the twenty-first regnal year of Ramses II the long period of hostility between Egypt and Hatti was brought to an end by means of a treaty of the pharaoh with Hattusili III. The treaty is known from several sources: from texts in Egyptian hieroglyphs preserved on the walls of the temple of Amon at Karnak and of the Ramesseum, and from three fragmentary Akkadian-language cuneiform tablets discovered at Boğazköy. The relationship of these versions to one another is complex. After the terms of the agreement had been settled upon by the diplomats of both states, each side had a version styled as the words of its own monarch inscribed in cuneiform and in the Akkadian language upon a tablet of precious metal. These documents were then exchanged. Thus it is the version composed by the Hittite chancellery, secondarily translated into Egyptian, which was carved into the walls of the Egyptian temples, while the tablets from Hattusa are copies which Hittite scribes made of the silver tablet dispatched by the Egyptians.

As might be expected, the mutual interference of three languages — Hittite, Egyptian, and Akkadian — has produced numerous difficulties for the philologist. On Egyptian grammatical influence on the Akkadian composition found at Boğazköy, see Spalinger 1981; Cochavi-Rainey 1990; Rainey and Cochavi-Rainey 1990.

Only the cuneiform tablets from the Hittite capital have been translated here, although in my treatment of §§12–19 I have made use of the work of Edel (in Kaiser 1983: 139–41), who has reconstructed this fragmentary portion of the Akkadian text with the aid of Egyptian-language material. Since the cuneiform texts show no paragraph divisions, I have broken up my translation according to sense, again largely following Edel's German rendering.

Preamble

§1 (A obv. 1–3) [The treaty which] Ramses, [Beloved] of Amon, Great King, King [of Egypt, Hero, concluded] on [a tablet of silver] with Hattusili, [Great King], King of Hatti, his brother, in order to establish [great] peace and great [brotherhood] between them forever.

The Parties

§2 (A obv. 3–7) Thus says Ramses, Beloved of Amon, Great King, King of Egypt, Hero of All Lands; son of Minmuarea (Seti I), Great King, King of Egypt, Hero; grandson of Minpahtarea (Ramses I), Great King, King of Egypt, Hero; to Hattusili, Great King, King of Hatti, Hero; son of Mursili, Great King, King of Hatti, Hero; grandson of Suppiluliuma, Great King, King of Hatti, Hero:

Purpose of Treaty; Previous Relations

§3 (A obv. 7–13) I have now established good brotherhood and good peace between us forever, in order likewise to establish good peace and good brotherhood in [the relations] of Egypt with Hatti forever. As far as the relations of the Great King, King of Egypt, [and] the Great King, King of Hatti, are concerned, from the beginning of time and forever [by means of a treaty] the god has not allowed the making of war between them. Ramses, Beloved of Amon, Great King, King of Egypt, is doing this in order to bring about the relationship which [the Sun-god] and the Storm-god established for Egypt with Hatti in accordance with their relationship from the beginning of time, so that for eternity he might [not permit] the making of war between [them].

Future Relations

§4 (A obv. 13–18) And Ramses, Beloved of Amon, Great King, King [of Egypt], has indeed created <it> (the relationship) [on] this [day] by means of a treaty upon a tablet of silver, with [Hattusili], Great King, King of Hatti, his brother, in order to establish good peace and good brotherhood [between them] forever. He is [my] brother, and I am his brother. <He is at peace with me>, and I am at peace with him [forever. And] we will create our brotherhood and our [peace], and they will be better than the former brotherhood and peace of [Egypt with] Hatti.

§5 (A obv. 19–21) Ramses, Great King, King of Egypt, is in good peace and good brotherhood with [Hattusili], Great King of Hatti. The sons of Ramses, Beloved of Amon, <Great King>, King of Egypt, will be at peace and [brothers with] the sons of Hattusili, Great King, King of Hatti, forever. And they will remain as in our relationship of brotherhood [and of] peace, so that Egypt will be at peace with Hatti and they will be brothers like us forever.

Non-aggression

§6 (A obv. 22–27) And Ramses, Beloved of Amon, Great King, King of Egypt, for all time shall not open hostilities against Hatti in order to take anything from it. And Hattusili, Great King, King of Hatti, for all time shall not open hostilities against Egypt in order to take [anything] from it. The eternal regulation which the Sun-god and the Storm-god made for Egypt with Hatti is intended <to provide> peace and brotherhood and to prohibit hostilities between them. And [Ramses], Beloved of Amon, Great King, King of Egypt, has taken it up in order to create peace from this day on. Egypt will be at peace and brotherly with Hatti forever.

Defensive Alliance

§7 (A obv. 27–30) And if someone else, an enemy, comes against Hatti, and Hattusili, [Great King, King of Hatti], sends to me: "Come to me, to my aid against him," then [Ramses, Beloved] of Amon, Great King, King of Egypt, must send his infantry and his chariotry, and they will defeat [his enemy and] take revenge for Hatti.

§8 (A obv. 31–33) And if Hattusili, Great King, King of Hatti, [becomes angry] with his own [subjects], after they have offended against him, and he sends to Ramses, Great King, King of Egypt, on account of this, then Ramses, Beloved of Amon, must send his infantry and his chariotry, [and] they will destroy all with whom he is angry.

§9 (A obv. 33–36) [And if] someone else, an enemy, comes against Egypt, and Ramses, Beloved of Amon, [King] of Egypt, your brother, sends to Hattusili, King of Hatti, his brother: "Come to my aid against him," then Hattusili, [King] of Hatti, shall send his infantry and his chariotry, and they will defeat his enemy.

§10 (A obv. 36–39) And if Ramses, Beloved [of Amon, King] of Egypt, becomes angry with his own subjects, after they have committed an offense against [him, and he sends] to Hattusili, King of Hatti, his(!) brother, on account of this, then Hattusili, [King] of Hatti, his brother, shall send [his] infantry and his chariotry, and they will destroy all [with whom] I am angry.

Succession

§11 (A obv. 40–43) And the son of Hattusili, King of Hatti, shall be made King of Hatti in place of Hattusili, his father, after the many years of Hattusili, [King] of Hatti. And if [the people] of Hatti commit an offense against him, then [Ramses], Beloved of Amon, must send [infantry] and chariotry to his aid and take revenge for him.

Fugitives

§12 (A obv. 43–46) [If a nobleman] flees from Hatti, or if a population in the territory of the King of Hatti [comes over] to Ramses, Beloved of

Amon, Great King, [King of Egypt], then I, Ramses, [Beloved of Amon, Great King, King of Egypt], must seize them and send [them into the hand of Hattusili, Great King, King of Hatti].

§13 (A obv. 46–48) [And if] a single man comes, or if two [obscure men come to Ramses, Beloved of Amon], in order to enter into [his] service, then [I, Ramses, Beloved of Amon, must seize them and send them to] Hattusili, King of Hatti.

§14 (A obv. 49–51) And if [a nobleman flees from Egypt, or] if a single population [comes to the King of Amurru, then Benteshina shall seize them] and send them to the King of Hatti, [his] lord. [And Hattusili, Great King, King of Hatti, shall send them to Ramses, Beloved] of Amon, Great King, King of Egypt.

§15 (A obv. 52–54) And [if a single man flees, or if two obscure men flee from the territory of the King] of Egypt, and [do not wish to continue in his service, then Hattusili, Great King, King of Hatti], shall give them into the hand of his brother and [not permit them to dwell in Hatti].

§16 (A obv. 54–57) [And if a dignitary flees from Hatti and comes to Egypt(?) — or if two] men — in order not [to continue in the service of Hattusili, Great King, King] of Hatti, [then Ramses, Beloved of Amon, must seize them] and send them to [Hattusili, Great King, King of Hatti], his brother.

§17 (A obv. 57–60) [And if] a single [dignitary] flees [from Egypt] and comes to [Hatti — or if two men — then] Hattusili, [Great] King, [King of Hatti, shall seize them and] send them(!) to [Ramses, Beloved] of Amon, [Great King, King of Egypt, his brother].

§18 (A obv. 60–64) [And if] a single man flees from [Hatti, or] two men, [or three men, and they come to] Ramses, Beloved [of Amon, Great King, King] of Egypt, his brother, [then Ramses], Beloved of Amon, Great King, [King of Egypt, must seize them and send them] to Hattusili, his brother [. . .] — for they are brothers. But [they shall not punish them for] their offenses. They shall [not] tear out [their tongues or their eyes]. And [they shall not mutilate(?)] their ears or [their] feet. [And they shall not destroy(?) their households, together with their wives] and their sons.

§19 (A obv. 65–70) And if [a single man flees from Egypt, or] two men, or three men, and [they come to Hattusili, Great King], King of Hatti, my brother shall seize them and send [them to me, Ramses, Beloved of Amon, Great King, King] of Egypt — for Ramses, Great King, King [of Egypt, and Hattusili are brothers. But they shall not punish them for their offenses. They shall] not [tear out their tongues] or their eyes. And [they shall not mutilate(?) their ears or their feet. And they shall not destroy(?) their households], together with their wives and their sons.

[*From this point a connected translation is impossible. The lines immediately following §19 seem to continue the discussion of the problem of fugitives. The sorry scraps of the reverse of Text A are sufficient to demonstrate that the treaty concluded with curses and blessings on the participants. The final two lines (A rev. 10'–11') indicate the presence on the original silver tablet sent from Egypt of two seals:* "Seal [of Ramses, Beloved of Amon, . . .], Seal [of the Sun-god(?) . . .]"]

No. 16
Treaty between Hattusili III of Hatti
and Benteshina of Amurru

With the reassertion of Egyptian power in western Asia under Seti I and Ramses II, Amurru was able or perhaps even forced to reconsider its loyalty to the Hittite empire. According to No. 17, §4, "the men of Amurru" decided to go over to the Egyptians. Although no ruler of Amurru is named in connection with this *volte face*, the king of the country at this time was in fact Benteshina, who was accordingly removed from office by Great King Muwattalli II after he had regained control of the area following the battle of Kinza/Qadesh. Benteshina was replaced on the throne by a certain Shapili, whose relation to the erstwhile royal house of Amurru remains uncertain.

Benteshina himself was carried off to Hatti, and in his exile he was taken under the protection of the future Hattusili III, who set him up in a household in the capital city of his central Anatolian appanage kingdom, Hakpis. Here Benteshina became part of the group that supported Hattusili when he ultimately deposed Muwattalli's son Urhi-Teshshup (Mursili III) and installed himself as Great King. In reward, Benteshina was re-established upon his own throne, an arrangement sealed not only by the present treaty, but also by a reciprocal marriage arrangement between the two royal houses (see §5). On the life and times of Benteshina, see Singer 1991a: 164–71; Klengel 1992: 168–72.

This Akkadian text belongs to the "Syrian group" discussed in the introduction to No. 5.

Preamble

§1 (obv. 1–3) [Thus says Labarna, Hattusili, Great King, King of Hatti, Hero; son of Mursili, King of Hatti, Hero; grandson] of Suppiluliuma, King of Hatti, Hero; [descendant of Hattusili], man [of Kussar].

Historical Introduction

§2 (obv. 4–6) In the time of my grandfather Suppiluliuma, Aziru, [king of the land of Amurru], revoked [his vassalage(?)] to Egypt, and [fell] at the feet of my grandfather Suppiluliuma. My grandfather had [compassion] for him and wrote a treaty tablet for him. He wrote out the borders of the land of Amurru of his ancestors and gave it (the tablet) to him.

§3 (obv. 7–10) When my grandfather Suppiluliuma died, my father Mursili, son of Suppiluliuma, took his seat upon the throne of kingship. In the land of Amurru, Ari-Teshshup acceded to kingship. Following Ari-Teshshup, Tuppi-Teshshup acceded to the throne of kingship. They shall keep to the tablet which my grandfather Suppiluliuma wrote for Aziru as a treaty.

§4 (obv. 11–15) Following my father, my brother Muwattalli acceded to the throne of kingship. To(!) my brother Muwattalli Benteshina was (politically) dead in [the land] of Amurru. Benteshina had acceded to the throne of kingship of the land of Amurru, but my brother Muwattalli removed Benteshina from the throne of kingship of the land of Amurru. He took him to Hatti. At that time I requested Benteshina from my brother Muwattalli and he gave him to me. I transported him to(!) the land of Hakpis and gave him a household. He did not suffer any harm. I protected him.

§5 (obv. 16–21) When Muwattalli, Great King, went [to] his fate, I, Hattusili, took my seat upon the throne of my father. I released Benteshina for a second time to(!) [the land of Amurru]. I assigned to him the household of his father and the throne of kingship. [We established] friendly relations between us [. . .] My son Nerikkaili will(!) take the daughter of Benteshina of the land of Amurru [as] his wife, [while I have given] Princess Gassuliyawiya to the land of Amurru, to the royal house, to Benteshina, [as] his wife. She now possesses queenship [in the land] of Amurru. In the future the son and grandson of my daughter shall [exercise] kingship in the land of Amurru.

Succession of Subordinate

§6 (obv. 22–27) Benteshina said this before My Majesty: "Say to my lord[22] — You are giving life to me, a dead man. You returned me [for a second time(?)] to(!) the land of Amurru, to the throne of my father. Like a dead man, you have given life to me. Let my lord make a tablet of treaty and of oath. Let him seal and write it, to the effect that Benteshina is king of the land of Amurru. In the future no one shall take the kingship of the land of Amurru from the hand of Benteshina or from the hand of his sons or the

hand of his grandsons." [Thus says] My Majesty: "I, My Majesty, will not
withhold from you(!) that which you, Benteshina, have requested from me."

§7 (obv. 28–33) [Now], I, Great King, <wrote> a treaty tablet for Benteshina, corresponding to the tablet which Suppiluliuma, Great King, . . .
for Aziru. I, Great King, wrote it for Benteshina, king of the land of
Amurru, according to the text of the treaty tablet of my grandfather, and I
gave it to him. No one shall take the kingship of the land of Amurru from
Benteshina, or from the hand of his son or his grandson, the progeny of
Benteshina and the progeny of my daughter. The son of Benteshina and his
grandson, the progeny of Benteshina and the son of my daughter, shall hold
the kingship of the land of Amurru. If someone seeks to harm Benteshina
or his son or grandson, he will be the enemy of the King of Hatti and of the
Hittites.

§8 (obv. 34–36) As long as Benteshina has not yet taken the princess
(Gassuliyawiya sexually) and has not yet gotten any sons, Benteshina may
elevate (to crown prince) either a prince of the land of Amurru, or his
brother, or his nephew, or any citizen of his land. The King of Hatti and the
Hittites shall not be anxious(?) concerning this matter.

Loyalty to Hittite Dynasty

§9 (obv. 37–44) Since I, My Majesty, have now treated you <well>, and I
have installed you in kingship [in the land] of Amurru, if from this day on
you, [Benteshina], do not protect Hattusili, Great King, [your lord, and]
Puduhepa, Great Queen, your lady, as well as the son and grandson of King
Hattusili and of [Queen] Puduhepa [as] overlords, the oath gods shall
oust(?) [you], and they shall burn(?) you! If someone <revolts against> my
son or my grandson — be he my [. . .], or my brother, or my nephew, or
[my] son-in-law, or another man — you, [Benteshina], shall not abandon
my son or my grandson. You shall not go elsewhere. And as [your soul, your
person], your wife, [your] sons, and your land are dear [to you], the soul
and person of the King(!) [and the sons of the King, and the land] of Hatti
[shall likewise be dear to you]. In the future [observe the treaty of the King
of Hatti, of his sons and grandsons, and of Hatti]. [*An uncertain number of
lines have been lost at the end of the obverse and the beginning of the reverse of our
single manuscript. The first four lines preserved on the reverse are too fragmentary
for translation.*]

Offensive Alliance

§10 (rev. 5'–11') [Be a friend to my friend]; be hostile [to] my enemy. [If
the King of Hatti goes against the land of . . .], or Babylonia, [or the land

of . . . — whatever] foreign [lands] located near your borders [are hostile to the King of Hatti, or whatever lands located near] the borders [of your land and friendly] to the King of Hatti, [turn and] become hostile [to] the King of Hatti — when [the King of Hatti] goes forth to attack, if Benteshina [does not set out wholeheartedly] with his infantry [and his chariotry], he will transgress the oath.

§11 (rev. 12'-17') And if [I send] a prince or a high-ranking nobleman together with his infantry and [his] chariotry [to the aid of Benteshina, or if] I send them to attack another land — [if Benteshina] does not set out [wholeheartedly with his infantry] and his chariotry, and [does not attack] the enemy, he will transgress the oath. [And if] he(!) commits some [misdeed], thinking as follows: "Although I [am under oath and bound by treaty, either let the enemy defeat him], or let him defeat the enemy. I don't want [to know anything about it]." — he will transgress the oath. [Or if] he writes [to that enemy], saying: "The troops of Hatti [are] now [coming to attack. Be on guard!" — he will transgress] the oath.

[*Three lines too fragmentary for translation.*]

Defensive Alliance

§12 (rev. 22'-26') If [some other enemy rises up] against [the King of Hatti and attacks Hatti, or if someone carries out] a revolt [against the King of Hatti, and Benteshina hears of it, then he must come immediately with his infantry and his chariotry] to [the aid of the Great King. But if it is not possible for Benteshina] to come, [his son or his brother shall come immediately with infantry and chariotry to the aid] of the King of Hatti.

§13 (rev. 27'-29') Or if [someone oppresses(?) Benteshina, either . . . , or anyone at all, and he sends to the King of Hatti: "Come] to [my] aid," [then the King will come to his aid. He will send either a prince or a high-ranking nobleman], together with infantry [and chariotry, and they will defeat that enemy].

[*There follow four lines too damaged for translation, after which the remainder of the tablet was apparently uninscribed. The text of the treaty must have continued on another tablet.*]

No. 17
Treaty between Tudhaliya IV of Hatti
and Shaushga-muwa of Amurru

This treaty is the last known document in the series of diplomatic agreements between Hatti and Amurru (see introduction to No. 5), and its historical introduction extends the account of events in the latter polity given in Nos. 5, 8, and 16, mentioning briefly the war between Hatti and Egypt which culminated in the battle of Kinza/Qadesh (§4; see Götze 1929). Shaushga-muwa, king of Amurru, was also a Hittite prince, brother-in-law (§6) as well as nephew (No. 16, §5), of his lord Tudhaliya (see Singer 1991a: 172–76). For this reason it was apparently not necessary to translate the treaty into Akkadian. In any event, both copies that have come down to us are in Hittite: Text A, which is shown to be a rough draft by its numerous erasures, insertions, and careless placement of text on the tablet, and Text B, which is extremely fragmentary.

The preserved provisions of the document deal exclusively with the loyalty demanded by Tudhaliya from Shaushga-muwa toward himself against other potential claimants to the Hittite throne, and toward Hatti against other great powers of the day. It is striking that Tudhaliya admonishes his treaty partner not to conduct himself like an earlier vassal and royal brother-in-law, whose treachery had helped Tudhaliya's own father seize power in Hatti (§§7–8). Also of interest is the trade embargo which the Hittite Great King seeks to impose on Assyria (§11).

Preamble

§1 (A i 1–7) [Thus says Tabarna, Tudhaliya], Great King, [King of] Hatti, Hero, Beloved of the Sun-goddess of Arinna; [son of Hattusili, Great King, King] of Hatti, Hero; [grandson of] Mursili, Great [King], King of Hatti, Hero; [descendant] of Tudhaliya, [Great King, King] of Hatti, Hero:

§2 (A i 8–12) I, My Majesty, [have taken you], Shaushga-muwa, [by the hand], and have made [you my] brother-in-law. And you [shall not alter the words] of the treaty tablet which [I have made] for you.

Historical Introduction

§3 (A i 13–27) [Earlier] the land of Amurru had not been defeated by the force of arms of Hatti. When [Aziru came] to the (great-)grandfather of My Majesty, [Suppiluliuma], in Hatti, the lands of Amurru were still [hostile]. They [were] subjects of the King of Hurri. Aziru accordingly gave him (Suppiluliuma) his allegiance, although he did [not] defeat him by force of arms. And Aziru, your (great-great-)grandfather, protected Suppiluliuma as overlord, and he protected Hatti. Later he also protected Mursili as overlord, and he protected Hatti. In no way did he commit an offense against Hatti.

§4 (A i 28–39) But when Muwattalli, uncle of My Majesty, became King, the men of Amurru committed an offense against him, informing him as follows: "We were voluntary subjects. Now we are no longer your subjects." And they went over to the King of Egypt. Then My Majesty's uncle Muwattalli and the King of Egypt fought over the men of Amurru. Muwattalli defeated him, destroyed the land of Amurru by force of arms, and subjugated it. And he made Shapili king in the land of Amurru.

§5 (A i 40–48) But when Muwattalli, the uncle of My Majesty, died, the father of My Majesty, Hattusili, became King. He deposed Shapili and made Benteshina, your father, king in the land of Amurru. He protected the father of My Majesty, and he protected Hatti. In no way did he commit an offense against Hatti.

Loyalty to Hittite Dynasty

§6 (A ii 1–6) [And] I, My Majesty, Great King, have taken you, Shaushga-muwa, by the hand [and] have made you my brother-in-law. I have given you my sister in marriage and have made you king in the land of Amurru. Protect My Majesty as overlord. And later protect the sons, grandsons, and progeny of My Majesty as overlords. You shall not desire some other overlord for yourself. This matter shall be placed under oath for you.

§7 (A ii 8–19) Because I have made you, Shaushga-muwa, my brother-in-law, protect My Majesty as overlord. And later protect the sons, grandsons, and progeny of My Majesty as overlords. You shall not desire anyone as overlord from among those who are legitimate brothers of My Majesty, sons of the concubines of the father of My Majesty, or even other royal progeny who are to be regarded by you as bastards. You shall not behave like Masturi: Muwattalli took Masturi, who was king of the land of the Seha River, and made him his brother-in-law, giving him his sister Massanuzzi in marriage. And he made him king in the land of the Seha River.

§8 (A ii 20–38) But when Muwattalli died, then Urhi-Teshshup, son of Muwattalli, became King. [My father] wrested the kingship away from Urhi-Teshshup. Masturi committed treachery. Although it was Muwattalli who had taken him up and had made him his brother-in-law, afterwards Masturi did not protect his son Urhi-Teshshup, but went over to my father, thinking: "Will I protect even a bastard? Why should I act on behalf of the son of a bastard?" Will you perhaps behave like Masturi? And if someone brings difficulties upon My Majesty, or upon the sons, grandsons, or progeny of My Majesty, and you, Shaushga-muwa, together with your wives, your sons, your infantry, and your chariotry, do not help wholeheartedly,

and are not ready to die for him, together with [your] wives and your sons
— This shall be placed under oath for you.

§9 (A ii 39–iii 5) Protect My Majesty as overlord. [And] later protect the
progeny of [My Majesty] as overlords. You shall not desire [anyone] else as
overlords. If [some conspiracy] breaks out [in Hatti . . .], then you shall not
[. . . Rather, together with your army] and your land, help [. . .] For My
Majesty [. . .] to My Majesty [. . .] [*The next six or seven lines have been
almost completely lost.*] [This shall be placed] under oath [for you].

§10 (A iii 6–18) [. . .] became involved with the Hittites. [. . .] If
[some] Hittite attaches himself to you — either a brother of the King, a
prince, a nobleman, or a man of the lowest or highest rank — and he brings
up again some slander concerning My Majesty, or he subjects My Majesty
to malice in some way before you, you shall not cover up the matter before
My Majesty. Tell it to My Majesty. [This] shall be placed under oath for
you.

[*Approximately twenty-five lines have been largely or totally lost.*]

Alliance

§11 (A iii 42–iv 18) . . . If [the King] of Egypt is My Majesty's [friend], he
shall be your friend. [But] if [he] is My Majesty's enemy, he shall be [your
enemy]. And the Kings who are my equals in rank are the King of Egypt,
the King of Babylonia, the King of Assyria, and the King of Ahhiyawa.[23] If
the King of Egypt is My Majesty's friend, he shall be your friend. But if he
is My Majesty's enemy, he shall be your enemy. And if the King of Babylonia is My Majesty's friend, he shall be your friend. But if he is My Majesty's
enemy, he shall be your enemy. Since the King of Assyria is My Majesty's
enemy, he shall be your enemy. Your merchant shall not go to Assyria, and
you shall not allow his merchant into your land. He shall not pass through
your land. But if he comes into your land, seize him and send him off to My
Majesty. This matter [shall be placed] under [oath] for you.

§12 (A iv 19–22) Because I, My Majesty, have begun war with the King
of Assyria, form for yourself, like My Majesty, an army and a unit of chariotry. Just as it is a matter of urgency and . . . for My Majesty, it shall likewise be a matter of urgency and . . . for you. With alacrity form for yourself
an army and a unit of chariotry. This matter shall be placed under oath for
you.

§13 (A iv 23–25) No ship [of] Ahhiyawa may go to him (the King of
Assyria?) [. . .] When he dispatches them [. . .] the deity of your land

[. . .] [*The remaining twenty or so lines of this column are too fragmentary for translation. About one-third of them have been lost completely.*]

§14 (A left edge 1–2) . . . Fortify and protect it continuously. In the face of the enemy for Hatti [. . .] You shall not protect [another man(?)]. This will be placed under oath for you.

[*The continuation of Text A onto another tablet has not been recovered. The reverse of Text B presents material which must be placed following the paragraphs of Text A rendered above. Unfortunately, the first seven partial lines preserved here cannot be translated. The remainder of the reverse of Text B contains an extensive but very fragmentary list of divine witnesses.*]

No. 18
Treaties between Hattusili III and Tudhaliya IV of Hatti and Kurunta/Ulmi-Teshshup of Tarhuntassa

These texts belong to a small group of documents concerned with dominion over the southern Anatolian land centered on the city of Tarhuntassa, which had for a short time under Muwattalli II been the capital of the Hittite empire. After Hattusili III usurped the Great Kingship of Hatti (see No. 18C, §2), he installed Muwattalli's son Kurunta — who had supported him against Urhi-Teshshup — as ruler of an appanage kingdom in Tarhuntassa. As head of a parallel, if junior, line of the Hittite royal family, Kurunta, like his distant cousin ruling in Carchemish, was preceded in rank only by the Great King of Hatti himself, and by the latter's heir apparent (see No. 18C, §18). Due to their peculiar position as both rulers of semi-independent countries and as members of the Hittite royal family, the kings of Tarhuntassa and of Carchemish received treaties which contain elements otherwise typical of Hittite international treaties, of instructions issued by the Great Kings to their own bureaucrats, and of land grants made by these Kings to their noblemen.

Since the upper portion of No.18B containing the preamble and historical introduction has been lost, it has long been uncertain whether this treaty was issued by Hattusili III or by his son and successor Tudhaliya IV. With the discovery in 1986 of No.18C, which is certainly the work of Tudhaliya, new light has been cast on the problem. In particular, it may now be seen that the boundary adjustment carried out by the father of the Hittite ruler of No. 18C (§5) is the same action as that described in the first person by the author of No. 18B (§3). Thus the latter text must be attributed to Hattusili. This being so, Kurunta and Ulmi-Teshshup must simply be two different names, Luwian and Hurrian respectively, for the same individual. (For this interpretation, see Klengel 1991: 231–32; Süren-hagen 1992: 350–58; Gurney 1993: 19–22; but cf. van den Hout 1989; Imparati 1991: 61–62).

Both treaties here are clearly dependent on earlier documents (see van den Hout 1989). In most cases these older texts have been lost, but in No.18A there is preserved the draft of a forerunner to No. 18B, §6 and No. 18C, §22. When the scribes adapted these earlier records, they did not always exercise sufficient care in harmonizing their source material with the later contexts. This accounts for the confusion of grammatical person particularly evident in No. 18B.

These treaties are noteworthy for the exceptionally full geographical detail provided in the descriptions of the frontiers of the land of Tarhuntassa, whose most important border area was the land of the Hulaya River (No. 18C, §§3–11 and No.18B, §§3–5).

Finally, it should be noted that No. 18C, which is inscribed upon a bronze tablet weighing some five kilograms, represents the sole example of a metal tablet yet recovered from Hatti, although such objects are else-where mentioned in Hittite diplomatic documents (No. 15, §1 and No. 18B, §14; see Watanabe 1989).

No. 18A
Edict of Hattusili III of Hatti
concerning Military Obligations of Kurunta
of Tarhuntassa

[Thus says Hattusili], Great [King], King [of Hatti: When the King and the Queen] made Kurunta king [in the land of Tarhuntassa, the King] and [the Queen examined] the divine obligations, [and] the divine obligations [had become too heavy] for him to manage. [Formerly, when] Muwattalli kept up Tarhuntassa and worshiped [the gods of Tarhuntassa] for himself, all [Hatti] cared [for them. But now the King] and the Queen [have made] Kurunta [king in] Tarhuntassa, and he has [not] been able to manage the divine [obligations from his land alone]. So [the King and the Queen] have made [this agreement] with you: [His Majesty] has remitted [the chariotry and infantry of the land of] the Hulaya [River for which the armory] in [Hatti] holds claim, and [in the future] only [200] of his [men] shall go on a Hittite military expedition. Additional [troops] shall not be sought from [him] for the armory. [These] troops have been remitted to him for the corvée [and dues] obligations. Some personnel [the King remitted] to him(!) for custodial duties in the temple, some [he remitted] to him for cultivation, and some [he remitted] to him for [guarding the salt lick. In the future no one shall contest this decision. But if] some [king should rise up against His Majesty, then the king of the land of Tarhuntassa] himself shall come to his assistance, but absolutely no [infantry shall be sought] from him. And [if] some equal should arise against the King, [then] the king of the land of Tarhuntassa himself [shall come] to his assistance, but [absolutely] no infantry or chariotry shall be sought from him.

No. 18B
Treaty between Hattusili III of Hatti and Ulmi-Teshshup of Tarhuntassa

[*The first approximately thirty lines which included the preamble and the historical prologue have been lost. The initial preserved lines are too fragmentary for connected translation. Here the Hittite King assures Ulmi-Teshshup that although he is* "only mortal and the day of your death will come," *his chosen successor will be installed in his place.*]

Succession

§1 (obv. 7'–14') I, My Majesty, will [not depose] your son. [I will accept] neither your brother nor anyone else. Later your son and grandson will hold [the land] which I have given [to you]. It may not be taken away from him. If any son or grandson of yours commits an offense, then the King of Hatti shall question him. And if an offense is proven against him, then the King of Hatti shall treat him as he pleases. If he is deserving of death, he shall perish, but his household and land shall not be taken from him and given to the progeny of another. Only someone of the progeny of Ulmi-Teshshup shall take them. Someone of the male line shall take them; those of the female line shall not take them. But if there is no male line of descent, and it is extinguished, then only someone of the female line of Ulmi-Teshshup shall be sought out. Even if he is in a foreign land, he shall be brought back from there and installed in authority in the land of Tarhuntassa.

Frontiers

§2 (obv. 15'–18') Protect the land which I have given to you, Ulmi-Teshshup, and the frontiers which I have established for you. Do not violate them. Your frontiers are established as follows: In the direction of the land of Pitassa, your frontier is Mount Hawa, the *kantanna* of the city of

Zarniya, and the city of Sanantarwa, but the *kantanna* of Zarniya belongs to the land of the Hulaya River, while Sanantarwa belongs to the land of Pitassa.

§3 (obv. 19'–32') In the direction of the border district of the land of Pitassa, his frontier is the sinkhole of the city of Arimmatta, but Arimmatta belongs to the land of Pitassa. In the direction of Mount Huwatnuwanta, his frontier is the *hallapuwanza*, but the *hallapuwanza* belongs to the land of the Hulaya River. Up behind the city of Kursawanta, <his> frontier is the Stone Monument of the Dog. In the direction of the city of Ussa, his frontier is the city of Zarata, but Zarata belongs to the land of the Hulaya River. In the direction of the city of Wanzataruwa, his frontier is the city of Harazuwa, but Harazuwa belongs to the land of Ussa. On the first treaty tablets his frontier in the direction of Mount Kuwakuwaliyatta was the city of Suttasna, but now I, the Great King, have made the city of Santimma his frontier. But Santimma belongs to the land of the Hulaya River. In the direction of the cities of Wanzataruwa and Kunzinasa, his frontier is Mount Arlanta and the city of Alana. Alana belongs to the land of the Hulaya River, but the water which is upon Mount Arlanta belongs jointly to Hatti and to the land of the Hulaya River. In the direction of the city of Sinnuwanta, his frontier is Mount Lula, but the city of Ninainta belongs to the land of the Hulaya River. However, the service estate of the golden charioteer, which is behind (the city), belongs to My Majesty. In the direction of the city of Zarnusassa, his frontier is the *harmima*, but the *harmima* belongs to <the land> of the Hulaya River. In the direction of the city of Zarwisa, his frontier is Mount Sarlaimmi and the sinkhole of water . . . In the direction of the mountain heights, his frontier is the city of Saliya, but Saliya belongs to Hatti. In the direction of foreign territory, his <frontier> is the city of Walwara and various dependencies(?) of Walwara — Mata, Sanhata, Surimma, Saranduwa, and Tattassi. In the direction of the city of Saranduwa, to whatever locality his armed force should reach — that belongs to the land of the Hulaya River. In the direction of the city of Walma, his frontier is the cities of Alluprata and Huhhura, but these cities belong to the land of the Hulaya River.

§4 (obv. 33'–37') That which is the border district of the land of Tarhuntassa — even a goatherd shall not enter the land. And if they drive their animals from the land of the Hulaya River to the great salt lick rock, they shall not take away his salt lick rights. They are given to the king of the land of Tarhuntassa; he shall always take the salt. I, Great King, have given the city of Sarmana, together with the fields, meadow, and sheep pasturage, and all the salt lick, to the king of the land of Tarhuntassa. No other city shall encroach upon the salt of Sarmana. In the city of Dunna, a single *kuwappala* is dedicated to the Storm-god of Lightning, and it belongs to [the king] of the land of Tarhuntassa. If Ulmi-Teshshup, king of the land of Tarhuntassa, later makes for himself another *kuwappala*, that shall be allowed him. [Whatever] royal protocol is allowed to the king of the land of Carchemish shall also be allowed to the king of the land of Tarhuntassa.

Deposition of Treaty

§5 (obv. 38'–39') This treaty tablet has already been made, and it shall be placed in Arinna in the presence of the Sun-goddess of Arinna. But his military obligation has not been treated on this tablet, so My Majesty has subsequently made a tablet of his military obligations as follows:

Military and Religious Obligations

§6 (obv. 40'–47') When I, My Majesty, came to Tarhuntassa and examined the divine obligations and regulation, they had become too heavy for him to manage. Formerly, when Muwattalli kept up Tarhuntassa and worshiped the gods of Tarhuntassa for himself, all Hatti cared for them. But now the King and the Queen have made Kurunta king in Tarhuntassa, and he has not been able to manage the divine obligations from his land alone. So the King and the Queen have made this agreement with you: My Majesty has remitted the chariotry and infantry of the land of the Hulaya River for which the armory in Hatti holds claim, and in the future only 200 of his men shall go on a Hittite military expedition; additional troops shall not be sought from him for the armory. These troops have been remitted to him for the divine corvée and dues obligations. Some personnel were remitted to him for custodial duties in the temple, some were remitted to him for cultivation, and some were remitted to him for guarding the salt lick. In the future no one shall contest this decision. But if some king of equal rank rises up against My Majesty, then the king of the land of Tarhuntassa himself shall come to his assistance, but absolutely no infantry or chariotry shall be sought from him.

Divine Witnesses

§7 (obv. 48'–49') In this matter the Storm-god of Lightning, the Sun-goddess of Arinna, the Storm-god of Hatti, the Storm-god of Nerik, Ishtar of Samuha, Ishtar of Lawazantiya, and the Thousand Gods of Hatti shall be witnesses.

§8 (obv. 50'–rev. 4) And in regard to the fact that I have made this treaty tablet for you, the Thousand Gods are now summoned to assembly. They shall observe and listen and be witnesses: The Sun-god of Heaven, the Sun-goddess of Arinna, the Storm-god of Heaven, the Storm-god of Hatti, the Storm-god of the Army, the Storm-god of Hisashapa, the Storm-god of Zippalanda, the Storm-god of Nerik, the Storm-god of Aleppo, the Storm-god of Uda, the Storm-god of Sapinuwa, the Powerful Storm-god, the *pihaimmi* Storm-god, the Storm-god of Lightning, Lulutassi, the Tutelary Deity, the Tutelary Deity of Hatti, Ayala, Karzi, Hapantaliya, Sharrumma, Zithariya, Hebat, Queen of Heaven, Ishtar, Ishtar of Nineveh, Ishtar of Hattarina, Ninatta, Kulitta, Nikkal, [Ishhara], the Moon-god, Lord of the Oaths, the Deity of Arusna, the War-god, the War-god of Hatti, the War-god of Illaya, the War-god of Arziya, Yarri, Zappana, Abara of Samuha, Hantitassu of Hurma, Katahha of Ankuwa, the Queen of Katapa, Ammamma of Tahurpa, Hallara of Dunna, Huwassanna of Hupisna, Lelwani, the mountain-dweller gods, the mercenary gods, the male deities, the female deities, the great sea, the mountains, rivers, and springs of Hatti and of the land of Tarhuntassa.

Curses and Blessings

§9 (rev. 5–7) And if you, Ulmi-Teshshup, <do not observe> these words of the tablet, or do not protect My Majesty, the Queen, and later the son of My Majesty as overlords, or should alter the words of this tablet, then these Thousand Gods shall eradicate your person, together with your wife, your sons, your land, your house, your threshing floor, your orchard, your fields, your oxen, your sheep, and all your possessions.

§10 (rev. 8–11) But if you observe the words of this tablet and protect My Majesty, the Queen, and later the son of My Majesty as overlords, and desire only My Majesty, the Queen, and later the son of My Majesty as overlords, then these oath gods shall benevolently protect your person, together with your wife, your son, your land, your house, your threshing floor, your orchard, your fields, your oxen, your sheep, and all your possessions. And you shall live to a good old age in the hand of My Majesty.

§11 (rev. 12–14) These oath gods shall eradicate from the Dark Earth, together with his progeny, whoever in this land brings difficulties upon Ulmi-Teshshup and takes it away from him(!), or [later] takes it away from the son or grandson of Ulmi-Teshshup, or diminishes his territory, or alters the words of this [tablet].

§12 (rev. 15–17) If My Majesty requests a city or some locality from Ulmi-Teshshup, he must give it to him with good grace. It is not a matter for coercion. This shall be exempted from the oath. Or if Ulmi-Teshshup requests something from My Majesty, My Majesty will give it to him. This shall also be exempted from the oath.

§13 (rev. 18–20) If he (His Majesty) does not wish to give some city or some locality to Ulmi-Teshshup, and the latter exerts himself and takes it by force, then these oath gods shall eradicate him from the Dark Earth, together with his progeny.

Succession (reprise)

§14 (rev. 21–27) I have engraved on a tablet of iron that which I, My Majesty, have given to Ulmi-Teshshup, king of the land of Tarhuntassa, the frontiers I have established for him, as well as that which I gave to him afterward. In the future no one shall take them away from the descendant of Ulmi-Teshshup, nor contest them with him at law. The King (of Hatti) shall not take them for himself. He shall not give them to his own son. Nor shall they be given to another descendant (of the Hittite royal family). In the future only a descendant of Ulmi-Teshshup shall hold the kingship of the land of Tarhuntassa. The Storm-god, King of Heaven; the Sun-goddess of Arinna, Lady of the Lands of Hatti; Sharrumma, son of the Storm-god; Ishtar; and the Thousand Gods of this tablet shall eradicate from Hatti — together with his progeny — whoever brings difficulties upon him and takes the land away from him, or alters a single word of this tablet.

Human Witnesses

§15 (rev. 28–32) This tablet <was written> in the city of Urikina in the presence of Crown Prince Nerikkaili; Prince Tashmi-Sharrumma; Prince Hannutti; Prince Huzziya; Ini-Teshshup, king of the land of Carchemish; Ari-Sharrumma, king of the land of Isuwa; AMAR.MUSHEN, uriyanni; Halpa-ziti, commander of the troops of the right; Prince Heshni; Prince Tattamaru; Prince Uppara-muwa, overseer of the golden grooms; Prince Uhha-ziti; Sahurunuwa, chief of the wooden-tablet scribes; Hattusa-Kurunta, general; Prince Tarhunta-piya; LUGAL.dLAMMA, commander of the troops of the left; Ali-ziti, chief of the palace servants; Tuttu, chief of the storehouse; Palla, lord of the city of Hurma; Walwa-ziti, chief of the scribes; Alalimi, chief of the cupbearers; Kammaliya, chief of the cooks; and Mahhuzzi, chief of the offering officials.

No. 18C
Treaty between Tudhaliya IV of Hatti
and Kurunta of Tarhuntassa

Preamble

§1 (i 1–5) Thus says Tabarna, Tudhaliya, Great King, King of Hatti, Hero; son of Hattusili, Great King, King of Hatti, Hero; grandson of Mursili, Great King, King of Hatti, Hero; great-grandson of Suppiluliuma, Great King, King of Hatti, Hero; descendant of Tudhaliya, Great King, King of Hatti, Hero:

Historical Introduction

§2 (i 6–13) When my father, Hattusili, began war with Urhi-Teshshup, son of Muwattalli, and deposed him from kingship, Kurunta was in no way guilty of offense. However the people of Hatti committed offense, Kurunta was not involved in any of it. Previously Muwattalli, the King, had entrusted him to my father, Hattusili, to raise, and my father had indeed previously raised him.

Frontiers

§3 (i 14–21) When my father deposed Urhi-Teshshup from kingship, my father took Kurunta and installed him in kingship in the land of Tarhuntassa. The treaty which my father made with him, and how he established the frontiers for him — concerning this my father made a written treaty with him, and it is in Kurunta's possession. His frontiers were established as follows: In the direction of the land of Pitassa, his(!) frontier is Mount Hawa, the *kantanna* of the city of Zarniya, and the city of Sanantarwa, but the *kantanna* of Zarniya belongs to the land of the Hulaya River, while Sanantarwa belongs to the land of Pitassa.

§4 (i 22–28) Previously, in the direction of the land of Pitassa, his frontier was the city of Nahhanta. My father pushed back his frontier, and on my father's treaty tablet the sinkholes of the city of Arimmatta are made the frontier. Now I, My Majesty, have reestablished the earlier frontier for him. In the direction of the land of Pitassa, in the direction of the border district of the city of Arimmatta, his frontier is the cities of Nahhanta and Hauttassa, but Nahhanta and Hautassa belong to the land of the Hulaya River.

§5 (i 29–42) In the direction of Mount Huwatnuwanta, his frontier is the *hallapuwanza*, but the *hallapuwanza* belongs to the land of the Hulaya

River. Up behind the city of Kusawanta, his frontier is the Stone Monument of the Dog. In the direction of the city of Ussa, his frontier is the city
of Zarata, but Zarata belongs to the land of the Hulaya River. In the direction of the city of Wanzataruwa, his frontier is the city of Harazuwa, but
Harazuwa belongs to the land of Ussa. In the direction of Mount
Kuwakuwaliyatta, the city of Suttasna was made his frontier on my father's
first treaty tablets, but it happened that later my father himself made the
city Santimma the frontier. But Santimma belongs to the land of the
Hulaya River. In the direction of the cities of Wanzataruwa and Kunzinasa,
his frontier is Mount Arlanta and the city of Alana. Alana belongs to the
land of the Hulaya River, but the water which is upon Mount Arlanta
belongs jointly to the land of the Hulaya River and Hatti.

§6 (i 43–47) In the direction of the city of Sinnuwanta, his frontier is
Mount Lula and the Sphinx Mountains, but the city of Ninainta belongs to
the land of the Hulaya River. However, the service estate of the golden
charioteer, which is behind (the city), belongs to My Majesty. In the direction of the city of Zarnusassa, his frontier was the *harmima*, but I, My
Majesty, have made the city of Uppassana his frontier. Uppassana belongs
to the land of the Hulaya River.

§7 (i 48–52) In the direction of the city of Zarwisa, his frontier is Mount
Sarlaimmi and the sinkhole of water . . . In the direction of the mountain
heights, his frontier is the cities of Hassuwanta, Mila, Palmata, Hashasa,
Sura, and Simmuwanta, but these cities belong to the land of the Hulaya
River.

§8 (i 53–67) In the direction of the border district of the city of
Hawaliya, his frontier is the cities of Walwara, Harhasuwanta, Tarapa, Sar-
nanta, Tupisa, Paraiyassa, and the dependency(?) of the city of Nata, but
these cities and the dependency(?) of Nata belong to the land of the
Hulaya River. In the direction of the sea, his frontier is the cities of Mata,
Sanhata, Surimma, Saranduwa, Istapanna, the dependency(?) of the city of
Sallusa, and the cities of Tatta and Dasa, but these cities belong to the land
of the Hulaya River. In the direction of the border district of the city of
Saranduwa, his frontier is the sea. In the direction of the border district of
the city of Parha, his frontier is the Kastaraya River. And if the King of
Hatti goes on campaign above it (the Kastaraya River) and seizes the land
of Parha by force of arms, then this too will belong to the King of
Tarhuntassa. In the direction of the border district of the city of Walma, his
frontier is the cities of Huwahhuwarwa, Alluprata, Kaparuwa, Hassuwanta,
Walippa, and Wala, but these cities belong to the land of the Hulaya River.

§9 (i 68–90) The cities and population groups within the land of Tarhuntassa which belonged to the King of Hatti were: Anta and its deserted settlements, the cities of Lahhwiyassi, Wastissa, Hadduwassa, Handawa, Daganza, Simmuwa, Sahita, the men of Kammama under service obligation, the golden charioteers of Walistassa, the cities of Inurta, Wattanna, Malhuwaliyata, Kasuriya, Sawiya, Pariyassa, Annauliliya, Puhanta, Gurtanassa, the pomegranate-growers(?) of the town of Aralla, the people of the city of Araunna, the city of Uppassana, and the bird breeders. Those who are in the border districts of the land are also given to him. Also the nomadic populations of the cities of Mattarwanta and Para, the depot administrators of the cities of Dagannunta and Munanta, the caretakers of young animals of the city of Ayara, the spearmen of the city of Tarapa, and the two service estates of the cities of Wattassa and Talwisuwanta. The potters are excluded, and the cupbearers are also excluded. They are turned over to the deities of Tarhuntassa. The *duddushialla*-men of the city of Iyasanta, the city of Azzuwassi, and the watchmen(?) of the city of Washaniya are included. The *warpatala*-men and the cupbearers of the city of Adara are included. Whatever *sarikuwa*-squads, craftsmen, and men under service obligation are in the land of Tarhuntassa and the land of the Hulaya River — my father gave him these cities with their bare walls. He did not give them to him together with their inhabitants. But I myself, Tudhaliya, Great King, interceded already in the reign of my father, so that he gave them to him together with their inhabitants. This is not set down, however, on my father's treaty tablet.

§10 (i 91–ii 3) Concerning the matter of the Eternal Rock Sanctuary, Marassanta made an oral appeal to my father, resulting in the ruling: "Kurunta shall not be found near the Eternal Rock Sanctuary." My father had a tablet made for Marassanta, and Marassanta has it in his possession. My father did not know this, however — how the text concerning the Eternal Rock Sanctuary is inscribed within the *kuntarra*-shrine of the Storm-god, and how for all time it should not be permitted for Kurunta to forfeit the Eternal Rock Sanctuary. But when it happened that my father heard the text, then my father himself reversed the decision. And when I, Tudhaliya, Great King, became King, I sent a man, and he saw how the text concerning the Eternal Rock Sanctuary is inscribed within the *kuntarra*-shrine of the Storm-god: "For all time it shall not be permitted for Kurunta to forfeit the Eternal Rock Sanctuary." If it happens that Marassanta brings the tablet which he holds, it shall not be accepted.

§11 (ii 4–20) That which is the border district of the land of Tarhuntassa — it is the land of the Hulaya River — even a goatherd shall not enter. And if they drive their animals from the land of the Hulaya River to the great salt lick rock, they shall not take away his salt lick rights. They are given to the king of the land of Tarhuntassa, and he shall always take the salt. My father, Hattusili, gave to Kurunta, king of the land of Tarhuntassa, the cities of Sarmana, Pantarwanta, and Mahrimma, together with fields, meadow, sheep pasturage, all the salt lick, and I, My Majesty, Tudhaliya, Great King, have also given it to him. No other person shall encroach upon the salt of Sarmana. In the city of Dunna a single *kuwappala* is dedicated to the Storm-god of Lightning, and it belongs to the king of the land of Tarhuntassa. If Kurunta, king of the land of Tarhuntassa, later makes another *kuwappala*, my father, Hattusili, Great King, allowed him that. I, My Majesty, Tudhaliya, Great King, have also allowed him that, and it shall indeed be allowed him.

Provisioning of Temples

§12 (ii 21–30) And although Hatti previously cared for all the gods of the land of Tarhuntassa, they shall not take those revenues and supplies for ceremonies for the gods of Tarhuntassa from that which my father gave to Kurunta, king of the land of Tarhuntassa, and that which I, My Majesty, have given him. If now I, My Majesty, designate some place for the raising of oxen and sheep, who should dun Kurunta for supplies for ceremonies of the gods? Then they will begin to give 200 oxen and 1,000 sheep yearly to the gods of Tarhuntassa (from this designated place). But if I do not give him any place, then the people of Hatti shall give 200 oxen and 1,000 sheep every year from the cattle deliveries(?) to the gods of Tarhuntassa.

Mutual Loyalty

§13 (ii 31–42) While I, Tudhaliya, Great King, had not yet become king, the god even then brought Kurunta and myself together in friendship, and even then we were esteemed and beloved by one another. We were sworn allies: "Let one protect the other." At that time my father had placed my elder brother in the office of crown prince, while he had not yet then designated me for kingship. But at that time Kurunta protected me and swore as follows concerning my person: "Even if your father does not install you in kingship, I will protect you alone in whatever position your father does install you, and I will be your subject." I swore to Kurunta as follows: "And I will protect you."

§14 (ii 43–52) But when my father deposed my brother whom he had placed in the office of crown prince and installed me in kingship, and when my father observed the respect and affection between Kurunta and myself, my father brought us together and had us swear an oath: "Let one protect the other." Thus my father had us swear an oath, and aside from that we were sworn allies. And Kurunta protected me and in no way broke the oaths which he had sworn to me. I, My Majesty, spoke to him as follows: "If the gods recognize me so that I become king, on my part there will be only good things for you."

§15 (ii 53–56) And when my father died, because lands entered into secession — at that time Kurunta would have died for me. He protected me and in no way broke the oaths which he had sworn.

§16 (ii 57–66) When the god took me and I became King, I made a treaty with Kurunta as follows: I have assigned to his service the cities which are not already set forth on the treaty tablet of my father, together with fields, dependent laborers, and everything else. Whoever is in the land of the Hulaya River — everything belongs to Kurunta, king of the land of Tarhuntassa. I have reestablished the frontiers for him favorably. I have returned the Eternal Rock Sanctuary to him. For all time no one shall take the Eternal Rock Sanctuary away from the progeny of Kurunta.

§17 (ii 67–78) And this treaty shall be valid for all time for Kurunta, king of the land of Tarhuntassa. While these <provisions remain in force>, Tudhaliya, King of Hatti, will protect <Kurunta>, in regard to kingship, and later the progeny of Tudhaliya shall likewise protect the progeny of Kurunta in regard to kingship in the land of Tarhuntassa. They shall not allow them to perish or be demoted. As I, Tudhaliya, Great King, protect Kurunta, later my son and grandson shall likewise protect the progeny of Kurunta. And as I protect Kurunta — if he is lacking something I compensate him — if something becomes difficult for the progeny of Kurunta, my son or grandson shall likewise always compensate him for it. He shall not allow him to perish or be demoted.

Relative Status of Subordinate

§18 (ii 79–83) Concerning the Great Throne (of Hatti), his protocol shall be the same as that of the king of the land of Carchemish. Only the crown prince shall be greater than the king of the land of Tarhuntassa; no one else shall be greater than he. Whatever royal ceremonial is allowed to the king of the land of Carchemish shall also be allowed to the king of the land of Tarhuntassa.

Succession

§19 (ii 84–94) And in regard to the fact that it is stipulated on the treaty
tablet of my father as follows: "Set in kingship in the land of Tarhuntassa
the son of the woman whom the Queen (of Hatti) will give you in marriage" — at the time when they made the treaty tablet in the reign of my
father, Kurunta had not yet even taken this woman for himself. If Kurunta
now takes this woman for himself, or if he does not take her for himself —
this matter will not be taken up further. Whichever son Kurunta approves,
whether he is the son of this woman or of some other woman, whichever
son Kurunta has in mind, and whichever son he approves, he shall install in
kingship in the land of Tarhuntassa. No one shall determine this matter for
Kurunta.

§20 (ii 95–iii 20) And this treaty shall be valid for Kurunta, for his son,
and for his grandson. I, My Majesty, will not depose your son. I will accept
neither your brother nor anyone else. Only your descendant may later hold
the land of Tarhuntassa which I have given to you. It may not be taken
away from him. But if any son or grandson of yours commits an offense,
then the King of Hatti shall question him. And if an offense is proven
against him, then he shall be treated as the King of Hatti pleases. <If he is
deserving of death, he shall perish>, but his household and land shall not be
taken from him, and he (the King of Hatti) shall not give them to another
descendant (of the Hittite royal family). Or concerning the problem of the
land of Tarhuntassa, because it is hereby stipulated subsequently (to my
father's treaty tablet), as follows: "For all time no one shall take the kingship of the land of Tarhuntassa away from the progeny of Muwattalli" — if
someone does do that, and gives it to another descendant of Muwattalli,
taking it away from the progeny of Kurunta, the Storm-god of Hatti and
the Sun-goddess of Arinna shall eradicate whoever should commit that
deed. For all time only a descendant of Kurunta shall hold the kingship of
the land of Tarhuntassa. Someone of the male line shall hold it; the progeny
of a daughter shall not be taken. And if some son or grandson of Kurunta
occupies the kingship in the land of Tarhuntassa, and if due to the word of
a deity the situation becomes unfavorable for that someone so that he abdi-
cates the kingship of the land of Tarhuntassa, only a descendant of Kurunta
shall be taken and installed in kingship in the land of Tarhuntassa. They
shall not give it to any other descendant (of the Hittite royal family). If
there is no male line of descent, then the progeny of the daughter of
Kurunta shall be sought out. Even if he is in a foreign land, he shall be
brought back from there and installed in kingship in the land of
Tarhuntassa.

§21 (iii 21–31) If some descendant of Tudhaliya occupies the kingship in Hatti, and something becomes difficult for him, whatever descendant of Kurunta occupies the kingship of the land of Tarhuntassa shall die for him. As Kurunta has protected Tudhaliya, later the progeny of Kurunta shall likewise protect the progeny of Tudhaliya. The progeny of Tudhaliya shall likewise protect the progeny of Kurunta and not allow them to perish or be demoted. If something becomes difficult for a descendant of Tudhaliya so that he withdraws from the kingship of Hatti, whatever descendant of Kurunta occupies the kingship in the land of Tarhuntassa shall begin war against the (new) King of Hatti and shall not be his subject!

Military Obligations

§22 (iii 32–42) My father, Hattusili, remitted the chariotry and infantry of the land of the Hulaya River for which the armory holds claim on you, and I, My Majesty, Great King, have also remitted them. And in the future only 100 of his foot soldiers shall go on a Hittite military expedition; (additional) troops shall not be sought from him by the armory. Whenever they raise troops from him, they shall raise 100 soldiers from him. He has no chariotry obligation. But if someone of equal rank rises up against the King of Hatti, or if My Majesty goes on campaign out of the Lower Land on this side, then they shall raise 200 soldiers from him. But they shall not do garrison duty.

§23 (iii 43–56) And in regard to the fact that the entire land belongs to him, and that absolutely all of it constitutes his forward frontier posts — if at some point a summons for assistance comes up, no one shall raise assistance from the land of the Hulaya River. There will be no corvée or dues obligations on the cities which are in Hatti, in the mountainous district of Huwatnuwanta, in the lands of Kizzuwatna, Hurniya, or Ikkuwaniya, or in the land of Pitassa — in any land at all — and which belong to the Storm-god of Lightning, to the deity of the city of Parsa, to Ishtar of the city of Inwita, to the Eternal Rock Sanctuary, to the King of the land of Tarhuntassa, or to his household. A summons for assistance shall not apply to them. No matter what corvée and dues obligations are in question, no one shall approach them. I have freed them in perpetuity for the service of the gods of Tarhuntassa.

Remission of Dues

§24 (iii 57–77) In the future no one shall alter that which my father gave to Kurunta, that which I, My Majesty, have given him, or the treaty which we have made with him. When I, My Majesty, examined the corvée and dues obligations of the king of the land of Tarhuntassa in regard to the gods of Tarhuntassa, they were too heavy for him to manage. The business of the gods which the king of the land of Tarhuntassa takes care of in Tarhuntassa corresponds to that in Hattusa, Arinna, and Zippalanda. That which my father gave to Kurunta, and that which I have given to him — because his expenditures for ceremonies and rites for the gods are heavy — I have remitted them to him for the sake of the Storm-god of Lightning; Sharrumma, son of the Storm-god; and all the gods of Tarhuntassa; and I have freed him. No one shall take anything away from him, and no one shall take him for corvée or dues obligations. The Sun-goddess of Arinna and the Storm-god of Hatti shall take away the kingship of the land of Hatti from whoever takes the kingship of the land of Tarhuntassa away from the progeny of Kurunta, or who demotes them or determines on their demise, or takes away from them(!) that which my father and I, My Majesty, have given to him, or alters a single word of this tablet.

Divine Witnesses; Curses and Blessings

§25 (iii 78–iv 15) And in regard to the fact that I have made this treaty for you, the Thousand Gods are now summoned to assembly in this matter. They shall observe and listen and be witnesses: The Sun-god of Heaven, the Sun-goddess of Arinna, the Storm-god of Heaven, the Storm-god of Hatti, the Storm-god of the Army, the Storm-god of Hisashapa, the Storm-god of Zippalanda, the Storm-god of Nerik, the Storm-god of Aleppo, the Storm-god of Uda, the Storm-god of Kizzuwatna, the Storm-god of Samuha, the Storm-god of Sapinuwa, the Powerful Storm-god, the Storm-god of Lightning, Lulutassi, the Tutelary Deity, the Tutelary Deity of Hatti, Ayala, Karzi, Hapantaliya, the Tutelary Deity of the Countryside, the Tutelary Deity of the Hunting Bag, Zithariya, Sharrumma, Hebat of Uda, Hebat of Kizzuwatna, Ishtar of Samuha, Ishtar of the Countryside, Ishtar of Lawazantiya, Ishtar of Nineveh, Ishtar of Hattarina, Ninatta, Kulitta, the Moon-god, King of the Oaths, Nikkal, Queen of the Oaths, Ishhara, the Deity of Arusna, the War-god, the War-god of Hatti, the War-god of Illaya, the War-god of Arziya, Yarri, Zappana, Hantitassu of Hurma, Abara of Samuha, Katahha of Ankuwa, Ammamma of Tahurpa, Huwassanna of Hupisna, Hallara of Dunna, Lelwani, the mountain-dweller gods, the mercenary gods, the male deities, the female deities, heaven, earth, the great sea, the mountains, rivers, and springs of Hatti and of the land of Tarhuntassa. And if you, Kurunta, do not observe these words of the tablet, and do not protect My Majesty and later the progeny of My Majesty con-

cerning overlordship, or if you even desire the kingship of Hatti for yourself, or if someone brings difficulties upon My Majesty or upon the progeny
of My Majesty concerning the kingship of Hatti, and you show him favor
and do not combat him, then these oath gods shall eradicate you together
with your progeny. But if you, Kurunta, hold to the words of this tablet and
desire My Majesty and later the progeny of My Majesty for overlordship,
and if you protect them, then these gods shall benevolently protect you.
And you shall live to an old age in the hand of My Majesty.

§26 (iv 16–29) These oath gods shall eradicate whoever in this land
brings difficulties upon Kurunta and takes it away from him, or later takes
it away from the progeny of Kurunta, or diminishes his territory, or takes
away from him that which I have given him, or alters a single word of this
tablet. In the future no one shall take away from the progeny of Kurunta
that which I have given to Kurunta, king of the land of Tarhuntassa, or the
frontiers which I have established for him. The <Great> King shall not take
them for himself. He shall not give them to his own son. Nor shall he give
them to any other descendant (of the Hittite royal family). No one shall
have a legal dispute with him. In the future the progeny of Kurunta alone
shall hold the kingship of the land of Tarhuntassa. These oath gods shall
eradicate whoever brings difficulties upon him and takes it away from him,
together with his progeny.

Human Witnesses

§27 (iv 30–43) Halwa-ziti, the scribe, son of Lupakki, man of the city of
Ukkiya, wrote this tablet in the city of Tawa in the presence of Prince
Nerikkaili; Huzziya, chief of the royal bodyguard; Prince Kurakura; Ini-
Teshshup, king of the land of Carchemish; Masturi, king of the land of the
Seha River; Shaushga-muwa, brother-in-law of the King; Uppara-muwa,
antuwasalli; Tattamaru, commander of the troops of the left; Prince Ehli-
Sharrumma; Aba-muwa, commander of the charioteers; Prince Heshmi-
Sharrumma; Prince Taki-Sharrumma; Prince Ewri-Sharrumma; Alalimi,
chief overseer of a thousand; Alantalli, king of the land of Mira; Benteshina, king of the land of Amurru; Sahurunuwa, chief of the wooden-
tablet scribes; Hattusa-Kurunta, general; Ura-Tarhunta, commander of the
charioteers; Hursaniya, general; Zuzuhha, commander of the grooms;
Saliqqa, commander of the troops of the right; Tapa-ziti, overseer of ten;
Tuttu, chief of the storehouse; Walwa-ziti, chief of the scribes; Kammaliya,
scribe and chief of the cooks; Nanizi, <chief> of the scribes and overseer of
the offering officials; and in the presence of all commanders of the army,
the overseer of the thousand dignitaries, and the entire royal family.

Deposition of Treaty

§28 (iv 44–51) This document is made in seven copies and is sealed with the seal of the Sun-goddess of Arinna and the seal of the Storm-god of Hatti. One tablet is deposited in the presence of the Sun-goddess of Arinna, one tablet in the presence of the Storm-god of Hatti, one tablet in the presence of Lelwani, one tablet in the presence of Hebat of Kizzuwatna, one tablet in the presence of the Storm-god of Lightning, and one tablet in the presence of Zithariya. And Kurunta, king of the land of Tarhuntassa, has one tablet in his residence.

Notes

1. For §§1–8 only significant variants from Text B have been noted.

2. Text B obv.¹ omits this paragraph.

3. Text B obv.¹ 12' adds: The wife and children of whoever conceals [him] will be given as restitution.

4. Text B obv.¹ 13'–16': [And if a slave] hides [a fugitive and] conceals him, [his master] must make restitution [on his behalf]. He must pay twelve unfree persons. But if he does not make restitution, [he will forfeit the slave himself]. If he does not have [the means, then his master] must swear an oath: "If this slave possesses anything [. . .]."

5. The scribe of Text A has indicated that the tablet he was copying had suffered damage in this section.

6. Since the initial cuneiform sign employed to write his name can be read as *kur* or *mat* as well as *šat*, modern scholars have also referred to this ruler as Kurtiwaza, or most often, as Mattiwaza. The reading Shattiwaza, however, best accords with the names of other rulers of Hurrian kingdoms — see Zaccagnini 1974. In any case, it seems that the colophon of No. 6B gives the Hurrian personal name of the Mittannian ruler, Kili-Teshshup, while the Indo-Iranian designation Shattiwaza was probably a throne name.

7. Text B has instead: his son treated him in an evil fashion.

8. Text B: Shuttarna.

9. Text B: Ishtar, Venus Star.

10. Text B: Ishtar, Venus Star.

11. In this section and §11 the term "Prince" certainly refers to the King of Hatti.

12. Akkadian text has: He came to my father, and my father made him his subject.

13. Akkadian text adds: He was friendly like a friend.

14. Akkadian text adds: yearly.

15. Akkadian text adds: He did not withhold tribute; he did not anger him.

16. Akkadian text adds: for a second time.

17. Lit.: "the day of the mother."

18. Text A omits.

19. Text C: from here, from the land of Lukka.

20. Possibly an error for Piyama-Kurunta.

21. This paragraph has been omitted in Text B.

22. As shown by this relic of an epistolary salutation, the quoted communication has been excerpted from a letter of Benteshina to Hattusili.

23. The scribe has erased the designation of this final ruler.

2

Diplomatic Correspondence

No. 19
Letter from Suppiluliuma I of Hatti
to Niqmaddu II of Ugarit

Suppiluliuma sent this letter to Niqmaddu before his armies had scored their great successes against the king of Mittanni and his vassals in western Syria. The Great King here attempts to induce the ruler of Ugarit to attack Nuhashshi and Mukish, which he disingenuously characterizes as rebels against Hatti, by promising him captives from these lands. In fact, Niqmaddu did not "take the initiative" against his neighbors but entered the Hittite camp only after the kings of Nuhashshi and Mukish had fallen upon Ugarit. The treaty offered by Suppiluliuma at the close of the letter was indeed concluded, and has been translated as No. 4.

§1 (lines 1–2) Thus says My Majesty, Great King: Say to Niqmaddu:

§2 (lines 3–18) While the land of Nuhashshi and the land of Mukish are hostile to me, you, Niqmaddu, shall not fear them. Trust in yourself! As previously your forefathers were at peace with Hatti and not hostile, now you, Niqmaddu, shall thus be hostile to my enemy and at peace with my friend. And if you, Niqmaddu, hear and observe these words of the Great King, your lord, then you shall surely experience the favor which the Great King, your lord, will show to you.

§3 (lines 19–29) Now you, Niqmaddu, observe the peace treaty with Hatti. In the future you will see how the Great King deals with the kings of the land of Nuhashshi and the king of the land of Mukish, who renounced the peace treaty with Hatti and became hostile to the Great King, their lord. In the future you, Niqmaddu, must trust in the words of the Great King, your lord.

§4 (lines 30–34) And if all of the kings release whatever troops they have for an attack on your land, you, Niqmaddu, shall not fear them. Send your messenger to me immediately. Let him come!

§5 (lines 35–52) And if you, Niqmaddu, take the initiative and attack the troops of the land of Nuhashshi or the troops of the land of Mukish by the force of your arms, no one shall take them away from you. Or if perhaps, in the absence of troops of the land of Nuhashshi, the troops of the land of Mukish enter your land as fugitives, no one shall take them from you. Or if perhaps cities of your region somehow become hostile to you, and you do battle with them and defeat them, no one shall later take them away from you. Or if perhaps in the future the Great King defeats these kings, then the Great King will give you a sealed treaty tablet.

No. 20
Copy of Letter from Sharri-Kushuh of Carchemish to Niqmaddu II of Ugarit

When much of the Hittite empire in Syria rose in revolt early in the reign of Mursili II, his brother and viceroy Sharri-Kushuh of Carchemish wrote to the king of Ugarit, who obviously remained loyal at this time, even if his land was perhaps compromised later (cf. introduction to No. 31). Sharri-Kushuh here urges Niqmaddu to attack his neighbor to the southeast, the land of Nuhashshi, which was among the rebels. As a reward he offers him captives from the enemy's army, much as Suppiluliuma had done earlier (see No. 19). The present text is a copy made under the authority of Sharri-Kushuh's grandson Ini-Teshshup, an impression of whose cylinder seal it bears (Schaeffer et al. 1956: 23–24, figs. 30–31).

§1 (lines 1–19) Thus says the king (of Carchemish): When the king of the land of Nuhashshi became hostile to me, I sent thus to Niqmaddu: If you begin war with Tette and you, Niqmaddu, take the initiative and attack before I draw near the land of Nuhashshi — if you attack the heart of the land of Tette — then whatever Niqmaddu takes [by the force of his arms] from the land of Nuhashshi, and [whatever troops] enter his land as fugitives <he shall retain>. If in the future Tette demands his subjects, Niqmaddu shall not return any of them. If Niqmaddu does not begin war with Tette and does not carry out the words which I have spoken, then the agreement on this tablet will be void.

§2 (lines 20–23) This tablet of the grandfather of the king was sealed, but broken. Now King Ini-Teshshup has sealed its replacement a second time.

No. 21
Letter from Prince Piha-walwi of Hatti
to Ibiranu of Ugarit

In this letter the high imperial official Piha-walwi warns the new Ugaritic king against neglecting two of his most important duties as a Hittite vassal: the ceremonial visit to the Great King and the payment of tribute. The prince stresses the subordinate position of Ibiranu by addressing him as "son," that is, his junior within the hierarchy of the Hittite state system.

§1 (lines 1–3) Thus says Prince Piha-walwi: Say to my son Ibiranu:
§2 (lines 4–5) At the moment all is well with His Majesty.
§3 (lines 6–20) Why have you not come before His Majesty since you have assumed the kingship of the land of Ugarit? And why have you not sent your messengers? Now His Majesty is very angry about this matter. Now send your messengers quickly before His Majesty, and send the king's presents together with my presents.

No. 22
Selections from the Correspondence
between the Hittite and Egyptian Courts
under Hattusili III and Ramses II

More than 100 letters, some very fragmentary, exchanged by the courts of Hatti and Egypt in the time of Ramses and Hattusili have been recovered from the ruins of Hattusa (Edel 1994: 2:17–18). Most of these had been sent from Egypt to Hatti, and were, of course, composed in Akkadian, the language usually employed for international diplomacy. But around twenty pieces (several still in the Hittite language) represent Hittite drafts or unsent corrected copies of letters addressed to the Egyptian ruler or persons in his entourage. Although the pharaoh and the Hittite Great King were the principal participants in this correspondence, other members of the royal family and high officials also took part. Indeed, a number of letters were composed in nearly identical pairs, of which Hattusili and Puduhepa each sent a copy to Ramses or each received one from him (Edel 1949; 1994: 2:19).

The main themes treated in this epistolary exchange were the establish-
ment of peace between the two empires (Nos. 22A–C), as codified in the
treaty translated here as No. 15; the Egyptian exile of Urhi-Teshshup, who
as Mursili III had ruled Hatti before his overthrow at the hands of Hattusili
(No. 22D); and the marriage of the daughter of Hattusili to Ramses (Nos.
22D–F). Note that most of these letters close with a list of the precious
goods sent along with them as "gifts of greeting."

No. 22A
Letter from Prince Sutahapshap of Egypt
to Hattusili III of Hatti

§1 (obv. 1–2) [Thus says] Sutahapshap, [son] of the Great King, the King
of Egypt:

§2 (obv. 3–4) Say [to] Hattusili, Great King, [King] of Hatti, my father:

§3 (obv. 5–7) May you, Great King, King of Hatti, my [father], be well,
and may your [lands] be [well]!

§4 (obv. 8–10) [Now I, your son], am well, and [the lands] of the Great
King, the King of Egypt, your brother, are well.

§5 (obv. 11–16) Now the Great King, the King of Hatti, my father, has
written to me inquiring about the health of his son, and I was overjoyed
that my father has written to me inquiring about my health.

§6 (obv. 17–rev. 4) The Sun-god and the Storm-god will inquire about the
health of the Great King, the King of Hatti, my father, and they will cause
peace and brotherhood to thrive forever between the Great King, the King
of Egypt, and the Great King, the King of Hatti, his brother. They will also
cause the years of the Great King, the King of Egypt, and the years of Hattusili, Great King, King of Hatti, his brother, to be prolonged,

§7 (rev. 5–7) since they (the Kings) are forever in a state of good peace
and good brotherhood.

§8 (rev. 8–10) I have now sent a present to my father in the care of Parihnawa as a gift of greeting for my father:

§9 (rev. 11–14) [One] drinking [cup] of good gold, inlaid, [with] the face
of an ox whose horns are of white stone, [and whose eyes] are of black
stone. [Its weight] is 93 shekels of good gold.

§10 (rev. 15) [One] new [. . . linen garment] of good fine thread.

§11 (rev. 16–17) [One] new two-sided [linen bed]spread of good fine
thread.

No. 22B
Letter from Queen Naptera of Egypt
to Puduhepa of Hatti

§1 (obv. 1–2) Thus says Naptera, Great Queen of Egypt: Say to Puduhepa, Great Queen of Hatti, my sister:

§2 (obv. 3) I, your sister, am well. My land is well.

§3 (obv. 4–11) May you, my sister, be well! May your land be well! I have now heard that you, my sister, wrote to me inquiring about my health, and that you are writing to me in regard to the relationship of good peace and the relationship of good brotherhood which exists between the Great King, the King of Egypt, and the Great King, the King of Hatti, his brother.

§4 (obv. 12–19) The Sun-god and the Storm-god will exalt you, and the Sun-god will cause peace to thrive and will provide good brotherhood forever between the Great King, the King of Egypt, and the Great King, the King of Hatti, his brother. And I am likewise in a condition of peace and brotherhood with you, my sister.

§5 (obv. 20–21) I have now sent you a present as a gift of greeting for you, my sister.

§6 (obv. 22–24) And may you, my sister, be informed about the present which I have sent you in the care of Parihnawa, the messenger of the King:

§7 (obv. 25–26) One very colorful necklace of good gold, made up of twelve strands. Its weight is 88 shekels.

§8 (obv. 27) One dyed cloak of byssus.

§9 (rev. 1) One dyed tunic of byssus.

§10 (rev. 2) Five dyed linen garments of good fine thread.

§11 (rev. 3) Five dyed linen tunics of good fine thread.

§12 (rev. 4) A grand total of twelve linen garments.

No. 22C
Letter from Ramses II of Egypt
to Prince Tashmi-Sharrumma of Hatti

§1 (lines 1–4) [Thus says Wasmuaria] satepnaria, [Great King, King of Egypt, son of the Sun-god, Ramses], Beloved of Amon, [Great King, King of] Egypt:

§2 (lines 5–6) [Say to] Tashmi-Sharrumma, my son:

§3 (lines 7–8) May you, son of the Great King of Hatti, my brother, be well!

§4 (lines 9–12) I have now sent a present to my son in the care of my messenger. May you be informed about it:

§5 (lines 13–14) One cup of good gold. Its weight is 49 shekels.

§6 (lines 15–17) Two dyed cloaks of byssus; two dyed tunics of byssus.

No. 22D
Letter from Ramses II of Egypt
to Kupanta-Kurunta of Mira-Kuwaliya

Since it was not appropriate for a vassal of one Great King to communicate directly with another, this letter for the ruler of Mira (a partner in treaty No. 11) was sent via the Hittite capital, where it remained until excavated in this century. Kupanta-Kurunta had apparently expressed some misgivings about Ramses' dealings with the deposed Urhi-Teshshup (§§3–4), leading the pharaoh to quote excerpts from his own correspondence with the Hittite Great King to demonstrate that he had brought the former ruler of Hatti to Egypt only at the urging of Hattusili himself (§§4–5), and that he remained loyal to the treaty established between them (§§6–7).

§1 (obv. 1–5) Thus says Wasmuaria satepnaria, Great King, [King of Egypt], son of the Sun-god, Ramses, Beloved of Amon: Say to Kupanta-Kurunta, king of the land of Mira: Now I [am well. My houses], my sons, my infantry, my horses, my chariots, and everything in all of my lands is exceedingly well.

§2 (obv. 6) May you, the king of Mira, be well! [May] your land [be well]!

§3 (obv. 7–13) Now I, Great King, King of Egypt, have heard all the matters which [you wrote] me about. No, concerning the affair of Urhi-Teshshup, I [have] not [done] that which you wrote me about. Now [. . .] The good relationship which I, Great King, King of Egypt, established with the Great King, [the King of Hatti], my brother, consists of good brotherhood and good peace. The Sun-god and [the Storm-god gave it] forever. Another thing: The affair of Urhi-Teshshup which you [wrote] me about — the Great King, the King of Hatti, has dealt with it in accordance with [my wishes].

§4 (obv. 14–27) He writes to me repeatedly about him as follows: "Let the Great King, the King of Egypt, have his infantry and [his chariotry] exert themselves, and let him expend his gold, his silver, his horses, his copper, [and his garments] in order to take [Urhi-Teshshup to Egypt. He shall not allow him to become strong] and to wage war [against Hatti . . ." That is what the Great King], the King [of Hatti, my brother, wrote to me . . .]

[*The remaining nine lines of the obverse and the first three preserved lines of the reverse are too fragmentary for translation.*]

§5 (rev. 4'–11') . . . Indeed, the Great King, the King of Egypt, immediately [wrote] about them (that is, charges of Egyptian collusion with Urhi-Teshshup) [to] the Great King, the King of Hatti: "What have I done? Where would I recognize Urhi-Teshshup (as ruler)?" That is what I [said]. But the Great King, the King of Hatti, did not write to me about this [matter]. Have *my* lips articulated plots? [The word] which men speak to you is worthless. Do not trust in it. I am happily in brotherhood and happily [at peace] forever with the Great King, the King of Hatti, my brother.

§6 (rev. 12'–16') Another thing: What is this matter which the Great King, the King [of Hatti], writes <me> about, and which you write [me] about? The written version of the oath which [I made] for the Great King, the King of Hatti, my brother, has been set at the feet of [the Storm-god] and before the Great Gods. They are the witnesses [to the words of the oath].

§7 (rev. 17'–19') And the written version of the oath which the Great King, [the King of Hatti, my brother], made for me [has been set] at the feet of the Sun-god of [Heliopolis] and before the Great Gods. They are the witnesses to the words [of the oath].

§8 (rev. 20'–24') I have taken the oath and will not abandon it. In your heart [do] not [trust] in the false words which you have heard. There is no sense in it. I am thus forever in the [good] relationship [of brotherhood] and peace in which I stand together with the Great King, [the King of Hatti, my brother].

No. 22E
Letter from Queen Puduhepa of Hatti
to Ramses II of Egypt

Since the beginning of this letter has been lost, scholars have long debated the identities of the correspondents (see Sommer 1932: 253; Helck 1963: 94–95 for the history of this discussion). Because the tablet was found in the Hittite capital, it is natural to assume that the female writer was a Hittite Great Queen, and the assertive role of the writer suggests that she was none other than Puduhepa, wife of Hattusili III and the most prominent Queen in Hittite history (see Otten 1975). The recipient was an independent ruler important enough to receive a Hittite princess in marriage, but is not monarch of Babylonia (see §10). Although it has been proposed that this letter was directed to the king of Amurru (Götze, introduction to the publication of the cuneiform copy), of Alashiya/Cyprus (Sommer 1932:

257), or of Ahhiyawa (Hagenbuchner 1989: 226), Helck's suggestion (1963: 95–96; cf. also Wouters 1989) that it forms part of the extensive "marriage correspondence" between the court of Hatti and that of Ramses II of Egypt (see Edel 1953; 1955) is certainly correct. Indeed, the discourse in §13 would be appropriate only in an exchange between the Hittite and Egyptian sovereigns, and the mention of Urhi-Teshshup in §2 also points to Egypt.

The fact that this piece is written in Hittite rather than Akkadian indicates that it is a preliminary draft. This judgment is supported by the presence on the tablet of many erasures, grammatical errors, and passages where words have been inserted.

The contents indicate that this letter was composed in response to an angry communication from the pharaoh, complaining of the delay in the dispatch of his Hittite bride. Puduhepa here attempts to justify the Hittite position, adducing a lack of resources due to a fire in the royal storehouse(?) (§2) and the onset of winter (§§4–5) as extenuating circumstances. Despite her occasional resort to sarcasm (see especially §3), the Queen is clearly at pains to smooth over the dispute.

[*The first one or two lines, which contained the heading of the letter giving the names of the recipient and sender, as well as the formulaic greetings, have been lost.*]

§1 (obv. 1'–6') [Concerning the fact that you, my brother, wrote to me as follows]: "At the time when your messengers [came to me], they brought me [back gifts], and I rejoiced." [When I heard] that, [I rejoiced likewise. The wife] of your brother (Puduhepa) [enjoys] full life. [May] the person of [my brother (Ramses) likewise] enjoy [full life! Send me . . .], and may they be set [with] lapis lazuli! Furthermore, my lands enjoy [full life]. <May> [your lands likewise] <enjoy> full [life]! [I have sent] my greetings and my ornaments [to my brother. May] my brother likewise [enjoy full life]!

§2 (obv. 7'–14') Concerning the fact that you, my brother, wrote to me as follows: "My sister wrote to me: '[I will give] a daughter to you.' [But you have withheld her. And] now you are angry [with me]. Why have you not now given her to me?" [I have indeed withheld my daughter.] You will not disapprove of it; you will approve of it. At the moment [I am not able to give] her to you. As you, my brother, know the storehouse(?) of Hatti, do I not [know that it is] a burned-out structure? And Urhi-Teshshup gave what remained to the Great God. Since Urhi-Teshshup is there, ask him if this is so, or not so. With whom should I compare the daughter of heaven and earth whom I will give to my brother? Should I compare her with the daughter of Babylonia, of Zulabi, or of Assyria? While I am not able to tie(?) her to them, up until now she [. . .]

§3 (obv. 15'–16') Does my brother not possess anything at all? Only if the Son of the Sun-god, the Son of the Storm-god, and the Sea have nothing, do you have nothing! But, my brother, you would enrich yourself somewhat at my expense! That is worthy neither of renown nor of lordliness.

§4 (obv. 17'–24') Concerning the fact that I wrote to my brother as follows: "What civilian captives, cattle, and sheep will I give (as a dowry) to my daughter? In my lands I do not even have barley. The moment that the messengers reach you, [let] my brother [send] a rider to me. Let documents be brought to the lords of my land so that the civilian captives, cattle, and sheep which are in their charge may be taken away and accommodated." [I] myself have sent messengers and tablets to them (my local subordinates). Later they arrived [at the palace(?)] of [His Majesty(?), together with] the messengers. But [your] rider did [not] come back promptly, and my messenger did not come either. Thereupon [I sent] Zuzu, charioteer and intimate of the king, [but] he was delayed. At the moment that Pihasdu did arrive, it [was] already [winter, and] I did not transfer the civilian captives again. My brother, ask your messengers [if this is so], or not so. The matter is not [. . .]

§5 (obv. 25'–33') Concerning the fact that you, my brother, wrote to me as follows: "Do not withhold the daughter from me any longer!" [. . .] Was she not approved by me? [Do I hold] back the daughter for myself? [Rather, I wish that she had] already arrived. When [I] myself for her [. . .] away, [. . .] If I had not at any time (sincerely) given my own daughter to you, [I would not have promised] you [the civilian captives, cattle, and sheep(?)]. But now not [. . .] And they (the bride and her party) will come down to spend the winter in Kizzuwatna [. . .] May His Majesty (that is, Hattusili) live for my sake! If (s)he should turn, [. . .] But Alalimi, overseer of the cupbearers, came, and your [rider arrived too(?)]. Let some of them (the marriage party) take possession of a single city, while others [. . .]

§6 (obv. 34'–40') Concerning the fact that you, my brother, wrote to me as follows: "I write to my sister that withholding the daughter [is not right . . .]" Whenever will we see [. . .]? You order [. . .]! May the gods [. . .] turn the withholding into haste for me! Let me not delay, let me hurry! [. . .] But my brother has [not accepted] in his own mind my status as a sister and my dignity, [saying: " . . .], and do what should not be done!" When should I alter the message [which] I am writing [to my brother] for the second time? Because I am(?) dear to you [. . .], should I [not(?)] alter [it]?

§7 (obv. 41'–43') Concerning the fact that you, my brother, wrote to me as follows: "[Your messengers] shall speak freely to the daughter." [I have]

thereupon [written] this word to my brother: "When in the future, condi-
tions are favorable, [they will come(?)]." That is why I have written [to] my
[brother].

§8 (obv. 44'-46') If [I had sent(?)] the daughter to my brother [precipi-
tously(?)], or if I had [not] given you the gifts appropriate for my brother or
for his sister, what would my brother even then [have said]? Perhaps: "May
the woman whom they gave to me have some support, and [may] it [be
generous] for her! That [would] be lordly behavior."

§9 (obv. 47'-52') The daughter of Babylonia and [the daughter] of
Amurru whom I, the Queen, took for myself — were they not indeed a
source of praise for me before the people of Hatti? It was I who did it. I
took each daughter of a Great King, though a foreigner, as daughter-in-law.
And if at some time his (the royal father's) messengers come in splendor to
the daughter-in-law, or one of her brothers or sisters comes to her, is this
not also a source of praise for me? Was there no woman available to me in
Hatti? Did I not do this out of consideration for renown?

§10 (obv. 53'-56') Did my brother have no wife at all? Did not my
brother make them (marriage arrangements) <out of consideration for>
his(!) brotherhood, my sisterhood, and our dignity? And when he did make
them, they were indeed settled in conformity with (the arrangements of)
the King of Babylonia. Did he not also take the daughter of the Great King,
the King of Hatti, the mighty King, for marriage? If you should say: "The
King of Babylonia is not a Great King," then my brother does not know the
rank of Babylonia.

§11 (obv. 57'-65') My personal deity who was responsible for this —
when the Sun-goddess of Arinna, the Storm-god, Hebat, and Shaushga
made <me> Queen — she joined me with your brother, and I produced
sons and daughters, so that the people of Hatti often speak of my experi-
ence(?) and capacity for nurture(?). My brother knows this. Furthermore,
when I entered the royal household, the princesses I found in the household also gave birth under my care. I [raised] them (their children), and [I]
also [raised] those whom I found already born. I made them military offi-
cers — may my personal deity [. . .]! And may [the gods likewise] endow
the daughter whom I will give to my brother with the Queen's experience(?)
and capacity for nurture(?)! And I, the Queen, spoke thereby: "Her brothers [will be concerned] for her." If this is not acceptable to my brother, will I
do anything displeasing to my brother?

§12 (rev. 1-6) Concerning the fact that you, my brother, wrote to me as
follows: "When you turn over the daughter to me, then write to me about
the matters which might be on your mind and which you might wish to

write to me about." This message is just what one would expect from my brother! Since the Queen is coming to Amurru, I will be in your vicinity, and from there I will write to my brother whatever matters are on the Queen's mind. You, my brother, will not disapprove of them; you will approve of them. When the daughter arrives at my brother's bed, these matters of the Queen will be settled.

§13 (rev. 7–16) Concerning the fact that you, my brother, wrote to me as follows: "My sister wrote to me: 'When messengers traveled to visit the daughter of Babylonia who had been given to Egypt, they were left standing outside!'" Ellil-bel-nishe, messenger of the King of Babylonia, told [me] this information. Because [I] heard this information — should I not have written of it to my brother? I will not again do anything about which my brother has now expressed his disapproval to me. I will not again do to my brother anything which displeases my brother. If I do not know something, then I might do such a displeasing thing to my brother. But because I already know, I certainly will not do anything displeasing to my brother. Now I know that Egypt and Hatti will become a single country. Even if there is not [now] a treaty with Egypt, the Queen knows thereby how [you] will conclude it out of consideration for my dignity. The deity who installed [me] in this place has not denied me anything. She has not denied me happiness. You, as son-in-law, [will take] my daughter [in marriage].

§14 (rev. 18–22) While my daughter [. . .] to an important [. . .] writes [. . .] And these to me [. . .] Which of my children [. . .] my [. . .]

No. 22F
Letter from Ramses II of Egypt
to Puduhepa of Hatti

After extended pleasantries, the first portion of this communication (§§8–9) presents Ramses' happy reaction to the joy expressed by Puduhepa at the successful conclusion of negotiations over the dispatch of a Hittite princess to the pharaoh's harem. There follows the report of a disagreement among the envoys sent from Hatti concerning whether Hattusili had indeed requested the return of some young Hittites who were apparently serving as pages at the Egyptian court (§§10–14).

§1 (lines 1–2) Thus says Wasmuaria satepnaria, Great King, King of Egypt, son of the Sun-god, Ramses, Beloved of Amon, Great King, King of Egypt:

§2 (line 3) Say to Puduhepa, Great Queen of Hatti, my sister:

§3 (lines 4–6) Now Ramses, Beloved of Amon, Great King, King of

Egypt, your brother, is well. His houses, his infantry, his horses, his chariots, and everything in [all of his lands] is exceedingly well.

§4 (lines 7–10) [May] you, [my sister], be exceedingly well! May [Hattusili], Great [King], King of Hatti, my brother, be well! May his [houses], his sons, his infantry, his horses, [his chariots], and his lands be well!

§5 (lines 11–18) Say to my sister: Now Tili-Teshshup, my sister's messenger, has arrived before me, accompanied by Reamasia, my sister's messenger; Parihnawa, my messenger; and Zinapa and Mania, also my messengers. They have told me of [the health] of my sister, of the health of [the Great King, the King of] Hatti, my brother, and [of the health of his sons]. And I was overjoyed

§6 (lines 19–25) [when] I heard of the health of my brother and of the health of my sister — "They are well, [safe], and healthy." And when I saw the tablet which [my sister] sent to me, when I heard all the matters which my sister wrote me about, when I received the present which my sister sent to me, and when I saw that it was secure and in good condition, I was indeed overjoyed.

§7 (lines 26–29) The Sun-god and the Storm-god will give us brotherhood and peace, even in this good relationship in which we find ourselves forever. And our messengers will travel continuously between us forever, fostering brotherhood and peace.

§8 (lines 30–36) [Say] to my sister: In respect to that which my sister wrote [to] me regarding her daughter: "The Sun-god has carried out my [wish] which I told him and has satisfied me." That is what my sister wrote to me. I am very pleased about this relationship which the Sun-god created when he satisfied [my] sister regarding the wish she expressed to him.

§9 (lines 37–43) The Sun-god and the Storm-god will see to the completion of all the arrangements which my sister desires be made for her daughter. They will install her in the household of the King, your brother, since she is intended for rule [in] Egypt. They will satisfy my sister and the King (of Egypt), your brother, with the arrangements which they will make for her.

§10 (lines 44–52) [Say] to my sister: Tili-Teshshup said to me: "Hattusili, Great King, [King] of Hatti, along with the Great Queen [of] Hatti, told me: 'Say to the Great King, King of Egypt, [our brother]: Send us the sons of Masniyalli.'" That is what he said. But Reamasia, the messenger of [my] sister, said: "My lady did not say to me: 'Say: [Send his sons,' and] I did not hear anything about it. And the Great King, the King of Hatti, did <not> speak [to] Tili-Teshshup." That is what he said.

§11 (lines 53–62) [And] Parihnawa said: "I did not hear anything about it. The Great King, [the King of Hatti], did not mention [the sons of] Mas-niyalli [to me], or say 'Speak to the King, [our brother, about them].' He did not mention them [to me], and I did not hear anything about it." And [he said] to Tili-Teshshup, "[No], he did not say anything!" [Zinapa] also said: "[Hattusili], Great King, King of [Hatti], and the Queen [did not say anything about the sons] of Masniyalli, such as '[Send them]!'" That is what he said. And Mania [said] the same thing about this situation. And they hold to this story. And [. . .]ri, the interpreter, also said the same thing about this situation.

§12 (lines 63–66) [I, the King], your brother, spoke to Tili-Teshshup, my sister's messenger: "You have indeed said: The Great King, the King of Hatti, told me, and the Great Queen of Hatti told me — 'Say to the King, our brother: Send the sons of Masniyalli.'"

§13 (lines 67–73) "Take them in charge and convey them to the Great King, the King of Hatti, [my] brother. And convey them to my sister." I said this to him, but he said: "No, I will not take them until the tablet of the Great King, the King of Hatti, together with the tablet of the Queen, arrives, saying 'Send them!'" That is what he said. Let my sister send clarification to me about the sons of Masniyalli.

§14 (lines 74–75) And if my sister says: "Send them!," then I will send them to my sister immediately.

§15 (lines 76–79) Say to my sister: I have now indeed dispatched my sister's messengers, together with my own messengers, so that they can travel immediately to my sister. And I have sent a very nice present to my sister in their care.

No. 22G
Letter from Ramses II of Egypt
to Hattusili III of Hatti

Here Ramses responds to a request from Hattusili for obstetric assistance for his sister Matanazzi (who is also mentioned as Massanuzzi in No. 17, §7). Since it was customary for Great Kings to exchange medical experts (cf. No. 23, §§12–13 and see Edel 1976), Ramses complies, although he indicates that only a miracle from the gods will allow a woman of Matanazzi's age to conceive (§§6–7).

§1 (obv. 1–3) [Thus says Wasmuaria] satepnaria, [Great King, King of Egypt], Son of the Sun-god, Ramses, [Beloved of Amon], Great King, King of Egypt:

§2 (obv. 4–5) [Speak to Hattusili, Great King, King] of Hatti, my brother:

§3 (obv. 6) Now I, [the Great King], your brother, am well.

§4 (obv. 7) May you, my [brother, be very well]!

§5 (obv. 8–14) Say to [my brother: That which my brother] wrote [to me concerning] his [sister] Matanazzi: "Let my brother send a man to prepare medicines for her, so that she might be caused to give birth." That is what my brother wrote to me.

§6 (obv. 15–rev. 5) Say to my brother: Now, I, the King, your brother, know about Matanazzi, my brother's sister. She is said to be fifty or sixty years old. It is not possible to prepare medicines for a woman who has completed fifty or sixty years so that she might still be caused to give birth.

§7 (rev. 6–8) O that the Sun-god and the Storm-god might command, so that the ritual which will be performed will be carried out fully for my brother's sister!

§8 (rev. 9–13) And I, the King, your brother, shall send a competent incantation priest and a competent [physician], and they will prepare medicines for her in order that she might give birth.

§9 (rev. 14–16) I have now sent a present to my brother in the [care of] this [messenger]:

§10 (rev. 17) [. . . cloaks] of byssus.

§11 (rev. 18) [. . . tunics] of byssus.

No. 23
Letter from Hattusili III of Hatti
to Kadashman-Enlil II of Babylon

Although this letter is addressed to the King of Babylonia, it was discovered at Hattusa; therefore it is either a draft or a corrected copy retained by the Hittite chancellery. The infrequency of erasures on the tablet favors the second alternative. In this long text Hattusili discusses a number of matters commonly attested in the international correspondence of the Late Bronze Age: the affairs of merchants (§§9–10), the relations of one Great King with the vassal of another (§11), the exchange of magico-medical experts and craftsmen among the major courts (§§12–13, 16), and the reciprocal dispatch of valuable animals and precious materials (§17 and damaged final lines).

But the primary concern of this letter is surely the attempt to repair the strains which had arisen between Hatti and Babylonia after the death of Kadashman-Enlil's father and predecessor, Kadashman-Turgu (§§4–6). According to Hattusili, his efforts to assure the legitimate succession of his ally's minor son (cf. No. 15, §11) had been maliciously misrepresented by

Kadashman-Enlil's advisors as unwarranted and humiliating interference in the internal affairs of Babylonia. The young king's vizier, Itti-Marduk-bal-atu, was particularly to blame for this calumny. Hattusili suggests that the recent interruption in diplomatic traffic between the two realms was in fact due to this cooling of relations, and not to the dangers allegedly posed to Babylonian envoys by Ahlamu Aramaean tribesmen and Assyrian forces. Whatever the true character of the Hittite monarch's intervention in the Babylonian succession, a note of condescension is apparent in his advice to Kadashman-Enlil (see especially §14).

Note also the discussion of relations between Babylonia and Egypt (§7). When the Egyptian monarch's refusal of Hattusili's demand for extradition of his "enemy" (almost certainly Urhi-Teshshup; cf. No. 22E, §2) led to tensions between Egypt and Hatti, Kadashman-Turgu had broken off relations with Ramses II and had even offered to send forces in support of his Hittite ally. Now, on the other hand, the new regime of Kadashman-Enlil had resumed diplomatic contacts with the pharaoh. See Rowton 1966: 243–49 for the dating of the present document after the conclusion of the peace between Hattusili and Ramses embodied in No. 15.

§1 (obv. 1–2) Thus says Hattusili, Great King, King of Hatti: Say [to] Kadashman-Enlil, Great King, King of Babylonia, my brother:

§2 (obv. 3–4) I am well. My household, my wife, my sons, my infantry, my horses, [my chariots], and everything in my land is well.

§3 (obv. 5–6) May you be well! May your household, your wives, your sons, your infantry, your horses, your chariots, and everything in your land be very well!

§4 (obv. 7–24) When your father and I established friendly relations and became affectionate brothers, we did not become brothers for a single day. Did we not establish brotherhood and friendly relations in perpetuity? We [then] set down [an agreement] with one another as follows: "We are mortal. The survivor shall protect the children of the one who goes first to his fate." Then when your father went to his fate while the gods prepared [longevity for me], I wept for him like a brother. [After] I had fulfilled [my mourning responsibilities] for your father, I dried my tears and [immediately] dispatched a messenger, writing to the noblemen of Babylonia as follows: "If you do not protect the progeny of my brother in regard to rule, I will become hostile to you. I will come and conquer Babylonia. But if an enemy somehow arises against you, or some matter becomes troublesome for you, write to me so that I can come to your aid." But my brother was a child in those days, and they did not read out the tablets in your presence.

Now are none of those scribes still living? Are the tablets not filed? Let them read those tablets to you now. I wrote these words to them with good intentions, but Itti-Marduk-balatu — whom the gods have caused to live far too long, and in whose mouth unfavorable words never cease — he froze my heart with the words he wrote to me: "You do not write to us like a brother. You pressure us as if we were your subjects."

§5 (obv. 25–35) Let me ask my brother: How did I pressure them as if they were my subjects? Have the people of Babylonia ever pressured the people of Hatti? Conversely, have the people of Hatti indeed ever pressured the people of Babylonia? I wrote to them with good intentions: "The progeny of my brother Kadashman-Turgu shall be protected," but Itti-Marduk-balatu wrote this to me. How did I write a malicious word to them, that Itti-Marduk-balatu should write these things to me? Indeed I wrote to them thus: "<If> you do not protect the son of your lord in regard to rule, and if an enemy land arises against you, I will not come to your aid." I have by no means taken the word of Itti-Marduk-balatu to heart. In those days my brother was a child, and Itti-Marduk-balatu, that evil man, spoke as he pleased. How should I take his word seriously?

§6 (obv. 36–54) Furthermore, my brother: Because my brother wrote to me: "Concerning my cutting off my messengers — since the Ahlamu are hostile, I have cut off my messengers" — how can this be, that you, my brother, have cut off your messengers on account of the Ahlamu? Is the might of your kingdom small, my brother? Or has perhaps Itti-Marduk-balatu spoken unfavorable words before my brother, so that my brother has cut off the messengers? In the land of my brother horses are more plentiful than straw. Should I indeed have dispatched a thousand chariots to meet your messenger in Tuttul, so that the Ahlamu would have kept their hands off? And if my brother should say [as follows]: "The King of Assyria will not allow my messenger [to enter] his land" — in infantry and chariotry the King of Assyria does not measure up to [the forces] of your land. Indeed your messenger by force [. . .] What is the King of Assyria who holds back your messenger [while my messengers] cross repeatedly? Does the King of Assyria hold back your messengers so that you, [my brother], cannot cross [to] my [land]? My brother, you are a Great King, and in a long life [may you be . . .]! Look, my brother, how I keep sending [my messengers] out of love for my brother, while my brother does not send his messenger. Does [my brother] not know [this]? Every word which my brother sent me I will retain. [Only if two kings] are hostile do their messengers not travel continually between them. Why, [my brother], have you cut off [your messengers]?

§7 (obv. 55–75) [Furthermore, my brother: Concerning] the messenger
of the King of Egypt of whom my brother wrote me — I write now as follows to my brother [concerning this messenger of the King] of Egypt:
[When your father] and I established friendly relations and became brothers, [we] spoke [as follows]: "We are brothers. To the enemy of one another
[we will be hostile, and with] the friend of one another we will be friendly."
And when the King of Egypt [and I] became angry [with one another], I
wrote to your father, Kadashman-Turgu: "[The King of Egypt] has become
hostile to me." And your father wrote to me as follows: "[If your troops] go
against Egypt, then I will go with you. [If] you go [against Egypt, I will send
you] such infantry and chariotry as I have available to go." Now, my
brother, ask your noblemen. They shall tell you [whether he would have
sent] infantry and chariotry to go with me, as many as he promised, [if I
had gone. But] what [did I ever] accept? My enemy who [had escaped] to
another country [left] and went to the King of Egypt. When I wrote to him:
"[Send me my enemy]," and he did not send me my enemy, [then, because
of this, I and the King of] Egypt became angry with one another. Then [I
wrote] to your father: "[The King of Egypt] is coming to the aid of my
enemy." [At that time your father] cut off [the messenger of the King of]
Egypt. When my brother [became King], you sent [your messenger to the
King of] Egypt, and the matter of the messenger [of the King of Egypt . . .
And the King of] Egypt [accepted] your [presents, and] you accepted [his
presents]. Now [you are an adult. If] you send [your messenger to the King
of Egypt], would I restrain you in any way?

§8 (obv. 76–rev. 8) [. . .] and now you are an adult [. . .] will come. The
health of my brother [. . .] they shall take. [. . .] I treat kindly. [. . .] three
or four times [. . .] son or daughter [. . . your father], Kadashman-Turgu,
and I [. . .] they complain as follows: [. . .] the kings of our vicinity [have
spoken as follows: "Because the King] of Babylonia and the King of Hatti
[established friendly relations and became affectionate brothers, since] the
King of Babylonia [went to his fate, will the King of Hatti] out of love for
his brother protect [the progeny of his brother?" Thus they have spoken,
and I wrote to them]: "Out of love for my(!) brother [I will protect the
progeny of my brother." And this word] was heard from east to west [. . .]
they shall hear.

§9 (rev. 9–13) [Furthermore, my brother: Because] my brother wrote to
me that I had provided a response <to> Adad-shar-ilani [. . .] brought it.
The king of Carchemish [decided . . .] the lawsuit of the merchants. My
brother, promptly send me another messenger, [so that] I can decide [their

lawsuit]. Or conversely, let me send their opponents at law, and [my brother] shall decide their lawsuit.

§10 (rev. 14–25) [Furthermore, my brother: Because] you wrote to me as follows: "My merchants are being killed in the land of Amurru, the land of Ugarit, [and the land of . . .]" — they do not kill (as punishment) in Hatti. [But . . .] they kill. If the King hears about it, [they pursue] that matter. They apprehend the murderer [and deliver him] to the relatives of the dead man, [but they allow] the murderer [to live. The place] in which the murder occurred is purified. If his relatives will not accept [the compensatory silver], they may make the murderer [their slave]. If a man who has committed an offense against the King [escapes] to another land, killing him is not permitted. Ask, my brother, and they shall tell you. [. . .] thus. Would those who do not kill a malefactor kill a merchant? [But in regard to] the Subarians, how should I know if they are killing people? Now [send] me the relatives of the dead merchants so that I can investigate their lawsuit.

§11 (rev. 26–33) Furthermore, my brother: Concerning Benteshina of whom my brother wrote to me: "He continually curses my land" — when I asked Benteshina, he replied to me as follows: "The Babylonians owe me three talents of silver." Right now a servant of Benteshina is on his way to you so that my brother can decide his lawsuit. And concerning the curses against the land of my brother, Benteshina swore an oath to my gods in the presence of Adad-shar-ilani, your messenger. If my brother does not believe this, let his servant who heard Benteshina when he continually cursed the land of my brother come here and oppose him in court. And I will put pressure on Benteshina. Benteshina is my subject. If he has cursed my brother, has he not cursed me too?

§12 (rev. 34–41) Furthermore, [my brother]: Concerning the physician whom my brother dispatched here — when they received the physician, he accomplished many [good] things. When illness befell him, I exerted myself constantly on his behalf. I performed many extispicies for him, but when his time [. . .] came, he died. And now my messenger will bring his servants so that my brother can [question] them, and they can relate to my brother the many things which the physician accomplished. And if they should make off with [the things which] I gave [to] their master, they will take fright and conceal the matter from my brother. [Let] my brother [pay special attention to] the chariot, the *attartu*-chariot, the horses, the refined silver, and the linen which I gave to the physician. They are written down, and I have sent the tablet to my brother so that my brother can hear it. When the time came [for the physician], he died. In no way would I have detained the physician.

§13 (rev. 42–48) Furthermore, [my brother]: When during the reign of my brother Muwattalli they received an incantation priest and a physician and detained them [in Hatti], I argued with him, saying: "Why are you detaining them? Detaining [a physician] is not right." And would I now have detained the physician? [Concerning the first] experts whom they received here: Perhaps the incantation priest died, [but the physician] is alive and proprietor of a fine household. The woman whom he married is a relative of mine. [If he says]: "I want to go back to my native land," he shall leave and go [to his native land]. Would I have detained the physician Raba-sha-Marduk?

§14 (rev. 49–55) [Furthermore, my brother]: I have heard that my brother has become a grown man and regularly goes out to hunt. [I rejoice] greatly that the Storm-god has exalted the name of my brother Kadashman-Turgu. [. . .] go and plunder an enemy land in this manner so that I might hear about it. [. . .] my [brother] defeated. Furthermore, my brother: They have said [that my brother is] a king whose weapons have been stowed and who just sits around. Do they not say this about him? [. . .] Do not keep sitting around, my brother, but go against an enemy land and defeat the enemy! [Against which land] should [my brother] go out? Go against a land over which you enjoy three- or fourfold numerical superiority.

§15 (rev. 56–57) [. . .] he made his father quake with rage. And now I have made him bring [. . .] to his wife and children.

§16 (rev. 58–61) [Furthermore, my brother]: I want to make [images] and place them in the family quarters. My brother, [send me] a sculptor. [When the sculptor] finishes the images, I will send him off, and he will go home. [Did I not send back the previous] sculptor, and did he not return to Kadashman-Turgu? [My brother], do not withhold [the sculptor].

§17 (rev. 62–66) [Furthermore, my brother]: Send me [horses], in particular tall stallion foals. The stallions which your father [sent me and the horses which] my brother has [up until] now sent me are good but too short. Old horses [. . . In Hatti] winters are harsh and an old horse will not survive. Send me, [my brother, horses], in particular foals. There are already many short horses in my land. [Ask your messenger, my brother], and he will tell you.

[*The final seventeen preserved lines of this letter are too damaged for connected translation. They deal with Hattusili's request for additional valuable materials:* "Why did you send me lapis lazuli of poor quality? The lapis lazuli which you sent me [. . .]"; "[Now] send me [the silver which] I need for my work . . ." ; *and with the gifts which he will still send to Babylonia:* "Anything else which my brother [needs] . . . let him write to me . . . Will I not [send] my brother that which is in my household?"]

No. 23A
Letter from a King of Hatti to an Anatolian Ruler

The date of this letter is not quite certain, since the Hittite Great King employs only his title in the salutation (§1), and the name of his correspondent has been lost. The subject matter, however, shows that it was written after the reign of Mursili II (Hoffner 1982: 134). Although the Hittite ruler addresses the recipient as his "son," he also refers throughout to the perfidy of the latter's father. Therefore this form of address indicates vassalage rather than biological relationship. Indeed, the Great King relates that he has installed his "son" in place of his father, despite the continuing hostility which this predecessor had displayed (§2).

The primary theme of this communication is that the younger ruler shall not follow the bad example of his father. In particular he shall resolve the dispute over hostages which had arisen between his father and the Hittite ruler (§9), and return fugitives to Hatti (§6).

He is also to turn over a certain Walmu to a Hittite envoy (§7), so that the former might be reestablished on his throne in the nearby land of Wilusa (cf. Greek (W)ilios). The implied contiguity of the vassal's domain to the Troad, combined with the fact that his submission allowed Hatti to extend its control to the seacoast (§2), indicates a location on the Aegean littoral of Anatolia. Note also that the Great King and the addressee of the letter had engaged in joint military action against the territory of Milawata, Greek Miletus (§8).

§1 (obv. 1) Thus says My Majesty: [Say] to [. . . , my son]:

§2 (obv. 2–19) [I], My Majesty, [have taken up] you, my son, an ordinary man, [and] you have recognized [me as overlord. I gave the land of your father] to you. [But your father . . .] had always desired my border territories. [. . .] When [. . .], and when your father [marched against the city of . . .], he subdued [the city of . . .], and [he . . .] My Majesty, [. . .] Then I, My Majesty, opened hostilities [and defeated your father]. But I, My Majesty, [took you up, . . . , my son], and treated you in a brotherly fashion. [. . .] Furthermore, under the Sun-god of Heaven [we swore an oath . . .] You [recognized] My Majesty [as overlord. I, My Majesty, thereby established] the sea once more [as my frontier . . .] Whatever evil [persons . . .] And furthermore, your father [. . .] he heard. [They became hostile] to the King of Hatti [and . . . , but] he kept quiet [about it. . . .] Your father [indeed . . .]

§3 (obv. 20–30) But now, because your father [. . . , you], my son, will protect my well-being. [. . . You] shall not [desire] my [land . . .] when your father [. . .] your father for [kingship(?) . . .] he [took(?)] to heart [. . . of(?)] my border territory they will attack, then [. . .] you will transgress [the oath]. And your father to me [. . .] you will do. And if [you] go away, [. . .] I, My Majesty, [will not lend] you [assistance(?)].

§4 (obv. 31–35) But whatever [evil] your father [committed] against me [. . .], this matter is a capital crime. The question of the cities of [Utima and Atriya . . .] he was not. I wrote to your father [. . .] concerning this matter of [Utima and Atriya], and [he did] not [resolve] it. [If you do not resolve it], you, my son, will commit an offense. It shall [be placed under oath].

§5 (obv. 36–38) But your father [. . .] in evil against me [. . .] the evil matter for My Majesty [. . .] they know [. . .] [*A total of fifteen to twenty lines has been lost at the bottom of the obverse and the top of the reverse.*]

§6 (rev. 1'–17') [. . .] But later you, my son, will say: "Your Majesty [did] not [. . .] How have I risen in revolt?" If, my son, the matter [of Agapurusiya . . .] has come up—I, My Majesty, have somehow [. . .] the matter of the fugitive. [. . .] Is it not right to return a fugitive? [. . .] We have placed something under (the oath of?) the Storm-god: "[We will return] a fugitive." Because your father [did not capture] the priest of the city of Talwisuwanta(?), he wrote [to me] later: "[He ran] away [. . ." And when he asked me for the fugitive so-and-so], did I not [release] him to him? If Agapurusiya were [. . .] At the time when Piyamaradu [. . .] "I will go away!" [. . .] Agapurusiya [. . .] If [you], my son, [knew . . . I] have informed him thus: [". . ."] And him in return [. . .] wholeheartedly [. . .] the matter [of Agapurusiya . . .]

[*Gap of approximately fifteen lines.*]

§7 (rev. 32'–44') [. . .] to him [. . .] But he [thus . . . And] furthermore the troops [. . .] he went [away]. Then by night he [. . .] down. [. . .] He did not [. . .] the land. And when his lord . . . [. . .] he fled to [. . . Then they took] for themselves another lord. [But] I did not recognize [. . .] the evil one. Kulana-ziti retained possession of the wooden tablets which [I made] for Walmu, and he has now brought them to you, my son. Examine them! Now, my son, as long as you look after the well-being of My Majesty, I, My Majesty, will put my trust in your good will. Turn Walmu over to me, my son, so that I may reinstall him in kingship in the land of Wilusa. As he was formerly king of the land of Wilusa, [he shall] now likewise be! As he [was] formerly our military vassal, he shall now likewise be our military vassal!

§8 (rev. 45'–47') As I, My Majesty, and you, my son, have plundered(?)

the border territory of the land of Milawata, you shall [not] withhold your [. . .] I, My Majesty, [will put my trust] wholeheartedly in your good will. [And the . . .] which I did not give to you along with the border territory of the land of Milawata [. . .]

§9 (lower edge 1–5) Your father [. . .], who always wished for my misfortune, and who was the primary factor in unfortunate affairs [for My Majesty, . . .] that to me. He boasted about my servants(?). And earlier, while he was boasting about the city of Arinna, [he said to me: ". . .] I will retain [them]." But when your father did not give me the hostages of the cities of Utima and Atriya, then I [. . .], and I sent Kulana-ziti.

§10 (left edge 1–6) And the matter of the cities of Awarna and [Pina(?) . . .] to you. I, My Majesty, [. . .] you, my [son . . .] Therein I did not see the [. . .] subdued by force of arms. [. . .] by means of mace and arrow [. . .] Out of consideration for [your] well-being I did not look [. . .] I looked away. [I wrote] to you concerning the matter of Awarna and Pina(?): "Give [me] the hostages of Awarna and Pina(?). I, [My Majesty], will give the hostages of the cities of Utima and Atriya over to you." I have given the hostages [of Utima and Atriya] over to you, but you still [. . .] me. It is not [at all right. And] your evil . . .

No. 24
Selections from the Correspondence
between the Hittite and Assyrian Courts

No. 24A
Letter from Urhi-Teshshup(?) of Hatti
to Adad-nirari I of Assyria

This fragmentary Hittite-language draft of a letter to an Assyrian monarch has no heading, so the identities of the correspondents must be deduced from its contents. Since the defeat of Wasashatta mentioned at the outset was the achievement of Adad-nirari I (Wilhelm 1982: 54–55), we may safely posit the latter as the recipient. Three Hittite rulers were contemporaries of Adad-nirari: Muwattalli II, Urhi-Teshshup (Mursili III), and Hattusili III. Muwattalli was probably too concerned with his war against Egypt to risk offending another great power through the dispatch of a letter as brusque as this text, and Hattusili is shown by No. 24B to have been more polite in his dealings with Adad-nirari. Therefore, the writer of No. 24A was most likely Urhi-Teshshup (Hagenbuchner 1989: 263).

While acknowledging that his subjugation of most of what remained of

Mittanni — here referred to as Hurri — now entitled the King of Assyria to style himself a Great King, the Hittite nonetheless expresses his displeasure at this development by refusing to address him as "brother," as was customary between rulers of equal rank. The reference to "seeing Mount Amanus" could refer either to a boast by the Assyrian that his forces had penetrated so far to the northwest, or to a proposed meeting of the two Great Kings in what was still Hittite territory.

(i 1–19) You continue to speak about [the defeat(?)] of Wasashatta [and the conquest(?)] of the land of Hurri. You indeed conquered by force of arms. And you conquered [. . .], and have become a Great King. But why do you still continue to speak about brotherhood and about seeing Mount Amanus? What is this, brotherhood? And what is this, seeing Mount Amanus? For what reason should I write to you about brotherhood? Who customarily writes to someone about brotherhood? Do those who are not on good terms customarily write to one another about brotherhood? On what account should I write to you about brotherhood? Were you and I born from one mother? As [my grandfather] and my father did not write to the King of Assyria [about brotherhood], you shall not keep writing to me [about brotherhood] and Great Kingship. [It is not my] wish.

[*The remaining six lines of column i and the preserved portions of columns ii–iv are too fragmentary for translation.*]

No. 24B
Letter from Hattusili III of Hatti
to Adad-nirari I of Assyria

Atypically for the Akkadian written at Hattusa, the language of this letter displays a number of features characteristic of the dialect of Assyria, which suggests that it was intended to be sent to that state. Indeed, it could very well have been written by an Assyrian in Hittite service (Goetze 1940: 32; cf. Beckman 1983b: 108, 111). Although the heading is lacking, the disparaging reference to the poor treatment of messengers under Urhi-Teshshup (§5) makes it very likely that the sender was Hattusili III, who would have had few qualms about criticizing the man whose throne he had usurped. The irregular circumstances of Hattusili's rise to power might also account for the failure of his correspondent to send him the proper presents upon his enthronement (§4). If this identification of the writer of the letter is correct, its recipient was certainly Hattusili's senior contemporary Adad-nirari I, for it is clear from §4 that he had been ruling for some time before the *coup d'état* in Hatti (see Rowton 1959; Hagenbuchner 1989: 267–68).

In addition to the discussion of the niceties of diplomatic practice in §§4–5, this text deals with the matter of the depredations of the population of the otherwise unknown city of Turira on Hittite territory (§1). The Assyrian having assured him that the city was subject either to himself or to Hatti — and by no means to Hanigalbat — Hattusili now proposes that one of the Great Kings act to chastise the troublemakers, respecting the interests of the other power in the process. The puzzling final line in this paragraph may contain a Hittite proverb about ingratitude (Beckman 1986: 24–25).

Finally, the request by the Assyrian for iron and iron weapons in §§2–3 has contributed to the modern misconception that the Hittites exercised a monopoly over the production of this metal during the Late Bronze Age. While there is no doubt that considerable use was made of iron in Hatti (see Košak 1986), there is ample evidence that other contemporary civilizations of the Near East also possessed this technology (Zaccagnini 1970; Muhly 1980: 50–51).

[*The upper portion of the obverse of this text has been lost. The first six preserved lines are too fragmentary for translation.*]

§1 (obv. 6'–19') [Furthermore, the people of] the city of Turira are constantly plundering my land. [They constantly plunder the land] of Carchemish [on that side], and the land [of Ashtata(?)] on this side. The king of Hanigalbat keeps writing to me: "[Turira] is mine." And from there, you(!) keep writing to me: "Turira is mine, or Turira is yours. It does not belong to the king of Hanigalbat." Do you not know about the matter of Turira? When Turira plunders the land, they keep taking the booty to Turira. My subjects who flee also keep going up to Turira. If Turira is yours, smash(?) it! But you shall not claim the possessions of my subjects who are dwelling in the city. If Turira is not yours, write to me, so that I may smash(?) it. The possessions of your troops who are dwelling in the city shall not be claimed. Why do the people of Turira sniff at(?) the gift of me, the lion?

§2 (obv. 20'–24') In regard to the good iron about which you wrote to me — good iron is not available in my armory in the city of Kizzuwatna. I have written that it is a bad time for making iron. They will make good iron, but they have not yet finished it. When they finish it, I will send it to you. For the moment I have sent you a dagger blade of iron.

§3 (obv. 25'–29') [In regard to] the suits of armor which you sent to me, saying: "[Send] blades [of iron in return for these]!" — they have not yet finished making [the iron. When they finish, I will send them] to you. I have become(?) like you. [. . .] the request which you wrote me about [. . .]

[The bottom of the obverse and the top of the reverse have been lost, resulting in a gap of uncertain length.]

§4 (rev. 2'–10') [. . .] Great King, King of Babylonia, [. . .] he wrote to you [. . .] to you. Did [my brother(?)][1] not send you appropriate gifts of greeting? But when I assumed kingship, [then] you did not send a messenger to me. It is the custom that when kings assume kingship, the kings, his equals in rank, send him appropriate [gifts of greeting], clothing befitting kingship, and fine [oil] for his anointing. But you did not do this today.

§5 (rev. 11'–19') Now, I have detained here my messenger whom I sent to you previously and Bel-qarrad. I have detained him because of this matter. I have sent [you] all of the requests which you wrote me about. Because of this matter [I have detained] him. The messengers whom you regularly sent here in the time of King Urhi-Teshshup often experienced [. . .] aggravation. Today, in [. . .], you should [not] say: "He is certainly experiencing aggravation as at that time." When he comes, you shall not need to ask Bel-qarrad whether I treated him well [. . .]

No. 24C
Letter from Tudhaliya IV of Hatti
to an Assyrian Nobleman

This Hittite-language draft of a letter to an official known from Mesopotamian sources to have occupied a high position at the courts of Adad-nirari I, Shalmaneser I, and Tukulti-Ninurta I (Weidner 1959), was included on a single tablet with drafts sharing similar concerns directed to another Assyrian courtier and to the Assyrian monarch himself. Unfortunately these other letters are fragmentary, and the names of their intended recipients have been lost. Once again the identification of the parties in a letter is dependent upon the analysis of its contents.

The mention here of a proposed campaign against the region of Papanhi, probably to be located somewhere in the mountains of southeastern Anatolia, should probably be connected with the claims of Tukulti-Ninurta to have fought against the land of Paphi early in his reign (Otten 1959: 46). Thus the new Assyrian ruler would be Tukulti-Ninurta, and the author of these letters Tudhaliya IV, who had already exercised power in Hatti for some time.

It is striking that Tudhaliya felt no compunctions about lending rather condescending advice to his Assyrian counterpart concerning his military undertakings, and also that he directed this advice not only to the young ruler himself, but to two of his advisors.

§1 (A rev. 8) Thus says My Majesty: Say to Baba-ahu-iddina:

§2 (A rev. 9–25) Because your lord died — as they have attributed manhood [to] the son of your lord who has been [elevated] over you, and as the god has given him heart, even in the time of his father [. . .] Those who are here on his behalf(?), Silli-Assur and Amurru-ashared, [have told] me about him, that he has just seated himself [upon] the throne of his father, and how to him, not even as to a bull, [. . . And] he keeps saying this: "I want to accomplish something! If the foreign [kings become hostile] to me, they would then come against me, and I could make a certain name for myself." Now very much [. . .] And because he has not yet . . . in the mountains in particular, let the enemy against whom he goes be brought down [. . .] at the command of the god. Because his father died, and he [has just seated himself] upon the throne [of his father], the campaign on which he goes for the [first] time should be one on which he enjoys three- or fourfold numerical superiority. If [it is . . .], or some strong position, then the first time they will [. . .] in this manner. But the lands which his father [had] conquered by force of arms [. . .] Because they keep telling me even this about the land of Papanhi: "[. . .], and the mountains are very treacherous," then vigor(?) [. . .] something. And because he even now continues to say [. . .] They shall not do it. The gods thus [. . .] And formerly, wherever he would go — if the population [. . .], or it is some troops of the land, [*Remainder too fragmentary for translation.*]

No. 25
Letter from a King of Hanigalbat
to a King of Hatti

Although the recipient and sender of this letter are referred to only by title, a key to their identification is provided by the mention of Ehli-Sharrumma (§4), who became king of Isuwa during the reign of Tudhaliya IV (Imparati 1992a: 310–11). Tudhaliya's contemporaries as King of Assyria were Shalmaneser I and Tukulti-Ninurta I (Otten 1959: 46). Since the former brought an end to Hanigalbat as an independent state, it must be his threatening behavior which is described here (Klengel 1963b: 287–90).

Therefore the writer is Shattuara II, final king of this weak successor to Mittanni (see introduction to No. 6).

Apparently the king of Hanigalbat, caught between the empires of Hatti and Assyria, has had to make concessions of some sort to the latter, which Hittite vassals in the region have reported to their lord as offenses against his rule (§4). In his defense, the Hanigalbatean likens his situation to that of a man pressed by two creditors, who must yield to the one presenting the most immediate challenge (§5). The mention of the Storm-god here is perhaps an attempt to deflect political responsibility onto the state deity.

Since the fragmentary second half of this letter seems to speak of "the enemy of my land," it may be that the real purpose of this communication was to secure Hittite aid against further Assyrian encroachments.

§1 (lines 1–2) Say to Your Majesty, my father: Thus says the king of Hanigalbat, your son:

§2 (line 3) May Your Majesty, my father, be well!

§3 (lines 4–6) I have put my trust in Your Majesty, my father. I say as follows: "May Your Majesty speak as my father, saying: '[. . .]'"

§4 (lines 7–9) In what respect have I now offended against my father, so that Halpa-ziti, king of Aleppo, and Ehli-Sharrumma, king of Isuwa, [have written(?)] to you?

§5 (lines 10–14) If a man has two legal opponents, and one man makes a claim while the other man does not [make a claim], . . .[2] Now the King of Assyria, my enemy, has made inquiries, and Your Majesty, my father, has heard how the Storm-god, my lord, acted.

§6 (lines 15–18) I was residing in the city of Shinamu, and Ehli-Sharrumma sent his messenger to me, saying: "May the subjects of His Majesty be . . . !"

§7 (lines 19–21) [And] I have come out to the city of Duruni[. . .] I have finished off [. . .] And he (the King of Assyria?) has come out to the city of [. . .]nama.

[*The twenty lines on the lower edge and reverse of this tablet are too fragmentary for translation.*]

No. 26
Letter from Mashuiluwa of Mira-Kuwaliya
to Mursili II of Hatti

When he fled his native land in western Anatolia as a consequence of palace intrigue directed against him, Mashuiluwa was welcomed in Hatti by Suppiluliuma I, who also gave him a Hittite princess in marriage (see del Monte 1974). However, it was left to Mursili II to install Mashuiluwa as ruler of the vassal kingdom of Mira-Kuwaliya. Therefore, we many conclude that the present letter was directed to the latter Great King. It deals with the ill health of a Hittite named Pazzu, suffering whose cause was thought to lie in the neglect of ancestral gods. Whether Pazzu was a messenger of the Hittite ruler or some sort of expert dispatched by the Hittite court to that of a vassal (see No. 23, §§12–13, 16) is unknown.

Say to His Majesty, My Lord: Thus says Mashuiluwa, your subject: Pazzu has recently become ill, and his ancestral deities have begun to trouble him. I have just sent him (back to Hatti) to worship his ancestral deities. When he finishes worshiping the deities, may My Lord send him back immediately. May My Lord also question him concerning the affairs of my land.

Notes

1. Or perhaps: [my father].
2. This seems to be a proverbial saying, to be completed by something like: "which opponent will draw his attention?"

Miscellaneous Texts

No. 27
Indictment of Madduwatta
by Arnuwanda I of Hatti

This document is the first portion of an extensive recounting of the duplicitous behavior of a Hittite vassal in western Anatolia. (For the geographic setting, see Bryce 1974.) That it is a draft is shown by the absence of a heading, as well as by an erasure in §30 and the inclusion of variant formulations of the same sentence in §19. It is also possible that the confusion of second- and third-person discourse employed for the vassal was eliminated in the final version.

Once thought to deal with events at the close of the thirteenth century B.C.E., this text has now been recognized as belonging in the Middle Hittite period of the late fifteenth century (Otten 1969; but cf. Heinhold-Krahmer 1977: 260–75). The unnamed author of the indictment was almost certainly Arnuwanda I, and the father of the writer, under whom many of the events discussed had actually occurred, would thus be Tudhaliya II. Note the awkward editing of citations from original documents of the reign of the earlier king so that he speaks of himself here as "the father of His Majesty" (for example in §§4 and 6–7)!

The purpose of this unusual text, which resembles the historical introductions to the treaties, is uncertain. Perhaps it was dispatched to Madduwatta in an effort to persuade him to reform and fulfill his obligations to his Hittite overlord. Unfortunately, no other texts dealing with this ruler have been recovered, so we can say nothing about the outcome of the dispute.

Of special interest is the mention of a ruler of Ahhiya, the older form of Ahhiyawa, a term that many scholars now believe refers in some manner to the Mycenaeans (Güterbock 1983; 1984; 1986; but cf. Sommer 1932; Steiner 1964). The broken final paragraph here apparently presents a proverb.

§1 (obv. 1–5) Attarissiya, the ruler of Ahhiya, chased [you], Madduwatta, out of your land. Then he harassed you and kept chasing you. And he continued to seek an [evil] death for you, Madduwatta. He [would] have killed you, but you, Madduwatta, fled to the father [of My Majesty], and the father of My Majesty saved you from death. He [got] rid of Attarissiya for you. Otherwise, Attarissiya would not have left you alone, but would [have killed] you.

§2 (obv. 6–9) When the father of My Majesty [got] rid of [Attarissiya] for you, [then] the father of My Majesty [took] you, Madduwatta, together with your wives, your sons, your infantry, and [your chariotry]. He gave you chariots, [. . .], barley(?), and seed(?) in heaps, and he gave you young wine, malt, beer-bread, rennet, and [cheese(?)] in heaps. And the father of My Majesty [saved] you, Madduwatta, together with your wives, your [sons], and your troops, when you were hungry.

§3 (obv. 10–12) And the father of My Majesty saved you from the sword of Attarissiya. The father of My Majesty saved you, Madduwatta, together with your wives, your [sons], your household servants, and together with your infantry and your chariotry. Otherwise, dogs would have devoured you from hunger. Even if you had escaped from Attarissiya, you would have died from hunger.

§4 (obv. 13–21) Furthermore, the father of My Majesty proceeded to make you, Madduwatta, his sworn ally. He caused [you] to swear an oath, and he placed these matters under oath for you, saying: "I, the father of His Majesty, have now saved [you], Madduwatta, [from the sword] of Attarissiya. Be a partisan of the father of His Majesty and of Hatti. I have [now] given you the land of Mount Zippasla [to occupy]. You, Madduwatta, occupy the land of Mount Zippasla, together with your [troops], and have your base of support established in the land of [Mount] Zippasla." The father of My Majesty repeatedly spoke as follows to you, Madduwatta: "Come, occupy the land of Mount Hariyati, so that you will be near Hatti." Madduwatta refused to occupy the land of Mount Hariyati, so the father of My Majesty proceeded to say again as follows to Madduwatta: "I have now given you the land of Mount Zippasla, so occupy it alone. You shall not occupy another river valley or another land in addition on your own authority. [The land of Mount] Zippasla shall be your border district. Be [my] subject, and your troops shall be my troops."

§5 (obv. 22–27) [But Madduwatta] said as follows to the father of My

Majesty: "You, my [lord], have given [me] the land of Mount [Zippasla] to occupy, [so that I am] the border guard [and] the watchman [of this land. And whoever] speaks of a matter [of hostility] before [me, or whenever I myself] hear of a matter of hostility from some land, [then I will not conceal that] person or that land [from the father of His Majesty], but I will indeed always write about them. But whatever land [begins war] against you, [while the troops] of Your Majesty [make war] — because I am nearby, I will attack it immediately, [and] I will immediately [bloody my hands]." You took an oath and [placed] these matters under oath.

§6 (obv. 28–36) And [the father] of My Majesty placed the following under oath for him: "The person who is an enemy to [the father of His Majesty] and [to] Hatti shall be an enemy [to you], Madduwatta. And as I, the father [of His Majesty] make war on him [without hesitation], you, [Madduwatta], and [your troops] shall likewise make war on him without hesitation. As Kupanta-Kurunta is an enemy [to the father of His Majesty], he shall likewise be an enemy [to you, Madduwatta], and as I, [the father of His Majesty], make war [on him] without hesitation, [you, Madduwatta], shall likewise make war on him without hesitation. [And] you shall not send anyone on a diplomatic mission to any [land on your own authority. You shall] not [be an enemy] to anyone [on your own authority], nor shall you practice . . . against anyone on your own authority. You shall not speak [. . .] repeatedly. [Whatever] fugitive of Hatti comes [to you], whether he is a craftsman, [or a . . .], you shall not conceal [him], nor [hide] him, nor [release] him to another land. Always [seize] him and [send] him back to the father [of His Majesty]."

§7 (obv. 37–41) "You shall not [conceal the person who] speaks an evil word before you, whether someone speaks of a matter of hostility before you, or someone slanders the kings and princes. Write about the matter to My Majesty. Seize the person and send [him to] the father of My Majesty. You shall not [send] someone [on a mission to] Attarissiya. If Attarissiya sends someone on a mission to you, seize the messenger and [send] him to the father [of My Majesty]. You shall not [conceal the matter about which] he writes [to you], but write about it scrupulously to the father of My Majesty. You shall not dispatch [the messenger] back to [Attarissiya] on your own authority."

§8 (obv. 42–48) You, Madduwatta, transgressed [the oaths] of the father of My Majesty. The father of My Majesty [gave] you the land of Mount Zippasla to occupy. Then he made you swear an oath, and placed the following under [oath] for you: "I have now given you the land [of Mount] Zippasla, [so] occupy [it alone]. You shall not occupy another land or [another] river valley in addition [on your own authority]." And [Madduwatta] seized the entire land, and then he mobilized [it en masse] with its troops. [He went in battle against] Kupanta-Kurunta, [but] when [Kupanta-Kurunta heard about it, he proceeded to turn loose(?)] the troops of the land [of Arzawa]. Then the troops of the land of Arzawa went against Madduwatta and disposed of all of the troops of Madduwatta. Madduwatta [fled alone. As for the army] — the few men who [escaped] — they disposed of all of it too.

§9 (obv. 49–52) And [Madduwatta's] wives, [his sons], their civilian captives and goods back [. . .] Then Kupanta-Kurunta [. . .] And he seized his household(?) [. . .], and took his wives, [his sons], their [civilian captives], and absolutely all the goods. [. . .] And Madduwatta [escaped] by himself, naked. [Only] a few men escaped, but they disposed of all of it (that is, the army).

§10 (obv. 53–57) And [when the father of My Majesty heard, then] he sent Piseni [. . . together with] infantry and chariotry to the aid of Madduwatta. And [. . . But] when [they came] to him, [they found] Madduwatta's [wives], <his sons>, their civilian captives and goods up in the city of Sallawassi, and [they gave] them back to him. [And they even found the wives, the sons], the civilian captives and goods [of] Kupanta-Kurunta up in Sallawassi, and these too they gave [to] Madduwatta. And [Kupanta-Kurunta] was kept apart by himself, and [Kupanta-Kurunta] fled [. . .] alone. All of this they disposed of, and [they installed] Madduwatta in his place once more.

§11 (obv. 58–59) Because the prominent noblemen Piseni and Puskurunuwa, son of [. . .], whom [I sent(?)] down to Sallawassi, made war on behalf of Madduwatta, they [could have] been killed for Madduwatta.

§12 (obv. 60–65) But [later] Attarissiya, the ruler of Ahhiya, came and was plotting to kill you, Madduwatta. But when the father of My Majesty heard, he dispatched Kisnapili, infantry, and chariotry in battle against Attarissiya. And you, Madduwatta, once more did not resist Attarissiya, but broke ranks before him. Then Kisnapili came and took charge of you [. . .] from Hatti. Kisnapili went in battle against Attarissiya. 100 [chariots and . . . infantry] of Attarissiya [drew up]. And they fought. One officer of Attarissiya was killed, and one officer of ours, Zidanza, was killed. Then Attarissiya [. . .] to Madduwatta, and he went off to his own land. And they installed Madduwatta in his place once more.

§13 (obv. 66–68) Later the city of Dalawa began [war], and Madduwatta wrote this to Kisnapili: "I will go to attack Dalawa. You go to the city of Hinduwa. I will attack Dalawa, and then the troops of Dalawa will not be able to come to the aid of Hinduwa, [so that] you can destroy Hinduwa." And Kisnapili sent troops to Hinduwa for battle.

§14 (obv. 69–72) Then because Madduwatta did not go to Dalawa for battle, but in fact wrote off to the men of Dalawa, saying: "[The troops] of Hatti have just gone to Hinduwa for battle. Block the route before them and attack them!" Then they deployed(?) [the troops] of Dalawa on the route. They proceeded to block the route [of our] troops and routed them. They killed Kisnapili and Partahulla. But [Madduwatta] laughed about them.

§15 (obv. 73–74) Furthermore, Madduwatta turned the people of Dalawa away from Hatti, and at the decision of their elders [they began] to march with him. [And] he made them swear an oath [to him], and finally they even began to pay him [tribute].

§16 (obv. 75–78) [But later Kupanta-Kurunta] was an enemy [to] the father of My Majesty, and you, Madduwatta, were at peace with him. [. . .] And you gave him your daughter in marriage. But you wrote as follows to My Majesty: "Now Kupanta-Kurunta [. . .], and I will write to him as follows: 'Come to me, and I will give you my daughter in marriage.' [If he comes to me], then [I will seize] him [and] kill him." And when Madduwatta wrote to me thus,

§17 (obv. 79–83) [then, I, My Majesty, thought(?) as follows]: "Madduwatta has sworn this to Kupanta-Kurunta: [' . . . ' Yet] he (Kupanta-Kurunta) has his [daughter] in marriage. [Will] he (Madduwatta) [plot evil against] his son-in-law and his own [daughter]? Will he arrange his death? And furthermore, will he proceed [to have] an emotional tie to an outsider? [. . . And] I have very much gotten to the heart of the matter(?), O Madduwatta." [. . . I wrote back to him as follows]: "Do as seems right to you."

[*The final five lines of the obverse, those of the lower edge, and the initial ten lines of the reverse, which are too fragmentary for translation, seem to have continued the discussion of Madduwatta's relationship to Kupanta-Kurunta. Also mentioned is Partahulla, the Hittite whose death was reported in §14.*]

§18 (rev. 11–18) [. . . And the father] of My Majesty [gave you] the land of the Siyanta River to occupy. [. . . But you, Madduwatta, were not] a border guard and a scout against the foreign lands. [And although you said to the father of My Majesty as follows]: "As soon as you, Your Majesty, my lord, summon me to a campaign, [I will come immediately," . . . When] the father of My Majesty gave [you] the land of the Siyanta River to occupy, and then [made] you [swear an oath, and placed the following under oath for you]: "The father of His Majesty has now given the land of the Siyanta River to you. Be [a border guard] and [a scout of the father of His Majesty(?)] for [the lands]. And hold off the foreign lands. [If a person speaks a] word [of hostility before you], you shall not conceal anything [from the father of His Majesty], but write me everything. [If a land begins war], attack [it immediately], and bloody your hands immediately."

§19 (rev. 19–24) "Furthermore, [you shall] not [occupy] another land or another river valley beyond [the land of the Siyanta River]." And Madduwatta transgressed the oath [to] the father of My Majesty, and he took all the land of Arzawa, and [. . .] it. But you placed the matter of the land of Hapalla under oath as follows — Madduwatta placed the matter of the land of Hapalla [under oath] as follows:[1] "Either I will defeat [the land] of Hapalla, or I will carry it off, together with civilian captives, cattle, and sheep, [and] I will turn [it] over [to] Your Majesty." But subsequently you did not defeat the land of Hapalla, and [you did not turn] it over to My Majesty. Madduwatta took it for himself.

§20 (rev. 25–28) He kept writing to the general: "I will approach the land of Hapalla through you (that is, your territory) alone. You [let] me through, saying: 'Go, smite the land of Hapalla, or carry it off!'" But when the general did let him through, he subsequently would have [blocked] his routes and would have attacked him in the rear. And in this matter even Antahitta, chief [of the . . .], and Mazlawa, the ruler of Kuwaliya, were informers against him.

§21 (rev. 29–33) In addition he took for himself [. . .] lands belonging to My Majesty: the land of Zumanti, the land of Wallarimma, the land of Iyalanti, the land [of Zumarri], the land of Mutamutassa, the land of Attarimma, the land of Suruta, and the land of Hursanassa. And furthermore, he did not allow [the messengers] of these lands to come before My Majesty. Finally, he did not allow the tribute which [had been imposed] on anyone to be brought before My Majesty, but always took it himself. And he set the horses of My Majesty which were [there to the plow(?)].

§22 (rev. 34–37) But you [occupied] the city of Upnihuwala on your own authority. And furthermore, you, Madduwatta, kept taking for yourself the fugitives of Hatti who [traveled] to you. [The father] of My Majesty and My Majesty wrote after them to you repeatedly, but you did not [give] them back. [And] we write to you [. . .] about this matter, but you do [not] subsequently [present] a defense to us in the matter. [And] you [write] about some other matters. You always write us back about other matters.

§23 (rev. 38–42) But later, I, My Majesty, brought infantry and chariotry out of the land of Salpa and [out of the land of . . . But] Madduwatta caused the chieftains [of] the land of Pitassa [and] the elders of Pitassa to swear an oath against [My Majesty], and led [them astray, saying]: "Be my partisans! Occupy [. . .]! Attack Hatti!" Then they proceeded [to attack the lands of My Majesty], and they burned down fortified cities. I, My

Majesty, [came back(?), and . . .] . . . <of?> my own troops. In those days Madduwatta hid his eyes and [. . .] forth to the people of Pitassa.

§24 (rev. 43–47) But [. . .] he wrote again and again to Kupanta-Kurunta: [". . . "] and led him astray. [. . .] And he (Madduwatta) himself placed it under oath as follows: "I am [now a border guard] and a watchman for these lands. And if a person [speaks] an evil word to me, I [will] not [conceal anything] from Your Majesty, [but] I will disclose [it] fully. If some <land> begins war, while the troops of Your Majesty [make war — because I am nearby], I will attack it immediately, and I will immediately bloody my hands."

§25 (rev. 48–54) [And] initially Madduwatta himself [placed the preceding] under oath. [Later he transgressed the oath.] Subsequently he did not attack them, but rather even hid his eyes. I, My Majesty, [. . .] to him [. . .] But Madduwatta repaid it with dishonesty. And of the land of Pitassa [. . .] he swore an oath earlier. I [released(?)] ten [teams] of horses and 200 infantrymen to Zuwa, the staff-bearer [. . .] The enemy drew up below the city of Marasa, [and] they killed Zuwa, the staff-bearer. [. . .] they have sworn. And they provided food and drink for his infantry and his [chariotry. . .] Then they went away and put the city of Marasa to the torch. [They burned] it [down].

§26 (rev. 55–58) But thereafter I, My Majesty, proceeded to send Mulliyara, the staff-bearer, on a mission to [Madduwatta], and [I instructed(?)] him as follows as a message for [Madduwatta]: "Why have you taken the land of Hapalla, which is a land of My Majesty? [Give] it back to me now!" [And Madduwatta] said as follows to [Mulliyara]: "The land of Hapalla is a [. . .] land, and it is on His Majesty's side, [but] I have conquered the land of Iyalanti, [the land] of Zumarri, and the land of Wallarimma [by] force of arms. They [belong] to me."

§27 (rev. 59–61) Niwalla, the huntsman of My Majesty, [ran off] and went to Madduwatta, and Madduwatta [took him in. Then] I, My Majesty, wrote after him initially: "Niwalla, the huntsman [of My Majesty], ran off and went to you. [Seize him and] give him back to me!" At first Madduwatta [. . .] kept saying: "No one [came] to me."

§28 (rev. 62–65) Now Mulliyara has come to him and found [the fugitive in his household]. He said [as follows] to [Madduwatta]: "The matter of a fugitive [is placed] under [oath] for you [as follows]: 'You [must always send] back to His Majesty whatever [fugitive] of [Hatti] comes to you.' [But Niwalla], the huntsman of His Majesty, [fled and came to you]. His Majesty has written to you repeatedly, but you conceal him [and hide him. Now seize him]!"

§29 (rev. 66–67) [Then] Madduwatta [replied as follows] to Mulliyara: "The huntsman [. . . and] he belongs to the household of Piseni. [. . .] the household of Piseni, my son [. . .]"

[*The next thirteen lines, which seemingly continue the discussion of Madduwatta with the Hittite envoy Mulliyara, are too fragmentary for translation.*]

§30 (rev. 84–90) [The report] of Mulliyara [which he delivered to me is as follows]: "I gave [him (Madduwatta) a tablet saying]: 'His Majesty said as follows [about the land of Alashiya]: "Because [the land] of Alashiya belongs to My Majesty, [and the people of Alashiya] pay [me tribute — why have you continually raided it?"' But] Madduwatta said as follows: '[When Attarissiya and] the ruler [of Piggaya] were raiding the land of Alashiya, I often raided it too.[2] But the father of His Majesty [had] never [informed] me, [nor] had His Majesty ever informed [me] to the effect: "The land of Alashiya is mine — recognize it as such!" If His Majesty now indeed demands the civilian captives back, I will give them back to him.'" And since Attarissiya and the ruler of Piggaya are rulers independent of My Majesty, while you, Madduwatta, are a subject of My Majesty — why have you joined up with [them]?

§31 (rev. 91–94) Furthermore, [. . .] brought [a message] as follows: "The stag doesn't cry out. He doesn't bite. He doesn't trample. [. . .] pursues the stag. But because the pig does cry out, the one who [. . .] to the pig [. . .] he kills. I will cry out like the pig, [and then] I shall die [. . .]"

Colophon

First tablet of the offense of [Madduwatta]
[*The text must have continued on a further tablet, now lost.*]

No. 27A
Indictment of Mita of Pahhuwa
and Treaty with the Elders of Several Anatolian Communities

This document datable on linguistic grounds to the Middle Hittite period is a curious hybrid: The first portion (§§2–10) presents a group of notables (§1) with an account of the unfaithfulness and misdeeds of a Hittite vassal in order to justify a demand for his extradition. The remainder of the text (§§11–19) is a treaty between an unidentified Great King of Hatti and the elders of a number of polities in southeastern Anatolia (§15). Topics covered by this agreement include the return of fugitives (§11), the mustering of troops for the Hittite army (§12), the behavior of these levies

(§18), a defensive alliance (§19), the renunciation of independent dealings with foreign states (§§12, 16), and loyalty to the Hittite ruling family (§16).

The communities in question were apparently small—most are not attested outside this document—so the Hittites have gathered their elders here for a collective oath, rather than conclude a separate treaty with each village or region.

Participants

§1 (obv. 1–5) [. . .] they will send Usapa. [And they sent(?)] Piggana, [son of Usapa], to Mita [. . .] And this is him. Lukiutta, [. . .], . . . , Arziukita, [. . .], . . . and Wartila, two [crafts]men(?); [. . .], Huwassata, a craftsman; [. . .], . . . and Hate, in place of two [crafts]men(?); [. . .], Piggana, son of Usapa; [and . . . , man of(?) the city] of Pahhuwa—[we have summoned] them to Hattusa.

Treachery of Mita

§2 (obv. 6–10) We have [. . .] Mita has now [. . .] sworn, and [he has placed these matters] under oath: "[Whoever is an enemy of His Majesty] is an enemy to me, [Mita]. He is my enemy, and I will [attack] him. [But whoever is a friend of His Majesty] is a friend to me, Mita. Now I, Mita, [will . . . I will relinquish the cities] of His Majesty [which] I hold— Aparhula, Hurla, Halmisna, [and Pahhura. And my troops] shall become the troops of His Majesty."

§3 (obv. 11–16) "[. . . and] I will deliver it all, and [. . . I will deliver(?) whatever is . . .] or stolen. [. . .] That man's messenger I(!) will not allow into my gate." [But when Mita] arrived [back in] Pahhuwa he transgressed the oaths. [. . .] he made, and he [committed an offense] even against My Majesty [and] against Hatti. [. . . Then] he married the daughter of my enemy Usapa.

§4 (obv. 17–20) [And concerning my civilian captives he said:] "Let them flee [from] Hatti and [come] to me!" [Then my civilian captives fled and went] to Mita. When I, My Majesty, [wrote to Mita]: "Send [them back to me]," he concealed them, saying as follows: "With my own eyes I [. . .] I didn't see anyone. No one came [to Pahhuwa]."

§5 (obv. 21–27) [Mita . . . did not] return anything [to me. They fled from Pahhuwa] into the land of Isuwa. [. . .] did not [return] anything [to me. Will the civilian captives] whom I, My Majesty, [demanded from Mita flee and go] to the ruler of Isuwa? [. . .] lord [. . .] He will either bring the person, [or . . .] he will bring the stolen goods. [. . . he will point out] the road to him once more. [. . .] he plans as follows:

§6 (obv. 28–33) "[. . .] each one for which we will make full restitution [. . . the cities of Halmisna], Pahhura, Hurla, and Aparhula [. . .]" He continually set back up [. . .] And the land of Isuwa [. . .] Then they went and attacked the cities of the land of Kummaha. [. . .] and the people of the city of Timmiya. And they [. . .], wherever there is an enemy of My Majesty.

§7 (obv. 34–40) [. . .] He admits that man into his city, and now [. . .] I, My Majesty, had just made [. . .] swear an oath. And back to the city of Pahhuwa [. . .] Piggana. And because Mita continued to cause great offense, [. . . He was] an evil person. That man regularly transgressed the oath. [. . .] he fought [with] the servants of My Majesty. And he called his father(-in-law?) by name. Furthermore, Mita and he keep for themselves the cities which belong to My Majesty, namely Halmisna, [Pahhura, Hurla, and Aparhula]. (He thinks:) "The Hassana who (previously) held [the cities] was a mere charioteer. But am I not indeed a ruler? I will not give them up!"

Demand for Extradition

§8 (obv. 41–48) Bring [to me, My Majesty, Mita and Piggana], their wives, their sons, their grandsons, their household slaves, their oxen, and their sheep, together with all their possessions. You shall not hold back as much as [a strand of wool]. Turn [over] the household of Kalimunaya, together with his wife, his sons, his oxen, his sheep, [and all his possessions]. And the people of the city of Arhita who escaped from the service of My Majesty, [as well as . . .], who is coming to you men of Pahhuwa—[capture] all of them, [together with their wives, their] sons, [and their grandsons]. In whatever city of yours [a fugitive(?)] takes refuge, [. . .] and [wherever] he is entering—[denounce(?)] straightaway(?) to My Majesty that city in which [he is taking refuge. Then] arrest [him] and turn [him] over immediately.

(The remainder of the obverse, perhaps fifty lines, has been largely lost.)

§9 (rev. 1–8) [We have summoned . . .], Arihpizzi, man of the city of Pittiyarik; Aissiya, man of the city of Duggama; [. . . , man of the city of . . .], and we have placed under oath for you as follows: Mita has now offended repeatedly. He has transgressed all of the matters which had been placed under oath. All of you have heard the [matters with which] I charged

[Mita]. And I, My Majesty, [. . .] have now written to the men of Pahhuwa. And if the men of Pahhuwa proceed [to act] loyally, [they will bring Mita], together with his wife, the daughter of [Usapa], and his [sons], together with his secondary wife, together with his household slaves, his oxen, and his sheep, [together with all his possessions. And] they will bring the household of Hassana and the household of [Kalimunaya], together with their wives, their sons, their household slaves, their oxen, their sheep, and [all their possessions]. They will turn [over everything]. They will not [hold back] as much as a strand of wool.

§10 (rev. 9–12) Five servants [of] Usapa are up in Pahhuwa with his daughter. And they too [. . .] They will release [the cities] of My Majesty [which] they hold—Halmisna, [Hurla], Pahhura, [and Aparhula]. They will arrest [the daughter] of Usapa and turn her over. If she [flees from Pahhuwa], then wherever she is entering, they will [denounce(?)] straightaway(?) to My Majesty the city in which she is taking refuge.

Return of Property

§11 (rev. 13–17) In regard to whatever they have in their possession belonging to the land of Isuwa—a person, oxen, sheep, or a fugitive coming to them [. . .]: A person who dies, or oxen and sheep which are eaten up [are of no consequence]. But they will give back everything which still exists and is visible to the eye. [They will not hold] back [as much as a strand] of wool, but will give it back. And [they will seize] everyone [who] has escaped and entered among the men of Pahhuwa.

Military Obligations; Foreign Envoys

§12 (rev. 18–26) Furthermore, they will provide troops yearly. And as the troops of the land of Isuwa and your troops are mobilized [. . .], the troops of Pahhuwa shall likewise march with your troops. Whatever call for help [comes] to you—as you rush out at the call for help, the men of Pahhuwa [shall] likewise [rush] forth. Whoever is an enemy of My Majesty shall be an enemy to the men of Pahhuwa. [They will not send a messenger] to the enemy, nor will they allow a messenger of the enemy into their gate. Whatever enemy sends a messenger to them, [they will arrest] his [messenger] and send him to My Majesty. They shall not turn him back on their own authority. Whatever word he [writes] to them, they will write that word straightaway(?) to My Majesty. They will not distort them. If the men of

Pahhuwa carry out [these words], then they will be the servants of My Majesty. But if the men of Pahhuwa do not carry out these words, but act with contempt for my authority and commence hostilities, then you shall [. . .] until the army arrives.

Suppression of Revolt

§13 (rev. 27–31) And on the day that you should hear a word of hostility among the men of Pahhuwa, go to Pahhuwa and attack Pahhuwa. Continue to attack it until My Majesty's army [arrives]. You shall bloody your hands immediately with the men of Pahhuwa. I, My Majesty, [will go] immediately against whoever does not bloody [his hands] with the men of Pahhuwa, even before I have gone against Pahhuwa. I will kill him immediately. Furthermore, I will likewise go in battle <against> Pahhuwa.

Participants

§14 (rev. 32–35) Santa-ziti and Muwattalli are their chiefs. Walwa-ziti, man of the city of Sullamma; Kasiyara, man of the city of Zanzaliya; Aritku, man of the city of Lillima; [. . .] and Mashuilu, men of the city of Hinzuta; Santa, man of the city of Wattarusna; Halpa and Siusa, men of the city of [. . .]; Usapa, man of the city of Tahhisa; Pahauwa, man of the city of Alatarma; Akarki, man of the city of Palisna; Piggana, [man of the city of . . .]; Huru, man of the city of Mararha; Agga, man of the city of Tahisna; Tahisalli, man of the city of Halma. These men [. . .]

Oath

§15 (rev. 36–37) We have placed everything under oath [for] the elders of the land of Isuwa, the elders of the land of Pahhuwa, the elders <of the land> of Zuhma, the elders of the land of [Hurri], the elders of the city of Maldiya, and for Arihpizzi, man of the city of Pittiyarik, [as follows]:

Loyalty to Hittite Dynasty; Foreign Envoys (reprise)

§16 (rev. 38–43) [All of you] are servants of My Majesty. [You shall be well-disposed(?)] to the King, the Queen, the sons of the King, and the grandsons of the King to the first and second generation [in regard to rule over you. But whoever is hostile to the King, the Queen, the sons] of the King, or the grandsons of the King to the first and second generation in regard to rule over you, and to Hatti in [regard to . . .] shall also be an enemy [to all of you]. And if I, My Majesty, make war upon him whole-heartedly, you [shall also make war upon him wholeheartedly]. You shall not allow [the messenger of an enemy into] your gate. [And you shall not . . .] the son-in-law(?) or relative by marriage [of] an enemy. [You shall] not [conceal(?)] the messenger of an enemy. [You shall] not [. . .] the messenger. [. . .] will come with him [. . .]

Reporting of Local Conditions

§17 (rev. 44–54) [. . .] to you [. . .] another [message(?) . . .] you shall not write [. . .] on the field [of battle] the man of the enemy [. . .] No one of his progeny or of his family shall [. . .] If even there on the field of battle, away [. . .], and furthermore conceals him, [then . . .] He will release a low-ranking person, and [. . . the man] of the enemy, then his [. . .] The custom of [the land] and the city is important [. . .] Why is [it] important? [. . .] How the springs and the roads are—you shall [report(?)] everything. [You shall not conceal] anything. You [shall not make an] unim-portant [matter urgent], nor shall you make an urgent matter unimportant. [. . .] Say what is accurate.

Conduct Following Military Campaign; Fugitives

§18 (rev. 55–60) [And when] you march [. . .], after the campaign you shall not violate the wife or daughter of a man, [nor] shall you injure [them]. After the campaign no one shall steal a man, woman, son, daugh-ter, slave, slave girl, ox, sheep, [horse], mule, ass, silver, gold, [. . .], bronze, or copper implements. And you shall seize a refugee [or a fugitive] who [comes] to you, whether he is a free man, a slave, or a slave girl, and [send] him to My Majesty. You shall not sell him to anyone—not [to] the enemy nor to [another] land. And you shall not turn his eyes [to the mountains. If] you hear an evil word from anyone, whether it is of [. . .] or of an enemy, you shall seize [the one responsible for] the word of hostility and send him to My Majesty.

Defensive Alliance

§19 (rev. 61–68) [But if] the population of some city [of] the enemy comes in peace, you shall [not slander(?)] Hatti before them. You shall not turn their [eyes to the mountains]. You shall not denigrate Hatti [. . .] before the lands. You shall not say [. . .] And if someone later [comes] against your lands and opens [hostilities], you shall [do battle] with that enemy [while] the infantry and chariotry of My Majesty have not yet arrived. You shall bloody [your hands immediately]. But when the infantry [and chariotry] of My Majesty [arrive . . .] in assistance, you [shall be] the vanguard [of] Hatti. You shall do battle [with the enemy. And when] I, My Majesty, summon you, no nobleman shall [remain] behind. [Only] free men [shall march]. No servant or hired substitute [shall report].

[*The final fourteen lines of the tablet are too fragmentary for translation. The colophon refers to the text as "Single tablet of the land of Pahhuwa* [. . .]."]

No. 28A
Edict of Suppiluliuma I of Hatti
concerning the Tribute of Ugarit

This document was issued by the Great King as a supplement to the treaty with Niqmaddu II presented in this volume as No. 4.

Preamble

§1 (A 1–2) Thus says His Majesty, Suppiluliuma, Great King, King of Hatti, Hero:

Historical Introduction; Tribute for Great King

§2 (A 3–24) When all of the kings of the land of Nuhashshi and the king of the land of Mukish were hostile to His Majesty, Great King, their lord, Niqmaddu, king of the land of Ugarit, was at peace with His Majesty, Great King, his lord, and not hostile. Then the kings of the land of Nuhashshi and the kings of the land of Mukish oppressed(?) Niqmaddu, king of the land of Ugarit, saying: "Why are you not hostile to His Majesty along with us?" But Niqmaddu did not agree upon hostilities against His Majesty, Great King, his lord, and His Majesty, Great King, witnessed the loyalty of Niqmaddu. Now Suppiluliuma, Great King, King of Hatti, has thus made a treaty for Niqmaddu, king of the land of Ugarit: Your tribute for His Majesty, Great King, your lord is as follows: 12 mina and 20 shekels[3] of gold and one golden cup one mina in weight as the primary portion of the tribute; four linen garments, one large linen garment, 500 shekels of blue-purple wool, and 500 shekels of red-purple wool for His Majesty, Great King, your(!) lord.

Tribute for Queen

§3 (A 25–26) One golden cup 30 shekels in weight, one linen garment, 100 shekels of blue-purple wool, 100 shekels of red-purple wool for the Queen.

Tribute for High Officials of Hatti

§4 (A 27–28) [One] golden cup 30 shekels in weight, one linen garment, 100 shekels of blue-purple wool, 100 shekels of red-purple wool for the crown prince.

§5 (A 29–30) One golden cup 30 shekels in weight, one linen garment, 100 shekels of blue-purple wool, 100 shekels of red-purple wool for the chief scribe.

§6 (A 31–32) One golden cup 30 shekels in weight, one linen garment, 100 shekels of blue-purple wool, 100 shekels of red-purple wool for the *huburtanuri*.

§7 (A 33) And the same for the second *huburtanuri*.

§8 (A 34–35) One linen garment, 100 shekels of blue-purple wool, 100 shekels of red-purple wool for the vizier.

§9 (A 36–37) One golden cup, one linen garment, 100 shekels of red-purple wool, 100 shekels of blue-purple wool for the *andubsalli*.

§10 (A 38–42) There is no one else to pay among the noblemen in the entourage of His Majesty, <Great> King, his lord. On the day when Niqmaddu brings his tribute, Niqmaddu shall not be obligated for any other gift.

Divine Witnesses; Curse

§11 (A 43–53) And His Majesty, Great King, witnessed the loyalty of Niqmaddu, when he himself came and threw himself at[4] the feet of His Majesty, Great King, his lord. And His Majesty, Great King, his lord, thus gave him this treaty. The Thousand Gods beginning with the Sun-god of Heaven, the Sun-goddess(!) of Arinna, the Storm-god of Heaven, and the Storm-god of Hatti shall be aware of the words written on this tablet. They will punish whoever alters the words of this tablet.

No. 28B
Inventory of Ugaritic Tribute to Hatti

Also found at Ugarit was an inventory of tribute due — or paid to(?) — the Hittite court. Since the name of neither the Hittite nor the Ugaritic monarch is included in the text, we cannot date this document precisely. In any event, the variation in quantities of goods presented by the Syrian vassal and the slight divergence in the list of recipients indicate that the tribute requirements had been revised from those given in the text just above.

§1 (obv. 1–10) [This tablet] records the tribute for His Majesty. [For His Majesty: one golden cup] 50 shekels in weight.

[For the Queen: one] golden [cup] and one silver cup.

[For the prince:] the same.

For the *huburtanuri*: the same.

For the (second) *huburtanuri*: the same.

For the chief scribe: the same.

For the lord of the storehouse: the same.

For the commander of the charioteers: one silver cup.

For the vizier: one [silver] cup.

§2 (rev. 1–2) 5 linen garments, 500 shekels [of blue-purple wool, and 500 shekels of red-purple wool] for His Majesty.

§3 (rev. 3) 2 linen garments, [200 shekels] of blue-purple wool, and 200 shekels of red-purple wool for [the Queen].

§4 (rev. 4) 2 linen garments, [200 shekels] of blue-purple wool, and 200 shekels of red-purple wool for the prince.

§5 (rev. 5) One linen garment, 100 shekels of blue-purple wool, and 100 shekels of red-purple wool for the chief scribe.

§6 (rev. 6) One linen garment, 100 shekels of blue-purple wool, and 100 shekels of red-purple wool for the *huburtanuri*.

§7 (rev. 7) One linen garment, 100 shekels of blue-purple wool, and 100 shekels of red-purple wool for the (second) *huburtanuri*.

§8 (rev. 8) [One linen garment, 100 shekels] of blue-purple [wool], and 100 shekels of red-purple wool <for> the lord of the storehouse.

§9 (rev. 9) [One linen garment, 100 shekels of blue-purple wool], and 100 shekels of red-<purple> wool for the commander of the charioteers.

§10 (rev. 10) [One linen garment, 100 shekels of blue-purple wool, and 100 shekels] of red-purple wool for the vizier..

No. 29
Edict of Mursili II of Hatti
recognizing the Status of Piyassili of Carchemish

Although the personal name of the Hittite king issuing this document has been broken away, the use of an epithet naming the Powerful Storm-god, the personal deity of Mursili II, leaves little doubt as to his identity. During the difficult initial decade of his rule, when he was confronted with a series of revolts throughout his realm, Mursili was dependent upon the support of his older brother Piyassili (also known by the Hurrian name Sharri-Kushuh), whom his father Suppiluliuma I had installed as king of Carchemish (see No. 6A, §10). This position of relative weakness in regard to the Syrian viceroy accounts for the tenor of this text, in which Mursili promises that within the Hittite empire only the Great King himself and his designated successor will outrank the descendants of Piyassili (cf. No. 18C, §18 and see Mora 1993).

§1 (obv. 1–5) [Thus says] His Majesty, [Mursili, Great King], King [of Hatti, Beloved] of the [Powerful] Storm-god; [son] of Suppiluliuma, [Great King], King of Hatti:

§2 (obv. 6–19) I have made this treaty for Piyassili, my dear brother, for his elevation, and for [his] sons and his grandsons in the future. Whatever son or grandson of Piyassili, or whatever descendant of Piyassili, should ascend the throne in the land of Carchemish — whoever is His Majesty's crown prince, and only he, [the crown prince (of Hatti)], shall be [greater than] the king of the land of Carchemish.

[*Five lines too fragmentary for translation.*]

§3 (rev. 3–12) [. . .] shall not have to get up from his seat [before] His Majesty. The word of Tabarna, Great King, is not to be discarded or broken. Whoever disregards it shall be the legal adversary of the Powerful Storm-god, my lord, of the Sun-goddess of Arinna, my lady, and of all the gods.

§4 (rev. 14–15) The scribe Tattiya wrote this tablet.

No. 30
Arbitration of Syrian Disputes
by Mursili II of Hatti

This text contains two separate documents recording intervention by the Hittite Great King in the affairs of his vassals in northern Syria. The first is a dispute over the possession of a city on the border between Nuhashshi and Barga (for the historical background see Bryce 1988: 23–24). Although Iyaruwatta had once been part of Barga, it had been given to Nuhashshi by a king of Mittanni two generations earlier. When Tette of Nuhashshi (see No. 7) later rebelled against the Hittites, the ruler of Barga, who remained loyal, seized the opportunity to request its reassignment to his own realm. Mursili promised to give him the settlement, but added that Iyaruwatta would remain with Nuhashshi should Tette be removed from rule by a palace coup before the city had been captured. Tette was indeed overthrown, but we are uncertain as to the disposition of Iyaruwatta since the present text is damaged and no other known composition discusses this matter. The document concludes with the imposition of peace between the contemporary rulers of the two vassal polities — Abiradda and Ir-Teshshup in Barga, and Shummittara and Huya in Nuhashshi. In each instance we are probably dealing with a vassal ruler and his chosen successor.

The second document is concerned with the division of spoils between Hatti and Amurru. In the time of Suppiluliuma I an agreement had been reached that civilian captives taken during campaigns in southern Syria should belong to the Hittites. Apparently the rulers of Amurru had been tardy in turning such persons over to the local Hittite authorities, who had finally taken matters into their own hands. Surprisingly, the Great King here takes the side of his vassal, disavowing an immediate interest in the captives and chastising his own subordinates for their independent action in taking possession of them.

The ruling made here, however, is provisional, pending the appearance before the Great King of all interested parties. In addition, the Syrians are told to submit their routine problems to "the Priest" for adjudication. This must refer to Mursili's brother Telipinu, who had been installed by Suppiluliuma as a subordinate ruler in the important Syrian city of Aleppo and who often bears this title (see Bryce 1992).

The Matter of Iyaruwatta

§1 (A i 1–2) Thus says My Majesty, Mursili, Great King, King of Hatti; son of Suppiluliuma, Great King, King of Hatti, Hero:

§2 (A i 3–17) Formerly the city of Iyaruwatta belonged to the land of Barga. Then it was taken away by force from the grandfather of Abiradda into the power of the king of the land of Hurri, who gave it to the grandfather of Tette, the *hapiru*. Then it happened that Tette and EN-urta fought a war with My Majesty, while Abiradda went over to My Majesty's side. He chased EN-urta, the enemy of My Majesty, out of the land, and himself came to the land of Hatti, to My Majesty. Kneeling at my feet, he said to me as follows: "Because the city of Iyaruwatta formerly belonged to my grandfather, give the empty city of Iyaruwatta back to me with its bare walls, gods, and ancestral spirits."

§3 (A i 18–25) I, My Majesty, made a commitment to him as follows: "If I, My Majesty, conquer Iyaruwatta by the sword with the infantry and chariotry of Hatti, I will take up its civilian captives and property and carry them off to Hatti. However, I will give the empty city of Iyaruwatta with its bare walls, gods, and ancestral spirits to you, Abiradda."

§4 (A i 26–34) But if not, and if before I, My Majesty, have conquered Iyaruwatta, a son or brother of Tette should anticipate and kill Tette, or capture him and [turn] him over to me, saying "I am the subject of Your Majesty in this place," then I, My Majesty, will not take Iyaruwatta away from him. [. . .] I will take. But if [no] one [anticipates] and kills Tette [. . .]

[*The remainder of this column is lost in the primary manuscript, and the duplicates partially covering this section do not provide sufficient context for translation. Mentioned are Tette, EN-urta, and the land of Aleppo. Better preserved, however, are three lines in Text B, immediately preceding the resumption of the main text:* "[. . .] was his brother. [. . .] turned [to] Hatti, and he became My Majesty's subject."]

§5 (A ii 1–9) And I, My Majesty, utterly destroyed EN-urta, together with his household and his land. But his kingship, throne, household, and land which I spared, I gave to Abiradda and made him king in the land of Barga. And Abiradda installed for himself his son Ir-Teshshup as their crown prince. In the future, when Abiradda dies, he shall leave to his son Ir-Teshshup his kingship, throne, land, and household.

§6 (A ii 10–18) And if Ir-Teshshup does not offend in any way against My Majesty and Hatti, then no brother or relative of his shall contest further with Ir-Teshshup in regard to the throne of kingship, his household, or his land. And if, while Abiradda is alive, his son Ir-Teshshup offends in some manner before his father Abiradda and seeks to harm his father, then the throne of kingship of Ir-Teshshup in Barga will tremble.

§7 (A ii 19–23) Because Huya and Shummittara went over to Hatti's side, Abiradda and Ir-Teshshup shall not seek to harm Shummittara and Huya and shall not engineer evil against them.

§8 (A ii 24–29) But if Abiradda and Ir-Teshshup do seek to harm Shummittara and Huya in some manner, engineer evil against them, or diminish them, then by this matter Abiradda and Ir-Teshshup will have offended against Hatti.

§9 (A ii 30–38) Shummittara and Huya shall not seek to harm Abiradda and Ir-Teshshup, shall not engineer evil against them, and shall not in any manner [diminish] them(!). [If] Shummittara [and Huya seek in any manner to harm Abiradda] and Ir-Teshshup and [engineer] evil against them, then Shummittara [and Huya] will have offended [against Hatti].

The Captives of Amurru

[*Here a double paragraph stroke marks the end of the first document. The second begins with the introductory lines:* "Tuppi-Teshshup, king of the land of Amurru, pleaded [his case] before My Majesty as follows." *A few poorly-preserved lines follow, in which mention is made of a certain Tudhaliya, as well as of Aziru and Tuppi-Teshshup of Amurru. The rest of column ii and the first half of column iii have been almost completely lost.*]

§10 (A iii 1–33) [" . . .] he keeps taking away from me [. . .] They continually resettle their cities." Why have you done this in this way, and continue to take his civilian captives away from Tuppi-Teshshup? Had I ever cared about those civilian captives, I, My Majesty, would personally have been concerned. I, My Majesty, would have taken those civilian captives for myself and carried them off to Hatti. On what basis do you continually concern yourselves and take them away on your own authority? The agreement concerning those civilian captives in the time of the father of My Majesty was as follows: The treaty of Aziru is set down on a tablet as follows: "If I, My Majesty, press upon some enemy land, and civilians of that enemy land pick up and come into your land, then seize them and turn them over!" And now, even if Aziru has not yet given those civilian captives back to My Majesty — if I had ever been concerned about them, I, My Majesty, would have taken them for myself. Why do you keep taking them for yourselves on your own authority? Now you shall not keep taking those civilian captives away from Tuppi-Teshshup. If there is some dispute, then the Priest shall intervene in the dispute. However, if some dispute is too important and you are unable to dispose of it, then refer it here to My Majesty so that My Majesty can dispose of it.

[*The upper portion of column iv has been lost.*]

§11 (A iv 2–13) The fact that this tablet of legal disputes has not now been sealed is because the king of the land of Carchemish, Tudhaliya, and Halpahi were not in the presence of My Majesty. For this reason this tablet has not now been sealed. When the king of the land of Carchemish, Tudhaliya, Halpahi, and Tuppi-Teshshup come into the presence of My

Majesty, they will come as a group before My Majesty, so that I, My Majesty, can question them concerning the disputes. And whoever makes some argument, I, My Majesty, will listen to it. Then at that time they will seal this tablet of legal disputes.

Colophons

Text A: By the hand of Tatigganza.

Text D: Single tablet of the regulation of the king of the land [of Amurru(?)].

No. 31
Edicts of Mursili II of Hatti
concerning the Frontiers and Tribute of Ugarit

It is clear from the expectations expressed by Sharri-Kushuh of Carchemish in No. 20 that Ugarit remained loyal to her Anatolian overlords during the initial stages of the Syrian uprising against Mursili II. The recipient of that letter, Niqmaddu II, was succeeded by his son Ar-Halba within a relatively short time of its dispatch. But the latter was not to sit long upon the throne of Ugarit. As part of his general reorganization of Syria after the suppression of unrest there (cf. No. 30), the Hittite king replaced Ar-Halba with his brother Niqmepa, to whom he granted a treaty (No. 9). This strongly suggests that Ar-Halba may have compromised himself, more likely through half-hearted support of the Hittites than through open participation in the revolt.

The two documents presented here support this surmise. The historical introduction to No. 31B relates how the southern portion of the realm of Ugarit, the land of Siyannu and Ushnatu, was removed from the control of Ugarit and placed directly under the jurisdiction of the king of Carchemish. This realignment to the detriment of Ugarit might well have been in retaliation for her bad behavior in the recent past. In No. 31A, the northern neighbors of Ugarit, the people of Mukish, ask for the return of territories granted to her by Suppiluliuma. If they had hoped to benefit from the punitive mood of the Hittite monarch, they were disappointed, for it seems that Mursili simply confirmed the borders established by his father.

No. 31A
Edict of Mursili II of Hatti
concerning the Frontiers of Ugarit

The primary importance of this document is that §3 allows us to restore the section of the Suppiluliuma-Niqmaddu treaty dealing with the frontiers of Ugarit (No. 4, §5). A stamp seal of Mursili (Schaeffer et al. 1956: 10, figs. 9–10) was impressed on Text A.

Preamble

§1 (A obv. 1–2) [Thus says] His Majesty, Mursili, Great King, King [of Hatti; son] of Suppiluliuma, Great King, Hero:

Historical Prologue

§2 (A obv. 3–16) [Concerning] the cities of the border districts of the land of Mukish [which] Suppiluliuma deeded over to Niqmaddu, [king] of the land of Ugarit, in a treaty tablet — Now when Niqmepa, son of Niqmaddu, had approached the Great King, saying: "The people of the land of Mukish have sued me, Niqmepa, at law concerning these cities," and when Mursili, Great King, investigated this case, he determined that these cities have belonged to the land of Ugarit since long ago. And now Mursili, Great King, has [accordingly(?)] given them to Niqmepa, king of the land of Ugarit.

Cities Allotted to Ugarit

[After probably only a short break, Text B continues with an enumeration of the settlements confirmed to Ugarit by Mursili. I have drawn the restorations, particularly at the beginning of the list, from the parallels and from No. 4, §5.]

§3 (B 1'–25') [. . . together with the territory of the Mountain of the Sun-god(?), . . . , . . . ratisa, . . .], Bituhuliwi together with its mountain territory [and the territory] of Mount Birzihe(?) up to the border, [Zimari] up to the Waters of Hundurashi, [. . .] together with Mount Heshmarashi, [. . .], Azaharuwa, Iyarqani, [. . .], Kanzata, Magdala [together with the] mountain [territory] of the Crossroads of Pithana, [the territory] of Kiburi, the territory of Mount Ashamtihe, [and] the territory of Mount Matrani, Huluri, Alulla, Yalda, Mirar, Nasha(?), Ulmuwa, Yatba, Yakuname, Henzuriwa, Nidabi, Kamaki, Hurbahulibi together with the territory [of . . .], Shanizula, Hala[. . .], Napshati, Baq[. . .], Ura(?) together with its moun-

tain territory, Pugule, [. . .], Sheta, Ya'niwa, [. . .] up to the territory of
Mount Igari-ayali together with Mount Hadamgi, [. . . itkitiya], Panishtai,
[Nakhati], Halpi, Shalma, [Gulbata], Zamirti, Sulada, [Maraili], and
Himulli in the midst of the sea.

Irrevocability

§4 (B 26'–30'; A rev. 2'–8') [Previously] Suppiluliuma, Great King, [King
of Hatti, Hero], gave his border districts to Niqmaddu, [king of the land of
Ugarit], together with their fields, [their mountains], and their [cities.
Now] Mursili, [Great] King, has thus given them [to Niqmepa], king of the
land of Ugarit, [and] to his sons [and grandsons forever]. In the future the
people of Mukish shall not make a [legal] complaint against Niqmepa and
his sons or grandsons [concerning] these [cities]. This tablet will answer
whoever makes a complaint.

Curse

§5 (A rev. 9'–15') [And] the Thousand Gods shall be aware of whoever
alters the words of this tablet. The Storm-god of Heaven, the Sun-god of
Heaven, the Storm-god of Hatti, the Sun-goddess of Arinna, Hebat of Kizzuwatna, Ishtar of Alalah, Nikkal [of Nubanni, and the Storm-god] of
Mount Hazzi shall be aware [of him].

No. 31B
Edict of Mursili II of Hatti
concerning the Tribute of Ugarit

Here Mursili apparently acknowledges the justice of Niqmepa's argument that the reduction of his territory by one-third should result in a low-
ering of his tribute. Note that under the Hittite system of measurement in
which the mina contained forty shekels, the 500 shekels of gold mentioned
in the broken portion of this text is the equivalent of the 12 mina and 20
shekels specified by Text 28A, §2.

The stamp seal of Mursili which was impressed on No. 31A is also found
on this tablet (Schaeffer et al. 1956: 8–9, figs. 7–8).

Preamble; Historical Introduction

§1 (lines 1–24) Thus says Mursili, Great King, King [of Hatti]; son of
Suppiluliuma, Great King, Hero: Since long ago the king of the land of

Ugarit and the king of the land of Siyannu have been as one. As the years passed, Abdi-Anati, king of the land of Siyannu, separated himself from Niqmepa, king of the land of Ugarit, and turned to the king of the land of Carchemish, so that now he is under his authority. And Mursili, Great King, transferred Abdi-Anati, king of the land of Siyannu, and his sons from the king of Ugarit and gave him as a subject to the king of the land of Carchemish. By means of a sealed tablet he deeded over Siyannu together with the cities in its vicinity and Ushnatu together with the cities in its vicinity, along with their border districts and their mountains, to the king of Carchemish. But when Niqmepa, king of the land of Ugarit, approached Mursili, [Great King], saying: "The Great King [has now made] this land two-thirds of its former size. The gold for the tribute and gifts [for the noblemen(?)] of Hatti are too heavy [for] the land."

[*The remaining five lines of the obverse, which are too fragmentary for transla-*
tion, mention "500 shekels of gold as tribute." *Three or four lines have been lost*
along with the lower edge, and the initial six lines of the reverse are fragmentary.
When translation again becomes possible, we find ourselves in the middle of a
description of payments due to high officials of the court, a list similar to those in
No. 28.]

Tribute for High Officials of Hatti

§2 (lines 40–41) . . . [One silver cup, one] linen garment, 100 shekels of red-purple wool, and [100 shekels] of blue-purple [wool] for the *huburta-nuri*.

§3 (lines 42–43) [One] silver [cup], one linen garment, 100 shekels of red-purple [wool], and 100 shekels of blue-purple wool for the (second) *huburtanuri*.

§4 (lines 44–45) One silver cup, one linen garment, 100 shekels of red-purple wool, and 100 shekels of blue-purple wool for the lord of the storehouse.

§5 (lines 46–51) One silver cup, one linen garment, and 100 shekels of red-purple wool for the vizier. The Great King thus imposed these gifts upon the king of the land of Ugarit. He shall not have to pay anything additional to the noblemen or to the princes.

§6 (lines 52–59) And if perhaps a prince or a nobleman from Hatti comes to the land of Ugarit among the messengers, if it pleases the king of the land of Ugarit, he (the king) may give him a present. If it is not his wish, he shall not give him a present. It is not an obligation.

Conclusion

§7 (lines 60–64) Mursili, Great King, King of Hatti, son of Suppiluliuma; Great King, Hero, has thus made this treaty for the land of Ugarit.

No. 32
Edict of Hattusili III of Hatti
concerning the Merchants of Ura at Ugarit

Merchants from the Kizzuwatnaean city of Ura (for its location see Beal 1992), probably working at least in part for the Hittite crown (see Klengel 1979: 78), threatened to disrupt the social and economic equilibrium of the Syrian port city through their mercantile and money-lending activities. Upon complaint from king Niqmepa of Ugarit, Hattusili seeks to moderate the effects of the merchants' presence by forbidding them to acquire real estate in the land of Ugarit and requiring them to return home for the winter. In any event, the cold season would have been unfavorable for their trading pursuits, since sea travel was highly limited during these months.

On Texts A and C are preserved fine impressions of a joint stamp seal of Hattusili and his Queen Puduhepa (Schaeffer et al., 1956: 12–21, figs. 13, 17, 18, 21).

§1 (A 1–4) Seal of Tabarna, Hattusili, Great King, King of Hatti. Say to Niqmepa:

§2 (A 5–37) Since you spoke as follows in my presence: "The men of the city of Ura, the merchants, are a heavy burden upon the land of your subject,"[5] His Majesty, Great King, has thus made a regulation concerning the men of Ura in their relations with the men of Ugarit. The men of Ura shall carry on their mercantile activities in the land of Ugarit during the summer, but they will be forced to leave the land of Ugarit for their own land in the winter. The men of Ura shall not live in the land of Ugarit during the winter. They shall not acquire houses or fields (in Ugarit) with their silver. Even if a merchant, a man of Ura, should lose his capital in the land of Ugarit,[6] the king of the land of Ugarit shall not permit him to live in his land. If men of Ugarit owe silver to men of Ura[7] and are not able to pay it off, the king of the land of Ugarit must turn over that man, together with his wife and his sons, to the men of Ura, the merchants. But the men of Ura, the merchants, shall not claim houses or fields of the king of the land of Ugarit. Now His Majesty, Great King, has thus made a regulation between the men of Ura, the merchants, and the men of the land of Ugarit.

No. 33
Edict of Hattusili III of Hatti
concerning Fugitives from Ugarit

The shortage of manpower in the Late Bronze Age is reflected in this decree as in a number of other Hittite diplomatic documents. The treaties often contain provisions calling for the return by one or both parties of individuals or groups fleeing the authority of the other (e.g., No. 1, §§1–2). Such emigrants might either seek service on terms more favorable than those they had fled, or in some instances form semi-autonomous bands of freebooters known as *hapiru*, In lesser polities, such as the small states of southern Syria and Palestine in the fourteenth century B.C.E., such groups constituted a danger to the rule of the princes within whose territories they operated, but in Hatti the *hapiru* were subject to royal control and even served as auxiliaries in the army.

Here the Hittite ruler renounces the services of anyone who should enter the territory of his *hapiru* from the realm of Ugarit. As recognized by several scholars (Nougayrol 1956: 107; Heltzer 1976a: 4–5; Diakonoff 1967: 365–66), the categories of person covered by this edict reflect the basic divisions of Ugaritic society: royal dependents ("subject of the king of Ugarit"), dependents of such dependents ("servant of a subject"), free citizens, and slaves purchased from foreign lands.

On its obverse this tablet bears a well-preserved impression of a stamp seal of Hattusili and Puduhepa (Schaeffer et al., 1956: 15, fig. 20; cf. Bittel 1976: 170, fig. 190).

§1 (lines 1–10) Sealed document of Tabarna, Hattusili, Great King: If some subject of the king of Ugarit, or a citizen of Ugarit, or a servant of a subject of the king of Ugarit departs and enters the territory of the *hapiru* of My Majesty, I, Great King, will not accept him but will return him to the king of Ugarit.

§2 (lines 11–19) If the citizens of Ugarit ransom someone from another country with their own silver and he flees from Ugarit and enters among the *hapiru*, I, Great King, will not accept him but will return him to the king of Ugarit.

No. 34
Edict of Puduhepa of Hatti
concerning Shipping Losses at Ugarit

Framed as an edict of "His Majesty," the text of this document does not mention the name of any Hittite king, but only that of the Ugaritic ruler

Ammistamru. On its upper left corner is found the seal of the Hittite Queen Puduhepa (Schaeffer et al., 1956: 13, fig. 16), who is known to have exercised significant power in Hatti during the reigns of both her husband Hattusili III and her (step?-)son Tudhaliya IV. Since the reign of Ammistamru II overlapped those of both of these Hittite kings, it is uncertain if Puduhepa here acts for the Hittite monarch while her husband is incapacitated (Otten 1975: 26), or during the minority of her son (Nougayrol 1956: 118).

The dispute presented to the Hittite court by an unnamed citizen of Ugarit and by Sukku, probably a Hittite, was decided in favor of the former, subject to the confirmation under oath by the harbormaster of Ugarit of his claim of damage to vessel and goods.

§1 (lines 1–3) Thus says His Majesty: Say to Ammistamru:

§2 (lines 4–22) When a citizen of Ugarit and Sukku came before His Majesty for judgment, Sukku spoke as follows: "His boat was crushed against the quay," while the citizen of Ugarit said as follows: "Sukku has recklessly(?) crashed my boat." His Majesty has decided their case as follows: The chief of the boatmen of Ugarit shall take an oath, and Sukku shall replace his boat and his goods which were stored in his boat.

No. 35
Edict of Ini-Teshshup of Carchemish
concerning the Banishment of the Brothers
of Ammistamru II of Ugarit

In the fourteenth and thirteenth centuries B.C.E. close family ties were established between the royal houses of the Hittite vassal states of Amurru and Ugarit (see also Nos. 36A, 36B, and 38). The earliest marriage was between Niqmepa of Ugarit and Ahat-milki, daughter of Ari-Teshshup of Amurru (see Lipiński 1981). The present document issued by the king of Carchemish confirms the banishment of two of the sons of the latter woman to Alashiya (Cyprus) in consequence of some unspecified offense against king Ammistamru II. Since Ahat-milki was also the mother of this monarch, the offenders were his brothers. They are here given their share of their patrimony, and they and their heirs are forbidden to challenge the settlement in the future. This incident undoubtedly took place at the beginning of Ammistamru's reign in connection with a struggle for succession to the Ugaritic throne.

The tablet has been impressed with a cylinder seal of Ini-Teshshup

(Schaeffer et al. 1956: 23–24, figs. 30–31). I have introduced the paragraph divisions.

§1 (lines 1–3) In the presence of Ini-Teshshup, king of the land of Carchemish; son of Sahurunuwa, king of the land of Carchemish; grandson of Sharri-Kushuh, king of the land of Carchemish, Hero:

§2 (lines 4–11) Heshmi-Sharrumma and ÌR-Sharrumma have committed an offense against Ammistamru, king of the land of Ugarit. Their mother Ahat-milki, queen of the land of Ugarit, has given them their inheritance portion, complete with silver and gold, complete with their utensils, and complete with all of their possessions, and she has sent them to the land of Alashiya.

§3 (lines 12–24) Before Ishtar of the Countryside she has imposed an oath upon them: "If in the future Heshmi-Sharrumma and ÌR-Sharrumma, their sons, or their grandsons, should make a complaint against Ammistamru, king of the land of Ugarit, or against his sons or his grandsons, concerning their inheritance portion, they shall transgress the oath." [In the future] Heshmi-Sharrumma and ÌR-Sharrumma, [their sons], and their(!) grandsons shall not make a complaint [against] Ammistamru, king of the land of Ugarit, [or] against his sons or his grandsons concerning [their] inheritance portion.

§4 (lines 25–27) If they make a complaint, this tablet will prevail over them. On this day the property is divided and separated.

No. 36A
Edict of Tudhaliya IV of Hatti
concerning the Divorce of Ammistamru II of Ugarit

Since this king of Ugarit was married to the daughter of another Hittite vassal, Benteshina of Amurru, his domestic difficulties were of concern to the imperial administration. Like any other Near Easterner of his time, Ammistamru was free to repudiate his wife, but the Great King took a role in the adjudication of property questions in order to head off strife between his Syrian subordinates. Tudhaliya also has an interest in the succession to the throne in Ugarit, and decrees that the divorced woman's son may maintain his position as crown prince only by renouncing all future contact with his mother. Some authorities (Kühne 1973; Singer 1991a: 174–75) connect this divorce with another dispute between the courts of Ugarit and Amurru, the so-called "Affair of the Daughter of the Great Lady," but this remains uncertain (Klengel 1992: 142).

This edict bears an impression of the stamp seal of Tudhaliya (Schaeffer et al. 1956: 19–21, figs. 24–26). The paragraph divisions are not present in the original document.

Preamble

§1 (lines 1–2) In the presence of His Majesty, Tudhaliya, Great King, King of Hatti:

Historical Introduction

§2 (lines 3–11) Ammistamru, king of the land of Ugarit, took as his wife the daughter of Benteshina, king of the land of Amurru, but she sought trouble for Ammistamru. Ammistamru, king of the land of Ugarit, has irrevocably divorced the daughter of Benteshina.

Division of Property

§3 (lines 12–21) Whatever possessions the daughter of Benteshina brought into the household of Ammistamru she shall take. She shall leave the household of Ammistamru. The citizens of Amurru shall swear an oath concerning whatever Ammistamru contests, and Ammistamru shall restore it to them in full.

Succession to the Throne

§4 (lines 22–42) Utri-Sharrumma is the crown prince of the land of Ugarit. If Utri-Sharrumma says: "I want to follow my mother," he shall place his garment on the stool and depart. Ammistamru, king of [the land] of Ugarit, [will install] another of his sons [in] the office of crown prince [in the land] of Ugarit. If [Ammistamru] goes to his fate, and Utri-Sharrumma takes his mother and returns her to the office of queen in the land of Ugarit, he shall place his garment on the stool and go where he pleases. His Majesty will install another son of Ammistamru in kingship in the land of Ugarit.

Sanctions

§5 (lines 43–50) In the future the daughter of Benteshina shall not make a complaint concerning her sons, her daughters, or her sons-in-law. They have been ceded to Ammistamru, king of the land of Ugarit. If she does make a complaint, this tablet will prevail over her.

No. 36B
Edict of Ini-Teshshup of Carchemish
concerning the Divorce of Ammistamru II of Ugarit

Also discovered at Ugarit was an accessory document issued by the viceroy of Syria, confirming the forfeiture of property in Ugarit by the divorced princess. A cylinder seal of Ini-Teshshup bearing only a cuneiform inscription was rolled on this document. As in the preceding texts, I have introduced the paragraph divisions.

§1 (lines 1–4) In the presence of Ini-Teshshup, king of the land of Carchemish; son of Sahurunuwa, king of the land of Carchemish; grandson of Sharri-Kushuh, king of the land of Carchemish, Hero:

§2 (lines 5–12) Whatever the daughter of Benteshina, king of the land of Amurru, accumulated in the land of Ugarit — whether silver, gold, copper, bronze utensils, tribute, gift, payment, male servant, female servant, garment, or linen — all of it has been ceded to Ammistamru, king of the land of Ugarit.

§3 (lines 12–19) In the future the daughter of Benteshina, king of the land of Amurru, shall not make a complaint concerning these goods against Ammistamru, king of the land of Ugarit, or against his sons or grandsons. If she does make a complaint, this tablet will prevail over her.

No. 37
Edict of Tudhaliya IV of Hatti
releasing Ammistamru II of Ugarit
from Participation in War against Assyria

The city of Ugarit was more important to Hatti for its wealth than for its military power. Thus in the course of his struggle with Assyria (see No. 17, §§11–12), Tudhaliya IV allowed Ugarit to contribute gold rather than soldiers to the war effort of the Hittite empire. This document affirming that arrangement was drawn up before the Great King's viceroy in Syria, Ini-Teshshup of Carchemish, one of whose cylinder seals was impressed on the tablet (Schaeffer et al. 1956: 24–25, figs. 32–33).

§1 (lines 1–16) [In the presence of] Ini-Teshshup, king of Carchemish; [son of Sahurunuwa], also king of Carchemish, I, [My Majesty, Tudhaliya], Great King, King of Hatti, released [Ammistamru, king of the land] of Ugarit, [his infantry and his chariotry. While the war with] Assyria has not come to an end, the infantry and the chariotry [of the king of the land] of Ugarit need not come [to my aid. In the future] suit shall not be brought [against] the king of the land of Ugarit. When the war with Assyria [has come to an end], if I, My Majesty, prevail over the king of Assyria, [then] we(!) will make peace with one another. Suit [shall not] be brought [concerning] his infantry and his chariotry, and even afterward [suit shall not] be brought against him.

§2 (lines 17–19) The king of the land of Ugarit has paid to My Majesty fifty mina of gold by means of ten shipments of the sealed storehouse.

No. 38
Edicts of Talmi-Teshshup of Carchemish
concerning the Divorce of Ammurapi of Ugarit

As had his great-grandfather(?) Ammistamru II (see No. 36), Ammurapi of Ugarit divorced a foreign wife. Ammurapi's unsatisfactory partner was Ehli-Nikkalu, daughter of a Hittite Great King, in all probability of the final Hittite monarch, Suppiluliuma II. Because of the implications of this action for the Hittite state system, the viceroy of Syria was once more involved in the adjudication of the details. The two edicts of Talmi-Teshshup of Carchemish translated here concern the disposition of real property in Ugarit and the return of the woman's dowry. Each edict was impressed with the same cylinder seal of Talmi-Teshshup (Schaeffer et al. 1956: 29–30, figs. 36–37). Nos. 38A and 38B have no paragraph strokes, so I have divided the text into sections myself.

No. 38A
Edict of Talmi-Teshshup of Carchemish
returning Property to Ammurapi of Ugarit

§1 (line 1) Edict of Talmi-Teshshup, king of the land of Carchemish.

§2 (lines 2–5) The king of the land of Carchemish has now returned to Ammurapi, king of the land of Ugarit, the fortified residence which Ehli-Nikkalu, daughter of His Majesty, has held.

§3 (lines 5–11) In the future, even in the time of(?) the grandsons of Ehli-Nikkalu, she shall not make a complaint against Ammurapi, king of the land of Ugarit, concerning this fortified residence. If she does make a complaint, this tablet will prevail over her. It has been ceded to Ammurapi, king of the land of Ugarit.

No. 38B
Edict of Talmi-Teshshup of Carchemish
returning Dowry to Ehli-Nikkalu

It seems that the matter of Ehli-Nikkalu's dowry was not settled until another marriage had been arranged for her, this time with the ruler of the otherwise-unattested city of Hapisse.

§1 (line 1) In the presence of [Talmi-Teshshup, king of the land of Carchemish]:

§2 (lines 2–14) Since [Ehli-Nikkalu has been promised in marriage(?)] to Tanhuwatassa, [. . .], king of the land of Hapisse, [he shall take] the women of [. . . , her female servants, her male servants], gold, silver, [oxen, copper utensils, asses, and] everything else which she brought to [the household (of Ammurapi)]. Ammurapi, king of the land [of Ugarit], has returned whatever women [of her . . .], her female servants, her male servants, [gold, silver], oxen, copper implements, her asses, and [everything else].

§3 (lines 14–21) In the future Ehli-Nikkalu shall not make a complaint [against] Ammurapi, king of the land [of Ugarit], and [Ammurapi], king of the land of Ugarit, must not make a complaint [against] Ehli-Nikkalu, [daughter of His Majesty]. This tablet will prevail over [whoever makes a complaint].

No. 38C
Letter of Talmi-Teshshup of Carchemish
to Ammurapi of Ugarit
concerning His Divorce

Although neither the king of Carchemish nor his Ugaritic counterpart are mentioned by name in this letter, there can be little doubt that it concerns the matter at hand, for we are aware of no other instance in which a daughter of the Hittite Great King was involved in a property dispute with a king of Ugarit. The sense of the proverbial saying adduced by the writer is probably that the Ugaritic ruler failed to exercise patience in the resolution of his domestic problem, but precipitously expelled his spouse from her home on his own authority, even after having been informed that a settlement was imminent.

§1 (lines 1–3) [Thus says] the king (of the land of Carchemish): Say [to] the king of Ugarit:

§2 (line 4) May you be well!

§3 (lines 5–19) A proverb of the Hittites: "A man was held in prison for five years. When they said to him, 'You will be released in the morning,' he was annoyed." Now you have acted in this way. Did the daughter of His Majesty perhaps remove herself from her estate? Or [did] *you* somehow [do it? You removed her!]

[*Remainder of tablet too fragmentary for translation.*]

Notes

1. Here the scribe has included two variant formulations of the same sentence.
2. The scribe erased this final clause.
3. Gloss: large shekels.
4. Texts B and F: fell at.
5. Text C: in the land of Ugarit.
6. Text C adds: and (wish to) live in the land of Ugarit.
7. Text C adds: the merchants.

Sources

1. *CTH* 26. Treaty between a King of Hatti and Paddatissu of Kizzuwatna (Akkadian)
   Text: KUB 34.1 + KBo 28.105a + 105b.
   Edition: Meyer 1953.
   Discussion: Bryce 1986: 95–96.
1A. *CTH* 133. Treaty between Arnuwanda I of Hatti and the Men of Ismerika (Hittite)
   Text: KUB 26.41 (+) KUB 23.68 + ABoT 58.
   Edition: Kempinski and Košak 1970.
2. *CTH* 41 and 131. Treaty between Tudhaliya II of Hatti and Sunashshura of Kizzuwatna (Hittite and Akkadian)
   Texts: Akkadian (*CTH* 41.I): A. KBo 1.5. B. KUB 3.4. C. KBo 28.106. D. KBo 28.75. Unplaced fragment: KBo 19.40; Hittite: A. (*CTH* 41.II) KUB 8.81 + KBo 19.39. B. (*CTH* 131) KUB 36.127.
   Editions: Weidner 1923: 88–111 (Akkadian); Götze 1924 (Hittite A); del Monte 1981: 215–29 (Hittite A and B).
   Translation: Luckenbill 1921: 180–87 (Akkadian).
   Discussions: Goetze 1940: 48–59; Petschow 1963: 241–49; Liverani 1973; Korošec 1982; Beal 1986; Bryce 1986: 96–97; Wilhelm 1988; Altman 1990; Desideri and Jasink 1990: 68–69, 78–84; Houwink ten Cate 1998.
3. *CTH* 42. Treaty between Suppiluliuma I of Hatti and Huqqana of Hayasa (Hittite)
   Texts: A. KBo 5.3 + KBo 19.43 + KUB 26.38 + KBo 5.12 + KBo 19.43a + KUB 40.35. B. KBo 19.44 + KUB 23.73 + KBo 19.44a + KUB 19.24 + KUB 26.37 + KUB 23.74 + KBo 19.44b + KUB 14.6 + KBo 22.40.
   Edition: Friedrich 1930: 103–63, 172–75.
   Discussions: Neu 1979; Carruba 1988.

4. *CTH* 46. Treaty between Suppiluliuma I of Hatti and Niqmaddu II of Ugarit (Akkadian)
    Texts: A. RS 17.340. B. RS 17.369A.
    Edition: Nougayrol 1956: 48–52.
    Translation: von Schuler in Kaiser 1983: 131–32.
    Discussion: Liverani 1962: 43–50; Klengel 1965: 349–56.

5. *CTH* 49. Treaty between Suppiluliuma I of Hatti and Aziru of Amurru (Hittite and Akkadian)
    Texts: Akkadian: A. KUB 3.7 + 122 + KUB 4.94. B. KUB 3.19 + KUB 48.71. C. KBo 28.140. D. Bo 9200. E. KBo 28.118. F. Bo 9201; Hittite: KBo 10.12 (+) 13 (+) 12a.
    Editions: Weidner 1923: 70–75, 146–49 (Akkadian); Freydank 1959 (Hittite); del Monte 1986: 116–41 (both).
    Translation: Goetze in Pritchard 1969: 529–30.
    Discussions: Klengel 1964c; 1977; Izre'el and Singer 1990: 144–50; Beckman 1997: 96–97.

6A. *CTH* 51. Treaty between Suppiluliuma I of Hatti and Shattiwaza of Mittanni (Hittite and Akkadian)
    Texts: Akkadian: A. KBo 1.1. B. KBo 1.2. C. KUB 3.1 a–d + KBo 28.111 + 112 + 114 (+) 113; Hittite: KUB 21.18 (+) KUB 26.34.
    Editions: Weidner 1923: 2–27 (Akkadian); Laroche 1969 (Hittite).
    Partial Translation: Goetze in Pritchard 1955: 205–6.
    Discussion: Yamada 1994.

6B. *CTH* 52. Treaty between Shattiwaza of Mittanni and Suppiluliuma I of Hatti (Hittite and Akkadian)
    Texts: Akkadian: KBo 1.3 (+) KUB 3.17; Hittite: KUB 23.50 + 219/w + 1472/u + HT 21 + KUB 8.80.
    Editions: Weidner 1923: 36–57 (Akkadian); Friedrich 1924 (Hittite).
    Discussions: Beckman 1993; 1997: 97–99.

7. *CTH* 53. Treaty between Suppiluliuma I of Hatti and Tette of Nuhashshi (Akkadian)
    Texts: A. KBo 1.4 + KUB 3.10 (+?) 9. B. KUB 3.2. C. KBo 1.16. D. KUB 3.3. E. KBo 28.98.
    Editions: Weidner 1923: 58–71; del Monte 1986: 142–55.

8. *CTH* 62. Treaty between Mursili II of Hatti and Tuppi-Teshshup of Amurru (Hittite and Akkadian)
    Texts: Akkadian: KUB 3.14; Hittite: A. KBo 5.9. B. KUB 3.119 (+) KUB 14.5 (+) KUB 19.48 + KUB 23.6 (+) KBo 22.39. C. KUB 21.49.
    Editions: Weidner 1923: 76–79 (Akkadian); Friedrich 1926: 1–48, 179–81 (Hittite); del Monte 1986: 156–77 (both).

Translations: Goetze in Pritchard 1955: 203–05; Lebrun 1992: 17–26.

Discussions: Cornil and Lebrun 1975–76: 96–100; del Monte 1985a; Singer 1991a: 150–51.

9. *CTH* 66. Treaty between Mursili II of Hatti and Niqmepa of Ugarit (Akkadian)

    Texts: A. RS 17.338 + RS 17.349B + RS 17.407 + RS 17.342 + RS 17.351A + RS 17.39 + RS 17.374. B. RS 17.353 + RS 17.357 + RS 17.04 + RS 19.101 + RS 17.450. C. RS 21.53.

    Editions: Nougayrol 1956: 84–101, 287–89; 1970: 127–29; Kestemont 1974b; del Monte 1986.

    Translation: Lebrun 1992: 43–47.

    Discussions: Kühne 1975; Klengel 1992: 135–36.

10. *CTH* 67. Treaty between Mursili II of Hatti and Targasnalli of Hapalla (Hittite)

    Text: KBo 5.4.

    Edition: Friedrich 1926: 52–94.

11. *CTH* 68. Treaty between Mursili II of Hatti and Kupanta-Kurunta of Mira-Kuwaliya (Hittite)

    Texts: A. KBo 4.3 + KUB 40.34 (+) KBo 19.62 + KBo 19.63 + KBo 19.64. B. KBo 4.7 + KBo 22.38 + 854/v + KBo 19.65 . C. KBo 5.13. D. KBo 19.66 + KUB 6.41 + KBo 19.67 (+) KBo 19.69. E. KUB 6.44 + KUB 19.53 + KUB 6.43 (+) KUB 6.42. F. KUB 19.54. G. KUB 6.48. H. KUB 19.51 + HFAC 1. I. KUB 19.52 + 242/w + KUB 40.53 (+) KUB 40.41. J. KUB 40.42. K. KBo 19.68.

    Edition: Friedrich 1926: 95–179.

    Partial Translation: Garstang and Gurney 1959: 89–90.

    Discussions: Heinhold-Krahmer 1977: 90–91; Beckman 1997: 99–100.

12. *CTH* 69. Treaty between Mursili II of Hatti and Manapa-Tarhunta of the Land of the Seha River (Hittite)

    Texts: A. KUB 19.49 + KUB 26.36 (+) KBo 19.70 (+) KUB 23.25 + KBo 23.41 + KBo 19.71 + KBo 22.34 + KBo 19.72. B. KUB 19.50 + KUB 26.59 + KUB 14.26 + KUB 48.74 + KUB 40.39. C. KUB 31.83. D. KUB 40.43.

    Edition: Friedrich 1930: 1–41.

    Partial Editions: Heinhold-Krahmer 1977: 88–90, 292–301; del Monte 1980.

13. *CTH* 76. Treaty between Muwattalli II of Hatti and Alaksandu of Wilusa (Hittite)

Texts: A. KUB 21.1 + KUB 19.6 + KBo 19.73 + FHL 57 + KBo 19.73a. B. KUB 21.5 + KBo 19.74. C. KUB 21.2 + KUB 48.95 (+) KUB 21.4 + KBo 12.36. D. KUB 21.3. E. HT 8. F. KBo 13.205.
Edition: Friedrich 1930: 42–102.
Discussions: Otten 1957; Heinhold-Krahmer 1977: 91; Güterbock 1986: 35–37.

14. *CTH* 75. Treaty between Muwattalli II of Hatti and Talmi-Sharrumma of Aleppo (Akkadian)
 Texts: A. KBo 1.6. B. KUB 3.6. C. KUB 3.5. D. KBo 28.120. E. KUB 48.72.
 Edition: Weidner 1923: 80–89.
 Translation: Luckenbill 1921: 188–90.
 Discussions: Götze 1928–29; Klengel 1964b; Na'aman 1980.

15. *CTH* 91. Treaty between Hattusili III of Hatti and Ramses II of Egypt (Akkadian)
 Texts: A. KBo 1.7 + KBo 28.115 (+) KUB 3.121. B. KBo 1.25 + KUB 3.11 VBoT 6 + KUB 48.73 + KUB 3.120.
 Editions: Meissner 1917; Weidner 1923: 112–23; Donbaz 1993; Edel 1994; 1997.
 Translations: Luckenbill 1921: 190–92; Goetze in Pritchard 1955: 201–6; Edel in Kaiser 1983: 135–43; Lebrun 1992: 48–53.
 Discussions: Rowton 1959; Kestemont 1981; Spalinger 1981; Sürenhagen 1985: 65–88; Rainey and Cochavi-Rainey 1990.

16. *CTH* 92. Treaty between Hattusili III of Hatti and Benteshina of Amurru (Akkadian)
 Text: KBo 1.8 + KUB 3.8 + KBo 28.116 + KBo 28.117.
 Editions: Weidner 1923: 124–35; del Monte 1986: 178–87.
 Translation: Lebrun 1992: 26–31.
 Discussions: Klengel 1992: 171–72; Houwink ten Cate 1994: 243–48.

17. *CTH* 105. Treaty between Tudhaliya IV of Hatti and Shaushga-muwa of Amurru (Hittite)
 Texts: A. 93/w (+) KUB 23.1 + KUB 31.43 (+) KUB 23.37 (+) 720/v (+) 670/v. B. 1198/u + 1436/u + 69/821 + KUB 8.82.
 Editions: Szemerenyi 1945; Kühne and Otten 1971.
 Discussions: Götze 1929; Sommer 1932: 320–27; Ranoszek 1950; Zaccagnini 1988; Singer 1991a: 172–73; 1991b; Klengel 1992: 173; 1995; Altman 1998.

18A. *CTH* 97. Edict of Hattusili III of Hatti concerning Military Obligations of Kurunta of Tarhuntassa (Hittite)

Text: ABoT 57.

Edition: Beckman 1989–90: 291–93.

Discussions: Imparati 1974: 158–60; 1991: 58–59; Sürenhagen 1992: 364–65 with note 100.

18B. *CTH* 106. Treaty between Hattusili III of Hatti and Ulmi-Teshshup of Tarhuntassa (Hittite)

Text: KBo 4.10 + KUB 40.69 + 1548/u.

Edition: van den Hout 1995.

Partial Edition: Forrer 1926: 6–9.

Partial Translations: Cavaignac 1932b; Garstang and Gurney 1959: 65–69; del Monte and Tischler 1978: 468–69; McCarthy 1963: 183–85.

Discussions: Garstang 1944; Laroche 1948; von Schuler 1965b: 455– 57; van den Hout 1984; 1989; Hoffner 1989; Sürenhagen 1992; Gurney 1993; Alp 1998.

18C. Treaty between Tudhaliya IV of Hatti and Kurunta of Tarhuntassa (Hittite)

Text: Bo 86/299.

Edition: Otten 1988.

Translation: Lebrun 1992: 31–42.

Discussions: Otten 1989; Watanabe 1989; Beckman 1989–90; Heinhold-Krahmer 1991–92; Imparati 1991, 1992a, 1992b; Sürenhagen 1992; Houwink ten Cate 1992; Beal 1993; Börker-Klähn 1993.

19. *CTH* 45. Letter from Suppiluliuma I of Hatti to Niqmaddu II of Ugarit (Akkadian)

Text: RS 17.132.

Edition: Nougayrol 1956: 35–37.

20. Copy of Letter from Sharri-Kusuh of Carchemish to Niqmaddu II of Ugarit (Akkadian)

Text: RS 17.334.

Edition: Nougayrol 1956: 54–55.

21. *CTH* 110. Letter from Prince Piha-walwi of Hatti to Ibiranu of Ugarit (Akkadian)

Text: RS 17.247.

Edition: Nougayrol 1956: 191.

22A. *CTH* 169. Letter from Prince Sutahapshap of Egypt to Hattusili III of Hatti (Akkadian)

Text: KUB 3.70.

Editions: Edel 1978: 129–36; 1994: 1:34–36, 2:59–61.

22B. *CTH* 167. Letter from Queen Naptera of Egypt to Puduhepa of Hatti (Akkadian)
   Text: KBo 1.29 + KBo 9.43.
   Editions: Edel 1978: 137–43; 1994: 1:40–41, 2:63–64.

22C. Letter from Ramses II of Egypt to Prince Tashmi-Sharrumma of Hatti (Akkadian)
   Text: KBo 28.44.
   Edition: Edel 1994: 1:46–47, 2:72–73.

22D. *CTH* 166. Letter from Ramses II of Egypt to Kupanta-Kurunta of Mira-Kuwaliya (Akkadian)
   Text: KBo 1.24 + KUB 3.23 + KUB 3.84.
   Edition: Edel 1994: 1:74–77, 2:125–30.

22E. *CTH* 176. Letter from Puduhepa of Hatti to Ramses II of Egypt (Hittite)
   Text: KUB 21.38.
   Editions: Helck 1963; Stefanini 1964–65; Edel 1994: 1:216–23, 2:322–44.
   Discussions: Sommer 1932: 253–60; Hagenbuchner 1989: 325–27; Wouters 1989: 233–34.

22F. *CTH* 158. Letter from Ramses II of Egypt to Puduhepa of Hatti (Akkadian)
   Text: KBo 28.23.
   Edition: Edel 1994: 1:106–9, 2:161–78.

22G. Letter from Ramses II of Egypt to Hattusili III of Hatti (Akkadian)
   Text: KBo 28.30.
   Editions: Edel 1976: 67–75; 1994: 1:178–81, 2:270–72.
   Discussion: Beckman 1983a: 253–54.

23. *CTH* 172. Letter from Hattusili III of Hatti to Kadashman-Enlil II of Babylon (Akkadian)
   Text: KBo 1.10 + KUB 3.72.
   Edition: Hagenbuchner 1989: 281–300.
   Partial Translations: Luckenbill 1921: 200–205; Friedrich 1925: 24–27; Oppenheim 1967: 139–46.
   Discussions: Edel 1958; Rowton 1966: 243–49; Naꞌaman 1998.

23A. *CTH* 182. Letter from a King of Hatti to an Anatolian Ruler (Hittite)
   Text: KUB 19.55 + KUB 48.90.
   Editions: Forrer 1926:233–61; Sommer 1932: 198–240.
   Translation: Garstang and Gurney 1959: 114–15.
   Discussions: Hoffner 1982; Bryce 1985.

24A. *CTH* 171. Letter from Urhi-Teshshup(?) of Hatti to Adad-nirari I of Assyria (Hittite)
Text: KUB 23.102.
Editions: Forrer 1926: 246–47; Hagenbuchner 1989: 260–64.
Discussion: Harrak 1987: 75–77.

24B. *CTH* 173. Letter from Hattusili III of Hatti to Adad-nirari I of Assyria (Akkadian)
Text: KBo 1.14.
Editions: Goetze 1940: 27–33; Harrak 1987: 68–75.
Translation: Luckenbill 1921: 205–7.
Discussions: Rowton 1959; Zaccagnini 1970; Hagenbuchner 1989: 267–69.

24C. *CTH* 178. Letter from Tudhaliya IV of Hatti to an Assyrian Nobleman (Hittite)
Text: A. KUB 23.103 rev. 8ff. B. KUB 23.92 rev. 9ff.
Editions: Otten 1959; Hagenbuchner 1989: 249–60.
Discussion: Harrak 1987: 147–48, 214.

25. *CTH* 179. Letter from a King of Hanigalbat to a King of Hatti (Akkadian)
Text: IBoT 1.34.
Editions: Klengel 1963b; Hagenbuchner 1989: 313–15.
Translation: Harrak 1987: 78–79.

26. *CTH* 202. Letter from Mashuiluwa of Mira-Kuwaliya to Mursili II of Hatti (Hittite)
Text: KBo 18.15.
Editions: Ehelolf 1937: 64–65; Hagenbuchner 1989: 367–69.

27. *CTH* 147. Indictment of Madduwatta by Arnuwanda I of Hatti (Hittite)
Text: KUB 14.1 + KBo 19.38.
Edition: Götze 1928.
Discussions: Sommer 1932: 329–49; Otten 1969; Heinhold-Krahmer 1977: 260–75; Güterbock 1983: 133–35; Hoffmann 1984; Schachermeyr 1986: 141–61.

27A. *CTH* 146. Indictment of Mita of Pahhuwa and Treaty with the Elders of Several Anatolian Communities (Hittite)
Text: KUB 23.72 + KUB 40.10 + 1684/u.
Translation: Gurney 1948.
Discussion: Hoffner 1976.

28A. *CTH* 47. Edict of Suppiluliuma I of Hatti concerning the Tribute of Ugarit (Akkadian)

Texts: A. RS 17.227. B. RS 17.300. C. RS 17.330. D. RS 17.347. E. RS 17.372B. F. RS 17.373. G. RS 17.446.

Editions: Nougayrol 1956: 40–44; Dietrich and Loretz 1964–66.

Translation: von Schuler in Kaiser 1983: 133–34.

Discussion: Klengel 1965: 352–53.

28B. *CTH* 48. Inventory of Ugaritic Tribute to Hatti (Akkadian)

Text: RS 11.732.

Editions: Virolleaud 1940: 253–59; Friedrich 1942: 471–78; Nougayrol 1955: 181–82; 1956: 47–48.

Discussions: Eissfeldt 1950; Goetze 1952: 1–2.

29. *CTH* 57. Edict of Mursili II of Hatti recognizing the Status of Piyassili of Carchemish (Hittite)

Text: KBo 1.28.

Edition: Klengel 1965: 53–55.

Discussions: Forrer 1926: 100–101; Otten 1956: 181; Gurney 1983: 100–101; Mora 1993: 67–70.

30. *CTH* 63. Arbitration of Syrian Disputes by Mursili II of Hatti (Hittite)

Texts: A. KBo 3.3 + KUB 23.126 + KUB 31.36 (+) 1459/u. B. KUB 19.41 + KUB 31.12 + 579/u. C. KUB 19.42 + KUB 40.9 (+?) KUB 21.30. D. KUB 19.44. E. KUB 19.45. F. KBo 16.23. G. KUB 19.43.

Edition: Klengel 1963a.

Translation: Cavaignac 1932a.

Discussions: Bryce 1988; Klengel 1992: 155.

31A. *CTH* 64. Edict of Mursili II of Hatti concerning the Frontiers of Ugarit (Akkadian)

Texts: A. RS 17.237. B. RS 17.62. parallels: RS 17.339A, RS 17.366.

Edition: Nougayrol 1956: 63–70.

Discussion: Astour 1969: 398–405.

31B. *CTH* 65. Edict of Mursili II of Hatti concerning the Tribute of Ugarit (Akkadian)

Text: RS 17.382 + RS 17.380.

Edition: Nougayrol 1956: 80–83.

Discussion: Klengel 1992: 136–37.

32. *CTH* 93. Edict of Hattusili III of Hatti concerning the Merchants of Ura at Ugarit (Akkadian)

Texts: A. RS 17.130. B. RS 17.461. C. RS 18.03.

Edition: Nougayrol 1956: 103–4.

Discussions: Gordon 1958; Klengel 1965: 360–70; 1979: 78; 1992: 138; Heltzer 1976b; Vargyas 1985.

33. *CTH* 94. Edict of Hattusili III of Hatti concerning Fugitives from Ugarit (Akkadian)
    Text: RS 17.238.
    Editions: Nougayrol in Bottéro 1954: 122–23; Nougayrol 1956: 107–8; Heltzer 1976a: 4–5.

34. *CTH* 95. Edict of Puduhepa of Hatti concerning Shipping Losses at Ugarit (Akkadian)
    Text: RS 17.133.
    Edition: Nougayrol 1956: 118–19.

35. Edict of Ini-Teshshup of Carchemish concerning the Banishment of the Brothers of Ammistamru II of Ugarit (Akkadian)
    Text: RS 17.352.
    Edition: Nougayrol 1956: 121–22.
    Discussion: Klengel 1992: 141.

36A. *CTH* 107. Edict of Tudhaliya IV of Hatti concerning the Divorce of Ammistamru II of Ugarit (Akkadian)
    Text: RS 17.159.
    Edition: Nougayrol 1956: 125–27.
    Translation: Röllig in Weiss 1985: 307–8.
    Discussions: Yaron 1963; Singer 1991a: 174–75; Klengel 1992: 141–42; Haase 1994: 68–69.

36B. Edict of Ini-Teshshup of Carchemish concerning the Divorce of Ammistamru II of Ugarit (Akkadian)
    Text: RS 17.396.
    Edition: Nougayrol 1956: 127–28.

37. *CTH* 108. Edict of Tudhaliya IV of Hatti releasing Ammistamru II of Ugarit from Participation in War against Assyria (Akkadian)
    Text: RS 17.59.
    Edition: Nougayrol 1956: 150–51.
    Translations: Schaeffer 1954–56: 98; Röllig in Weiss 1985: 306–7.

38A. Edict of Talmi-Teshshup of Carchemish returning Property to Ammurapi of Ugarit (Akkadian)
    Text: RS 17.226.
    Edition: Nougayrol 1956: 208.
    Discussions: Astour 1980; Klengel 1992: 148.

38B. Edict of Talmi-Teshshup of Carchemish returning Dowry to Ehli-Nikkalu (Akkadian)
    Text: RS 17.355.
    Edition: Nougayrol 1956: 209–10.
    Discussion: Astour 1980.

38C. Letter of Talmi-Teshshup of Carchemish to Ammurapi of Ugarit con-
cerning His Divorce (Akkadian)
Text: RS 20.216.
Edition: Nougayrol et al. 1968: 108–10.
Discussions: Nougayrol 1960; Astour 1980: 103–5.

Concordance
to Laroche, *Catalogue des textes hittites* (1971)

CTH	No.		
26	1	93	32
41	2	94	33
42	3	95	34
45	19	97	18A
46	4	105	17
47	28A	106	18B
48	28B	107	36A
49	5	108	37
51	6A	110	21
52	6B	131	2
53	7	133	1A
57	29	146	27A
62	8	147	27
63	30	158	22F
64	31A	166	22D
65	31B	167	22B
66	9	169	22
67	10	171	24A
68	11	172	23
69	12	173	24B
75	14	176	22E
76	13	178	24C
91	15	179	25
92	16	182	23A
		202	26

Bibliography

Alp, Sedat
1998   "Zur Datierung des Ulmitešup-Vertrags." *AoF* 25:54–60.

Altman, Amnon
1984   "The 'Deliverance Motif' in the 'Historical Prologues' of Šuppiluli-uma I's Vassal Treaties." Pp. 41–76 in *Confrontation and Co-exis-tence*. Ed. by Pinhas Artzi. Bar-Ilan Studies in History 2. Ramat-Gan: Bar-Ilan University Press.

1990   "On the Legal Meaning of Some of the Assertions in the 'Historical Prologue' of the Kizzuwatna Treaty (KBo I, 5)." Pp. 177–206 in *Bar-Ilan Studies in Assyriology dedicated to Pinhas Artzi*. Ed. by Jacob Klein and Aaron Skaist. Ramat-Gan: Bar-Ilan University Press.

1998   "On Some Assertions in the 'Historical Prologue' of the Šaušga-muwa Vassal Treaty and Their Assumed Legal Meaning." Pp. 99–107 in *XXXIVème Rencontre Assyriologique Internationale. Kongreye Sunulan Bildirler*. Ed. by H. Erkanal, V. Donbaz and A. Uğuroğlu. Ankara: Türk Tarih Kurumu.

Astour, Michael
1969   "The Partition of the Confederacy of Mukiš-Nuhašše-Nii by Šup-piluliuma: A Study in Political Geography of the Amarna Age." *Or* n.s. 38:381–414.

1979   "The Kingdom of Siyannu-Ušnatu." *UF* 11:13–28.

1980   "King Ammurapi and the Hittite Princess." *UF* 12:103–8.

Barré, Michael L.
1983   *The God-List in the Treaty between Hannibal and Philip V of Macedo-nia: A Study in Light of the Ancient Near Eastern Literary Tradition*. Baltimore: Johns Hopkins University Press.

Beal, Richard
1986   "The History of Kizzuwatna and the Date of the Šunnaššura Treaty." *Or* n.s. 55:425–45.

1992 "The Location of Cilician Ura." *AnSt* 42:65–73.

1993 "Kurunta of Tarhuntašša and the Imperial Hittite Mausoleum: A New Interpretation of §10 of the Bronze Tablet." *AnSt* 43:29–39.

Beckman, Gary

1983a *Hittite Birth Rituals*. Studien zu den Boğazköy-Texten 29. Wiesbaden: Otto Harrassowitz.

1983b "Mesopotamians and Mesopotamian Learning at Ḫattuša." *JCS* 35:97–114.

1986 "Proverbs and Proverbial Allusions in Hittite." *JNES* 45:19–30.

1989–90
Review of Otten 1988. *WO* 20–21:289–94.

1993 "Some Observations on the Šuppiluliuma-Šattiwaza Treaties." Pp. 53–57 in *The Tablet and the Scroll: Near Eastern Studies in Honor of William W. Hallo*. Ed. by Mark E. Cohen et al. Bethesda: CDL Press.

1997 "New Joins to Hittite Treaties." *ZA* 87:96–100.

Bittel, Kurt

1976 *Die Hethiter*. Universum der Kunst. Munich: Beck.

Börker-Klähn, Jutta

1993 "Zum Kolophon der Bronzetafel aus Boğazköy." *AoF* 20:235–37.

Bottéro, Jean

1954 *Le problème des Ḫabiru*. Paris: Imprimerie Nationale.

Bryce, Trevor R.

1974 "The Lukka Problem — and a Possible Solution." *JNES* 33:395–404.

1985 "A Reinterpretation of the Milawata Letter in the Light of the New Join Piece." *AnSt* 35: 12–23.

1986 "The Boundaries of Hatti and Hittite Border Policy." *Tel Aviv* 13:85– 102.

1988 "Tette and the Rebellions in Nuhassi." *AnSt* 38:21–28.

1992 "The Role of Telipinu, the Priest, in the Hittite Kingdom." *Hethitica* 11:5–18.

Canfora, Luciano, Mario Liverani, and Carlo Zaccagnini, eds.

1990 *I trattati nel mondo antico: Forma, ideologia, funzione*. Rome: "L'ERMA" di Bretschneider.

Carruba, Onofrio

1988 "Die Hajasa-Verträge Hattis." Pp. 59–75 in *Documentum Asiae Minoris Antiquae: Festschrift für Heinrich Otten zum 75. Geburtstag*. Ed. by Erich Neu and Christel Rüster. Wiesbaden: Otto Harrassowitz.

Cavaignac, Eugène
1932a "L'affaire de Iaruvatta." *RHA* 6:189–200.
1932b "Dadasa-Dattassa." *RHA* 9:65–76.
Cochavi-Rainey, Zipora
1990 "Egyptian Influence in the Akkadian Texts Written by Egyptian Scribes in the Fourteenth and Thirteenth Centuries B.C.E." *JNES* 49:57–65.
Cornil, Piet, and René Lebrun
1975–76
   "Fragments hittites relatifs à l'Égypte." *OLP* 7–8:83–108.
del Monte, Giuseppe
1974 "Mashuiluwa, König von Mira." *Or* n.s. 43:355–68.
1980 "Neue Bruchstücke zum Manapa-ᵈU-Vertrag." *Or* n.s. 49:58–66.
1981 "Note sui tratti fra Ḫattuša e Kizuwatna." *OA* 20:203–21.
1985a "Muršili II e l'Egitto." Pp. 161–67 in *Studi in onore di Edda Bresciani.* Ed. by S. F. Bondì et al. Pisa: Giardini Editori.
1985b "Nuovi frammenti di trattati hittiti." *OA* 24:263–69.
1986 *Il trattato fra Muršili II di Hattusa e Niqmepa' di Ugarit.* Oriens Antiqui Collecto 18. Rome: Istituto per l'Oriente C. A. Nallino.
del Monte, Giuseppe, and Johann Tischler
1978 *Die Orts- und Gewässernamen der hethitischen Texte.* Répertoire Géographique des Textes Cunéiformes 6. Wiesbaden: Ludwig Reichert.
Desideri, Paolo, and Anna Margherita Jasink
1990 *Cilicia. Dall'età di Kizzuwatna alla conquista macedone.* Turin: Casa Editrice Le Lettere.
Diakonoff, Igor
1967 "Die hethitische Gesellschaft." *MIO* 13:313–66.
Dietrich, Manfried, and Oswald Loretz
1964–66
   "Der Vertrag zwischen Šuppiluliuma und Niqmandu: Eine philologische und kulturhistorische Studie." *WO* 3:206–45.
Donbaz, Veysel
1993 "Some Observations on the Treaty Documents of Qadesh." *IM* 43:27–37.
Edel, Elmar
1949 "Die Rolle der Königinnen in der ägyptisch-hethitischen Korrespondenz von Boğazköy." *IF* 60:72–85.

1953 "KUB III 63: Ein Brief aus der Heiratskorrespondenz Ramses' II." *JKF* 2:262–73.

1955 "Weitere Briefe aus der Heiratskorrespondenz Ramses' II: KUB III 37 + KBo I 17 und KUB III 57." Pp. 29–63 in *Geschichte und Altes Testament: Festschrift A. Alt*. Ed. by G. Ebeling. Tübingen: J. C. B. Mohr.

1958 "Die Abfassungszeit des Briefes KBo I 10 (Hattušil — Kadaš-man-Ellil) und seine Bedeutung für die Chronologie Ramses' II." *JCS* 12:130–33.

1976 *Ägyptische Ärzte und ägyptische Medizin am hethitischen Königshof*. Rheinisch-Westfälische Akademie der Wissenschaften, Vorträge G 205. Opladen: Westdeutscher Verlag.

1978 *Der Brief des ägyptischen Wesirs Pašijara an den Hethiterkönig Hattušili und verwandte Keilschriftbriefe*. Nachrichten der Akademie der Wissenschaften in Göttingen. I. Philologisch-historische Klasse. Jahrgang 1978, Nr. 4. Göttingen: Vandenhoeck & Ruprecht.

1994 *Die ägyptisch-hethitische Korrespondenz aus Boghazköi in babylonischer und hethitischer Sprache*. Rheinisch-Westfälische Akademie der Wissenschaften, Abhandlungen 77. Opladen: Westdeutscher Verlag.

1997 *Der Vertrag zwischen Ramses II. von Ägypten und Ḫattušili III. von Ḫatti*. Wissenschaftliche Veröffentlichung der Deutschen Orient-Gesellschaft 95. Berlin: Gebr. Mann.

Ehe, lof, Hans

1937 "Vorläufiger Bericht über die Ausgrabungen in Boğazköy 1936. 3. Schrifturkunden. B. Die Tontafeln." *MDOG* 75:61–70.

Eissfeldt, Otto

1950 "Zu den Urkunden über den Tribut Niqmads, Königs von Ugarit, an den hethitischen Grosskönig Schuppiluliuma." Pp. 147–57 in *Festschrift Alfred Bertholet*. Ed. by W. Baumgartner et al. Tübingen: J. C. B. Mohr.

Fensham, Charles

1963 "Clauses of Protection in Hittite Vassal-Treaties and the Old Testament." *VT* 13:133–43.

Forrer, Emil

1926 *Forschungen*. Erkner bei Berlin: Selbstverlag.

Freydank, Helmut

1959 "Eine hethitische Fassung des Vertrages zwischen dem

Hethiterkönig Šuppiluliuma und Aziru von Amurru." *MIO* 7:356–81.

Friedrich, Johannes
1924   "Ein Bruchstück des Vertrages Mattiwaza-Šuppiluliuma in hethitischer Sprache?" *AfO* 2:119–24.
1925   *Aus dem hethitischen Schrifttum*, 1. Heft. Der Alte Orient 24/3. Leipzig: Hinrichs.
1926   *Staatsverträge des Ḫatti-Reiches in hethitischer Sprache* I. Mitteilungen der Vorderasiatisch-Ägyptischen Gesellschaft 31/1. Leipzig: Hinrichs.
1930   *Staatsverträge des Ḫatti-Reiches in hethitischer Sprache* II. Mitteilungen der Vorderasiatisch-Ägyptischen Gesellschaft 34/1. Leipzig: Hinrichs.
1942   "Hethitisch-Ugaritisches." *ZDMG* 96:471–94.

Garstang, John
1944   "The Hulaya River Land and Dadassa: A Crucial Problem in Hittite Geography." *JNES* 3:14–37.

Garstang, John, and O. R. Gurney
1959   *The Geography of the Hittite Empire*. Occasional Publications of the British Institute of Archaeology in Ankara 5. London: British Institute of Archaeology at Ankara.

Goetze (Götze), Albrecht
1924   "Das hethitische Fragment des Šunaššura-Vertrags." *ZA* 36:11–18.
1928   *Madduwattaš*. Mitteilungen der Vorderasiatisch-Ägyptischen-Gesellschaft 32/1. Leipzig: Hinrichs.
1928–29
        "Die historische Einleitung des Aleppo-Vertrages (KBo I, 6)." *MAOG* 4:59–66.
1929   "Zur Schlacht von Qadeš." *OLZ* 832–38.
1933   *Die Annalen des Muršiliš*. Mitteilungen der Vorderasiatisch-Ägyptischen Gesellschaft 38. Leipzig: Hinrichs.
1940   *Kizzuwatna and the Problem of Hittite Geography*. Yale Oriental Series, Researches 22. New Haven: Yale University Press.
1952   "Hittite Courtiers and their Titles." *RHA* 54:1–14.

Gordon, Cyrus
1958   "Abraham and the Merchants of Ura." *JNES* 17:28–31.

Grayson, A. Kirk
1987   "Akkadian Treaties of the Seventh Century B.C." *JCS* 39:127–60.

Gurney, O. R.
1948 "Mita of Paḫḫuwa." *Liverpool Annals of Art and Archaeology* 28:32–47.
1983 "The Hittite Title *tuhkanti-*." *AnSt* 33:97–101.
1993 "The Treaty with Ulmi-Tešub." *AnSt* 43:13–28.

Güterbock, Hans G.
1983 "The Hittites and the Aegean World: Part 1. The Ahhiyawa Problem Reconsidered." *AJA* 87:133–38.
1984 "Hittites and Akhaeans: A New Look." *PAPS* 128:114–22.
1986 "Troy in Hittite Texts? Wilusa, Ahhiyawa, and Hittite History." Pp. 33–44 in *Troy and the Trojan War*. Ed. by Machteld J. Mellink. Bryn Mawr: Bryn Mawr College.

Gutgesell, Manfred
1984 *Der Friedensvertrag: Ramses und die Hethiter: Geheimdiplomatie im Alten Orient*. Hildesheim: Bernward.

Haase, Richard
1994 "Drei Kleinigkeiten zum hethitischen Recht." *AoF* 21:65–72.

Hagenbuchner, Albertine
1989 *Die Korrespondenz der Hethiter*. 2. Teil. Texte der Hethiter 16. Heidelberg: Carl Winter.
1993 "Schutz- und Loyalitätsverpflichtungen in hethitischen Staatsverträgen." *Bulletin of the Middle Eastern Culture Center in Japan* 7:99–118.

Harrak, Amir
1987 *Assyria and Hanigalbat*. Hildesheim: Georg Olms.
1998 "Sources épigraphiques concernant les rapports entre Assyriens et Hittites à l'âge du Bronze Recent." Pp. 239–52 in *XXXIVème Rencontre Assyriologique Internationale. Kongreye Sunulan Bildirler*. Ed. by H. Erkanal, V. Donbaz and A. Uğuroğlu. Ankara: Türk Tarih Kurumu.

Heinhold-Krahmer, Suzanne.
1977 *Arzawa: Untersuchungen zu seiner Geschichte nach den hethitischen Quellen*. Texte der Hethiter 8. Heidelberg: Carl Winter.
1991–92 "Zur Bronzetafel aus Boğazköy und ihrem historischen Inhalt." *AfO* 38–39:138–58.

Helck, Wolfgang
1963 "Urhi-Tešup in Ägypten." *JCS* 17:87–97.

Heltzer, Michael

1976a *The Rural Community in Ancient Ugarit.* Wiesbaden: Ludwig Reichert.

1976b "Über die staatsrechtliche Regelung der Einfuhr fremdländischer Sklaven in Vorderasien des II. Jahrtausends v. u. Zeitalter." *UF* 8:443–45.

1982   *The Internal Organization of the Kingdom of Ugarit.* Wiesbaden: Ludwig Reichert.

Hillers, Delbert

1969   *Covenant: The History of a Biblical Idea.* Baltimore: Johns Hopkins University Press.

Hoffmann, Inge

1984   "Einige Überlegungen zum Verfasser des Madduwatta-Textes." *Or* n.s. 53:34–51.

Hoffner, Harry A., Jr.

1976   "A Join to the Hittite Mita Text." *JCS* 28:60–62.

1982   "The Milawata Letter Augmented and Reinterpreted." Pp. 130–37 in *Vorträge gehalten auf der 28. Rencontre Assyriologique Internationale in Wien 6.–10. Juli 1981.* Ed. by Hans Hirsch. Horn, Austria: Ferdinand Berger & Söhne.

1989   "The Ulmitešub Treaty (KBo 4.10 = CTH 106) with a New Join." Pp. 199–203 in *Anatolia and the Near East: Studies in Honor of T. Özgüç.* Ed. by K. Emre et al. Ankara: Türk Tarih Kurumu.

1990   *Hittite Myths.* Atlanta: Scholars Press.

Hoffner, Harry A., Jr., and Hans G. Güterbock, eds.

1980— *The Hittite Dictionary of the Oriental Institute of the University of Chicago.* Chicago: The Oriental Institute.

Houwink ten Cate, Philo H. J.

1992   "The Bronze Tablet of Tudhaliyas IV and its Geographical and Historical Relations." *ZA* 82:233–70.

1994   "Urhi-Tessub revisited." *BiOr* 51:233–59.

1998   "An Alternative Date for the Sunassuras Treaty (KBo 1.5)." *AoF* 25:34–53.

Imparati, Fiorella

1974   *Una concessione di terre da parte di Tudhaliya IV.* Paris: Klincksieck.

1991   "Le relazioni politiche fra Hatti e Tarhuntassa all'epoca di Hattusili III e Tuthaliya IV." Pp. 23–68 in *Quatro studi ittiti.* Ed. by F. Imparati. Florence: Elite.

1992a "A propos des témoins du traité avec Kurunta de Tartuntassa." Pp. 305–22 in *Hittite and Other Anatolian and Near Eastern Studies in Honour of Sedat Alp*. Ed. by H. Otten et al. Ankara: Türk Tarih Kurumu.

1992b "Significato politico della successione dei testimoni nel trattato di Tuthaliya IV con Kurunta." *Istituto per gli studi micenei ed egeoanatolici, Seminari* 1991:59–86.

Izreʾel, Shlomo

1991 *Amurru Akkadian: A Linguistic Study*. Atlanta: Scholars Press.

Izreʾel, Shlomo, and Itamar Singer

1990 *The General's Letter from Ugarit: A Linguistic and Historical Reevaluation of RS 20.33 (Ugaritica V, No. 20)*. Tel Aviv: The Chaim Rosenberg School of Jewish Studies.

Kaiser, Otto, ed.

1983 *Rechts- und Wirtschaftsurkunden. Historisch-chronologische Texte*. Texte aus der Umwelt des Alten Testaments, I/2. Gütersloh: Gerd Mohn.

Kalluveettil, P.

1982 *Declaration and Covenant: A Comprehensive Review of Covenant Formulae from the Old Testament and the Ancient Near East*. Rome: Biblical Institute Press.

Kempinski, Aharon, and Silvin Košak

1970 "Der Išmeriga-Vertrag." *WO* 5:191–217.

Kestemont, Guy

1974a *Diplomatique et droit internationale en Asie Occidentale (1600–1200 av. J. C.)*. Louvain-La-Neuve: Institut Orientaliste.

1974b "Le traité entre Mursil II de Hatti et Niqmepa d'Ugarit." *UF* 6:85– 127.

1976 "Le panthéon des instruments hittites de droit public." *Or* n.s. 45:147–77.

1981 "Accords internationaux relatifs aux ligues hittites (1600–1200 av. J. C.)." *OLP* 12:15–78.

Klengel, Horst

1963a "Der Schiedesspruch des Muršili II. hinsichtlich Barga und seine Übereinkunft mit Duppi-Tešup von Amurru (KBo III 3)." *Or* n.s. 32:32–55.

1963b "Zum Brief eines Königs von Hanigalbat (IBoT I 34)." *Or* n.s. 32:280–91.

1964a "Aziru von Amurru und seine Rolle in der Geschichte der Amarnazeit." *MIO* 10:57–83.

1964b "Ein neues Fragment zur historischen Einleitung des Talmišar-
       ruma Vertrages." *ZA* 56:213–17.
1964c "Neue Fragmente zur akkadischen Fassung des Aziru-Ver-
       trages." *OLZ* 59:437–45.
1965   *Geschichte Syriens im 2. Jahrtausend v. u. Z. Teil I — Nordsyrien.*
       Berlin: Akademie-Verlag.
1969   "Syrien in der hethitischen Geschichtschreibung." *Klio* 51:5–14.
1977   "Zwei neue Fragmente zum akkadischen Aziru-Vertrag." *AoF*
       5:259–61.
1979   "Handel und Kaufleute im hethitischen Reich." *AoF* 6:69–80.
1991   "Tuthalija IV. von Hatti: Prolegomena zu einer Biographie." *AoF*
       18:224–38.
1992   *Syria. 3000 to 300 B. C.* Berlin: Akademie Verlag.
1995   "Historischer Kommentar zum Šaušgamuwa-Vertrag." Pp. 159–
       72 in *Studio Historiae Ardens. Ancient Near Eastern Studies Pre-
       sented to Philo H. J. Houwink ten Cate on the Occasion of his 65th
       Birthday.* Ed. by Theo P. J. van den Hout and Johan de Roos.
       Leiden: Nederlands Instituut voor het Nabije Oosten.

Korošec, Viktor
1931   *Hethitische Staatsverträge. Ein Beitrag zu ihrer juristischen Wertung.*
       Leipzig: Theodor Weicher.
1982   "Über den nichtparitätischen Charakter des Šunaššura-Ver-
       trages (KBo I, 5)." *AfO Beiheft* 19:168–72.

Košak, Silvin
1986   "'The Gospel of Iron.'" Pp. 125–35 in *Kaniššuwar: A Tribute to
       Hans G. Güterbock on his Seventy-Fifth Birthday.* Ed. by H. A.
       Hoffner, Jr., and G. Beckman. Chicago: The Oriental Institute.

Kühne, Cord
1973   "Ammistamru und die Tochter der 'Grossen Dame.'" *UF*
       5:175–84.
1975   "Zum neu gewonnenen Niqmepa' Vertrag." *UF* 7:239–51.

Kühne, Cord, and Heinrich Otten
1971   *Der Šaušgamuwa-Vertrag.* Studien zu den Boğazköy-Texten 16.
       Wiesbaden: Otto Harrassowitz.

Laroche, Emmanuel
1948   "Un point d'histoire: Ulmi-Teššub." *RHA* 48:40–48.
1969   "Fragments hittites du traité mitannien de Šuppiluliuma Ier."
       Ugaritica 6:369–73.
1971   *Catalogue des textes hittites.* Paris: Klincksieck.

Lebrun, René
1992 "Les traités hittites." Pp. 15–59 in Jacques Briend, René Lebrun, and Émile Puech, *Traités et serments dans le proche-orient ancien*. Supplément au Cahier Évangile 81. Paris: Impressions Dumas.

Lipiński, Edward
1981 "Ahat-milki, reine d'Ugarit, et la guerre de Mukiš." *OLP* 12:79–115.

Liverani, Mario
1962 *Storia di Ugarit nell'età degli archivi politici*. Studi Semitici 6. Rome: Centro di Studi Semitici.
1973 "Storiografia politica hittita — I. Šunaššura, ovvero: della reciprocità." *OA* 12:268–97.
1983 "Aziru, servitore di due padroni." Pp. 93–121 in *Studi orientalistici in ricordo di Franco Pintore*. Ed. by O. Carruba et al. Pavia: Gianni Iuculano Editore.
1990 *Prestige and Interest: International Relations in the Near East ca. 1600–1100 B.C.* Padua: Sargon srl.

Luckenbill, D. D.
1921 "Hittite Treaties and Letters." *AJSL* 37:161–211.

McCarthy, D. J.
1963 *Treaty and Covenant: A Study in Form in the Ancient Oriental Documents and in the Old Testament*. Analecta Biblica 21. Rome: Pontifical Biblical Institute.

Meissner, Bruno
1917 "Der Staatsvertrag Ramses' II. von Ägypten und Ḫattušils von Ḫatti in akkadischer Fassung." *Sitzungsberichte der königlicher preussischen Akademie der Wissenschaften* 20:282–95.

Mendenhall, George
1954 "Covenant Forms in Israelite Tradition." *BA* 17/3:50–76.
1990 "The Suzerainty Treaty Structure: Thirty Years Later." Pp. 85–100 in *Religion and Law: Biblical-Judaic and Islamic Perspectives*. Ed. by E. B. Firmage et al. Winona Lake: Eisenbrauns.

Meyer, Gerhard R.
1953 "Zwei neue Kizzuwatna-Verträge." *MIO* 1:108–24.

Mora, Clelia
1993 "Lo 'status' del re di Kargamiš." *Or* n.s. 62:67–70.

Moran, William L.
1992 *The Amarna Letters*. Baltimore: Johns Hopkins University Press.

Muhly, James D.
1980 "The Bronze Age Setting." Pp. 25–67 in *The Coming of the Age of*

Iron. Ed. by T. A. Wertime and J. D. Muhly. New Haven: Yale University Press.

Naʾaman, Nadav
1980 "The Historical Introduction of the Aleppo Treaty Reconsidered." *JCS* 32:34–42.
1998 "The Closing Paragraphs of Letter KBo I 10." *AoF* 25:61–67.

Neu, Erich
1979 "Zum sprachlichen Alter des Ḫukkana-Vertrages." *KZ* 93:64–84.

Nougayrol, Jean
1955 *Le palais royal d'Ugarit III: Textes accadiens et hourrites des archives est, ouest et centrales.* Paris: Klincksieck.
1956 *Le palais royal d'Ugarit. IV: Textes accadiens des archives sud.* Paris: Klincksieck.
1960 "Une fable hittite." *RHA* 67:117–19.
1970 *Le palais royal d'Ugarit VI: Textes en cunéiformes babyloniens des archives du Grand Palais et du palais sud d'Ugarit.* Paris: Klincksieck.

Nougayrol, Jean, et al.
1968. *Ugaritica V.* Paris: Geuthner.

Oppenheim, A. Leo
1967 *Letters from Mesopotamia.* Chicago: University of Chicago Press.

Otten, Heinrich
1951 "Ein althethitischer Vertrag mit Kizzuvatna." *JCS* 5:129–32.
1956 "Hethitische Schreiber in ihren Briefen." *MIO* 4:179–89.
1957 "Zusätzliche Lesungen zum Alakšandu-Vertrag." *MIO* 5:26–30.
1959 "Ein Brief aus Hattuša an Bâbu-aḫu-iddina." *AfO* 19:39–46.
1967 "Ein hethitischer Vertrag aus dem 15./14. Jahrhundert v. Chr. (KBo XVI 47)." *IM* 17:55–62.
1969 *Sprachliche Stellung und Datierung des Madduwatta-Textes.* Studien zu den Boğazköy-Texten 11. Wiesbaden: Otto Harrassowitz.
1971 "Das Siegel des hethitischen Grosskönigs Taḫurwaili." *MDOG* 103:59–68.
1975 *Puduḫepa: Eine hethitische Königen in ihren Textzeugnissen.* Akademie der Wissenschaften und der Literatur, Abhandlungen der Geistes- und Sozialwissenschaftlichen Klassen, Jahrgang 1975, Nr. 1. Mainz: Franz Steiner.
1981 *Die Apologie Hattusilis III: Das Bild der Überlieferung.* Studien zu den Boğazköy-Texten 24. Wiesbaden: Otto Harrassowitz.
1988 *Die Bronzetafel aus Boğazköy: Ein Staatsvertrag Tutḫalijas IV.* Stu-

dien zu den Boğazköy-Texten, Beiheft 1. Wiesbaden: Otto Harrassowitz.

1989 *Die 1986 in Boğazköy gefundene Bronzetafel: Zwei Vorträge*. Innsbrucker Beiträge zur Sprachwissenschaft, Vorträge und kleinere Schriften 42. Innsbruck: Institut für Sprachwissenschaft der Universität Innsbruck.

Parpola, Simo, and Kazuko Watanabe
1988 *Neo-Assyrian Treaties and Loyalty Oaths*. State Archives of Assyria 2. Helsinki: Helsinki University Press.

Petschow, Herbert
1963 "Zur Noxalhaftung im hethitischen Recht." *ZA* 55:237–50.

Pintore, Franco
1978 *Il matrimonio interdinastico nel Vicino Oriente durante i secoli XV–XIII*. Rome: Istituto per l'Oriente.

Preiser, Wolfgang
1996 "Zur Ausbildung einer völkerrechtlichen Ordnung in der Staatenwelt des Alten Orients." Pp. 227–39 in *Vom Halys zum Euphrat. Thomas Beran zu Ehren*. Ed. by U. Magan and M. Rashad. Münster: Ugarit-Verlag.

Pritchard, James B., ed.
1955 *Ancient Near Eastern Texts relating to the Old Testament*. 2d ed. Princeton: Princeton University Press.

1969 *The Ancient Near East: Supplementary Texts and Pictures relating to the Old Testament*. Princeton: Princeton University Press.

Rainey, Anson, and Zippora Cochavi-Rainey
1990 "Comparative Grammatical Notes on the Treaty between Ramses II and Hattusili III." Pp. 796–823 in *Studies in Egyptology presented to Miriam Lichtheim*, vol. 2. Ed. by Sarah Israelit-Groll. Jerusalem: Magnes Press.

Ranoszek, R.
1950 "A propos de KUB XXIII 1." *ArOr* 18/4:236–42.

Rowton, Michael
1959 "The Background of the Treaty between Ramses II and Ḫattušiliš III." *JCS* 13:1–7.

1966 "The Material from Western Asia and the Chronology of the Nineteenth Dynasty." *JNES* 25:240–58.

Schachermeyr, Fritz
1928 "Zur staatsrechtlichen Wertung der hethitischen Verträge." *MAOG* 4:180–86.

1986 *Mykene und das Hethiterreich*. Vienna: Verlag der Österreichischen Akademie der Wissenschaften.

Schaeffer, Claude F.-A.
1954–56
   "Ugarit und die Hethiter." *AfO* 17:93–99.
Schaeffer, Claude F.-A., et al.
1956   *Ugaritica III*. Paris: Geuthner.
Singer, Itamar
1991a   "A Concise History of Amurru." Pp. 135–95 in Vol. 2 of Izre'el 1991.
1991b   "The 'Land of Amurru' and the 'Lands of Amurru' in the Šaušga-muwa Treaty." *Iraq* 53:69–74.
Sommer, Ferdinand
1932   *Die Aḫḫiyava-Urkunden*. Abhandlungen der Bayerischen Akademie der Wissenschaften. Philosophisch-historische Abteilung n.F. 6. Munich: Beck.
Spalinger, Anthony
1981   "Considerations on the Hittite Treaty between Egypt and Hatti." *SAK* 9:299–358.
Stefanini, Rugiero
1964–65
   "Una lettera della regina Puduhepa al re di Alasiya (KUB XXI 38)." *AttiAccTosc* 29:3–69.
Steiner, Gerd
1964   "Die Aḫḫijawa-Frage heute." *Saeculum* 15:365–92.
Sürenhagen, Dietrich
1985   *Paritätische Staatsverträge aus hethitischer Sicht*. Pavia: Gianni Iuculano Editore.
1992   "Untersuchungen zur Bronzetafel und weiteren Verträgen mit der Sekundogenitur in Tarḫuntašša." *OLZ* 87:341–71.
Thieme, Paul
1960   "The 'Aryan' Gods of the Mitanni Treaties." *JAOS* 80:301–17.
Szemerenyi, Oswald
1945   "Vertrag des Hethiterkönigs Tudhalija IV. mit Ištarmuwa von Amurru (KUB XXIII 1)." *Oriens Antiquus* (Budapest) 9:113–29.
van den Hout, Theo P. J.
1984   "Kurunta und die Datierung einiger hethitischen Texte." *RA* 78:89–92.
1989   "A Chronology of the Tarhuntassa-Treaties." *JCS* 41:100–14.
1994   "Der Falke und das Kücken: der neue Pharao und der hethitische Prinz?" *ZA* 84:60–88.
1995   *Der Ulmitesub-Vertrag: Eine prosopographische Untersuchung*. Stu-

dien zu den Boğazköy-Texten 38. Wiesbaden: Otto Harrassowitz.

Vargyas, P.
1985 "Marchands hittites à Ugarit." *OLP* 16:71–79.

Virolleaud, C.
1940 "Lettres et documents administratifs provenant des archives d'Ugarit." *Syria* 21:247–76.

von Schuler, Einar
1965a *Die Kaškäer.* Berlin: Walter de Gruyter.
1965b "Sonderformen hethitischer Staatsverträge." *JKF* 2:445–64.

Watanabe, Kazuko
1989 "Mit Gottessiegeln versehene hethitische 'Staatsverträge.'" *Acta Sumerologica* 11:261–76.

Watkins, Calvert
1986 "The Language of the Trojans." Pp. 45–62 in *Troy and the Trojan War.* Ed. by M. J. Mellink. Bryn Mawr: Bryn Mawr College.

Watson, Alan.
1993 *International Law in Ancient Rome: War and Religion.* Baltimore: Johns Hopkins University Press.

Weidner, Ernst
1923 *Politische Dokumente aus Kleinasien: Die Staatsverträge in akkadischer Sprache aus dem Archiv von Boghazköi.* Boghazköi-Studien 8 and 9. Leipzig: Hinrichs.
1959 "Der Kanzler Salmanassars I." *AfO* 19:33–39.

Weinfeld, Moshe
1973 "Covenant Terminology in the Ancient Near East and its Influence on the West." *JAOS* 93:190–99.
1976 "The Loyalty Oath in the Ancient Near East." *UF* 8:379–414.
1990 "The Common Heritage of Covenantal Traditions in the Ancient World." Pp. 175–91 in Canfora et al. 1990.

Weiss, Harvey, ed.
1985 *Ebla to Damascus.* Washington: SITES.

Wilhelm, Gernot
1982 *Grundzüge der Geschichte und Kultur der Hurriter.* Darmstadt: Wissenschaftliche Buchgesellschaft.
1988 "Zur ersten Zeile des Šunaššura-Vertrages." Pp. 359–70 in *Documentum Asiae Minoris Antiquae: Festschrift für Heinrich Otten zum 75. Geburtstag.* Ed. by Erich Neu and Christel Rüster. Wiesbaden: Otto Harrassowitz.

Wouters, Werner
1989 "Urḫi-Tešub and the Ramses-Letters from Boghazköy." *JCS* 41:226–32.
1998 "Boğazköy: Royal Correspondence between Assur and Hatti." Pp. 269–73 in *XXXIVème Rencontre Assyriologique Internationale. Kongreye Sunulan Bildirler.* Ed. by H. Erkanal, V. Donbaz and A. Uğuroğlu. Ankara: Türk Tarih Kurumu.

Yamada, Masamichi.
1994 "The Northern Border of the Land of Aštata." *Acta Sumerologica* 16:261–68.

Yaron, R.
1963 "A Royal Divorce at Ugarit." *Or* n.s. 32: 21–31.

Zaccagnini, Carlo
1970 "KBo I 14 e il 'monopolio' hittita del ferro." *RSO* 45:11–20.
1974 "Šattiwaz(z)a." *OA* 13:25–34.
1983 "Patterns of Mobility among Ancient Near Eastern Craftsmen." *JNES* 42:245–64.
1988 "A Note on Hittite International Relations at the Time of Tudḫaliya IV." Pp. 295–99 in *Studi di storia e di filologia anatolica dedicati a Giovanni Pugliese Carratelli.* Ed. by F. Imparati. Florence: Edizioni Librarie Italiane Estere.
1990 "The Forms of Alliance and Subjugation in the Near East of the Late Bronze Age." Pp. 37–79 in Canfora et al. 1990.

Indexes

Proper names appearing in the titles and genealogies of rulers and in the epithets of deities have normally not been indexed. However, I have included those instances where the mention of, for instance, "the king of Isuwa" is the only indication of the participation of a polity in a particular context. While the spelling of proper names in Hittite texts may vary considerably, for the convenience of the general reader a single form of each name —sometimes chosen quite arbitrarily — has been employed throughout this volume. Entries in this index have been alphabetized normally and not according to Hittitological practice by which all dentals are placed under t, etc.

Persons

212

Deities

Cities

Countries, Districts, Peoples
(Hatti has not been indexed.)

Mountains

Rivers

Topics